Lecture Notes in Computer Sci

Commenced Publication in 1973
Founding and Former Series Editors:
Gerhard Goos, Juris Hartmanis, and Jan van Leeuw

T0238158

Stephen W. Gilroy   Michael D. Harrison (Eds.)

Interactive Systems

Design, Specification, and Verification

12th International Workshop, DSVIS 2005
Newcastle upon Tyne, UK, July 13-15, 2005
Revised Papers

 Springer

Volume Editors

Stephen W. Gilroy
Michael D. Harrison
University of Newcastle upon Tyne
School of Computing Science
Newcastle upon Tyne, NE1 7RU, UK
E-mail: {steve.gilroy,michael.harrison}@ncl.ac.uk

Library of Congress Control Number: 2006925462

CR Subject Classification (1998): H.5.2, H.5, I.3, D.2, F.3

LNCS Sublibrary: SL 2 – Programming and Software Engineering

ISSN	0302-9743
ISBN-10	3-540-34145-5 Springer Berlin Heidelberg New York
ISBN-13	978-3-540-34145-1 Springer Berlin Heidelberg New York

Springer is a part of Springer Science+Business Media

springer.com

© Springer-Verlag Berlin Heidelberg 2006
Printed in Germany

Typesetting: Camera-ready by author, data conversion by Scientific Publishing Services, Chennai, India
Printed on acid-free paper   SPIN: 11752707   06/3142   5 4 3 2 1 0

Preface

The 12th year of this workshop brought further development to familiar themes but also welcomed inclusion of less familiar topics such as "experience" and "quality-based design." The two keynote speakers, Cliff Jones and Peter Wright, described contrasting research and in so doing added zest to the meeting, emphasizing the interdisciplinary breadth of the problems of interactive system design and verification. Cliff Jones, taking an approach that is familiar to the workshop faithful, discussed the role that a careful formal framing plays in specifying how an interactive system relies on its environment, including users. Peter Wright, in contrast, discussed the nature of human experience and how new conceptions of user experience can critically inform interaction design theory, principles and practice.

As usual, the submitted papers placed a strong emphasis on task representation as a means of modelling the requirements for the interactive system. CTT appears to be emerging as a defacto standard for describing tasks within this community and several papers describe model-orientated approaches based on task representation. Montero et al. address a broad framework rendered in terms of a tool, while Ponsard et al. give a specific example of model-based design and Nobrega et al. deal with the more specific issue of mapping CTT to UML. Other papers consider different aspects of conceptualizing the design. Paterno and Volpe consider how to move from sketches or informal descriptions to task representations, while Paquette and Schneider deal with templates that ease the process of producing task descriptions. Naghsh et al. on the other hand consider annotations and paper prototypes. A further set of papers deals with the peculiar and novel requirements of mobile and migratory applications. Hence there are papers about platform fusion (Dupuy-Chessa et al.), a taxonomy of migratory user interfaces (Berti et al.). As usual there are papers that concern the modelling and analysis of properties such as moding (Gow et al.), menus (Zhang et al.), the verification of haptic algorithms (de Boeck et al.) and group interactions (ter Beek et al.).

Other papers hint at the more radical agenda suggested by Peter Wright's keynote address. The paper by Dix et al. addresses a framework for thinking about the design of computer interfaces that support performance. Two papers discuss how distributed cognition issues might be addressed in design. Blandford and Furniss's paper draws on claims analysis and distributed cognition, while Campos and Doherty fold an analysis of information resources into a formal approach. Finally, Lee et al. address an approach to measuring user preferences using utility trade-offs.

The workshop stimulated new ideas, working groups reflected on present and future issues in the community. We fully expect that the meeting triggered significant collaborations. The location of the workshop, the North East of England, is an area full of character and history. Overall the workshop was a rewarding and illuminating experience.

From the 60 or so papers that were submitted to the conference, the reviewers worked hard to get down to the 20 papers included in these proceedings. Submissions came from a range of countries, including the UK, Italy, France, Belgium, Spain, Korea, Canada, USA, Portugal, Ireland, Brazil and Switzerland.

The papers are organized into six themes reflecting common issues and approaches explored by the accepted papers. In addition, four papers summarize break-out discussions. These center on issues that the workshop participants chose as being important in future research that might be presented in later DSVIS meetings. In summary, we hope that the proceedings will give the reader a feeling for the values and goals of the community and provide a context that links all of the papers presented here.

Stephen Gilroy
Michael Harrison

Organization

Conference

Programme Chair
Michael Harrison   University of Newcastle upon Tyne, UK

Reviews and Proceedings
Stephen Gilroy   University of Newcastle upon Tyne, UK

Conference Support
Annabel Bixby   University of Newcastle upon Tyne, UK
Christine Wisher   University of Newcastle upon Tyne, UK

Programme Committee

Remi Bastide	LIIHS-IRIT, France
Ann Blandford	UCL, UK
José C. Campos	University of Minho, Portugal
Anke Dittmaar	University of Rostock, Germany
Alan Dix	Lancaster University, UK
Gavin Doherty	University of Dublin, Trinity College, Ireland
Peter Forbrig	University of Rostock, Germany
T.C. Nicholas Graham	Queen's University, Kingston, Canada
Philip Gray	University of Glasgow, UK
Chris Johnson	University of Glasgow, UK
Joaquim A Jorge	IST-UTL, Portugal
Rick Kazman	Carnegie Mellon University, USA
Karsten Loer	Germanischer Lloyd AG, Germany
Panos Markopoulos	Technische Universiteit Eindhoven, Netherlands
Mieke Massink	CNR-ISTI, Italy
Laurence Nigay	Université Joseph Fourier, France
Phillippe Palanque	LIIHS-IRIT, France
Fabio Paternò	CNR-ISTI, Italy
Chris Roast	Sheffield Hallam University, UK
Kevin Schneider	University of Saskatchewan, Canada
Harold Thimbleby	University of Wales, Swansea, UK
Jean Vanderdonckt	Université Louvain-La-Neuve, Belgium

Additional Reviewers

Patrick Olivier	University of Newcastle upon Tyne, UK
Shamus Smith	Durham University, UK

Supporting Societies

British Computing Society
British HCI Group
IFIP Working Group
Informatics Research Institute, University of Newcastle upon Tyne

Table of Contents

Migration and Mobility

Analysis Tools

Model-Based Design Processes and Tools

Group Discussions

User Experience and the Idea of Design in HCI

Peter Wright[1], Mark Blythe[1], and John McCarthy[2]

[1] Department of Computer Science,
University of York, Heslington, York YO10 5DD, UK
{peter.wright, mark.blythe}@cs.york.ac.uk
[2] Department of Applied Psychology,
University College Cork, Cork, Ireland
john.mccarthy@ucc.ie

Abstract. In this paper we argue that the idea of design in HCI is changing. For many years the design-as-engineering approach has dominated HCI research and practice, but now technological developments and new conceptions of 'the user' require more interdisciplinary conceptions of design. In particular, the turn to experience in HCI has lead us to consider a design-as-craft perspective which we exemplify in this paper by the work of digital jeweller, Jayne Wallace. But our aim is not to supplant one design perspective with an other. On the contrary, we argue that experience design requires a new form of radically interdisciplinary dialogue between different design perspectives that span the arts, sciences and humanities. However, such radically interdisciplinary dialogue is not without its problems and points of contention. We conclude by arguing that not only new conceptual tools but also new HCI curricula may be helpful in achieving this interdisciplinary dialogue.

1 Introduction

Fifteen years ago the idea of design in HCI was taken for granted and not a point of concern or discussion. Design meant the process of modelling users and systems and specifying system behaviour such that it fitted the users' tasks, was efficient, easy to use and easy to learn. In short, design in HCI was about engineering usability. Research agendas around this idea involved how best to model the user and to overcome the technical problems with specifying interactive programs in a way that promoted usability. The translation from the specification of user tasks to the specification of system dialogues presented significant technical interest and research opportunities but was not seen as fundamentally problematical. It was simple to see that designing the behaviour and visual appearance of a system to match the user's tasks, goals and action possibilities was a fundamentally sound proposition, which could be progressed not only as a human factors enterprise (task modeling, cognitive functional analysis, etc.) but also a formal software engineering enterprise [17].

But more recently various technological developments have led to a questioning of this idea of design in HCI. The confluence of information and communications technologies, and the reconceptualisation of interactive systems as new media [5] brings a much broader set of ideas about what it means to design an interactive system and

S.W. Gilroy and M.D. Harrison (Eds.): DSVIS 2005, LNCS 3941, pp. 1–14, 2006.

indeed what it is that is being designed. Just consider for example, some common terms that permeate text books and research papers in HCI:

- User-centred design
- Dialogue design
- Information design
- Interaction design
- Emotional design
- Experience design

What is clear is that design has always been a central concern, but when Norman and others [23] introduced the idea of user-centred design there was little argument about what it was that was being designed—PCs and other desk-based computer interfaces. But the remainder of the list speaks to changing concerns. It appears we no longer design dialogue but interactions, information spaces, affect and now, user experience. Moving down the list also reveals differences in our understanding of 'the user'—the user as someone who engages in dialogue through to someone who has an experience with- or through- the technology. This raises the broader question of whether design means the same thing with these different conceptions of the user. Can we design experiences in the same way as we design dialogues? So the question is whether these changes to the focus of study in HCI have any implications for what our idea of design is or should be? Our recent research programme exploring theory and method for experience-centred design has led us to conclude that we need to change our ideas about design in HCI. Within HCI research there is a tendency to simplify accounts of the idea of design, the most common of which is a simplification to a single, linear developmental trajectory wherein one technique, tool or viewpoint, overwrites its earlier predecessor. For example,

- First came batch processing, then command line, then GUI...
- First came task analysis, then scenario-based design, then personae-based design...
- First came the user as human factor then as human actor then...
- First the user was a cog in a virtual machine now the user is a consumer....
- First came psychology, then ethnomethodology, then phenomenology...

These simplifications are often pedagogically useful but potentially misleading. It seems more appropriate (certainly as we view HCI practice as it is on the ground today) to understand these as coexisting perspectives, but where at certain times or in certain situations, one view, one metaphor, or one practice, is more central than another, one argument or one discourse is the dominant discourse for a while. Such a multi-perspectival view leads us to consider the boundaries between these accounts and encourages a dialogue between them. The quality of that dialogue will determine the effectiveness of our multi-disciplinary approach. A dialogue that tries to reduce ideas on the margins to more central ideologies will tend to stifle creativity, dialogues which at least for a time try to reverse centre and margin, or dialogues which strive to avoid replicating centre-margin distinctions, tend to foster creativity [1]. A number of different perspectives on HCI design already exist, ranging from engineering through to design as arts and crafts. If practitioners and researchers with these different perspectives can be helped to work together in some way then the new challenges of HCI design will be more easily met. We want to argue that this can be best done by a kind of radical interdisciplinary research programme. By radical interdisciplinarity, we mean not just psychologists, electronic engineers and computer scientists talking together and collaborating, for these groups fundamentally share a common idea of design. We mean psychologists, computer scientists, and electronics engineers talking to visual and performance artists, industrial designers, product designers and so on. A kind of cross-faculty collaboration that Buchanan refers to as a liberal arts of design [7]. But in order for such radical interdisciplinarity to work and in order to be able to engage meaningfully and productively across these radically interdisciplinary boundaries we need a much deeper critical understanding of what design thinking or design practice is both within the discipline of HCI (which is broad enough as it is) and within these other disciplines. We also need to explore ways in which the difficult job of dialogue across boundaries can be achieved.

2 Design-as-Engineering

One perspective on design that has held a central position in HCI at times is what we have termed the design-as-engineering perspective but which some authors have referred to as the conservative view of design [12]. In this account design is seen as going from a fixed problem statement (or requirements specification), to an abstract specification of the solution that is then refined down into an actual implemented solution through a sequence of well-prescribed steps. The design problem, which is seen as given when design begins, may be broken down into smaller parts in order to divide and conquer. This breakdown is followed by a synthesis stage in which solutions to problem parts are aggregated into an overall design solution. This approach is at the heart of most software engineering and formal approaches to system design. Within this approach the emphasis is on proceduralising as much of the design process as possible to ensure knowledge is independent of individual designers and hence the process is replicable. Fallman [12] describes it as the conservative account to emphasise the idea that system properties and behaviours specified first at the abstract level are conserved throughout the subsequent refinement steps. Fallman describes the approach thus:

"According to this account of design, the design process is supposed to progress gradually from the abstract (requirements specifications) to the concrete (resulting artifacts). Progress is achieved through following a sequence of well-described, discrete and rational and structured methodological steps. A good designer in this tradition is someone who is able to follow prescribed action. This tends to de-emphasise the role of the designer, striving towards a disembodied design process built on structured methods and externalised guidelines rather than on the skills and judgment of individual designers." p. 226.

Within HCI, the kinds of approaches to design that seem to fit this account very well are exemplified by methodologies such as MUSE [19] and approaches to usability engineering proposed by both Nielsen [22] and Whiteside et al [28]. Within the more formal software engineering world of HCI, the engineering account is exemplified by approaches to specification based on abstract modelling of the user and the system followed by refinement through to implementation, in which users goals are refined into task sequences which are then mapped to dialogues. Even some scenario-based design view of design [24]. The key features which unite these under the engineering approach are

- Representation of the user or use context as a fixed set of well defined goals, tasks, or needs
- Relatively abstract representations of typical users
- Adherence or orientation to a task or scenario procedural methodology
- An attempt to encapsulate usable design in terms of principles, guidelines or methods that can be re-produced by engineers who are not HCI specialists
- A tendency to see usability as a property of the interface
- An attempt to control the interaction with the user through design

The design-as-engineering approach to HCI can be highly successful. Particularly where the domain of application is well regulated, relatively closed and the user's role and goals in the system can be well defined and adequately captured in for example, a task analysis of tractable size. In these situations there are relatively uncontentious criteria as to what counts as an improved design [16]. But there are limits to this ap-proach and there are other disciplines which offer equally valuable perspectives on HCI. One new area of HCI research that offers challenges to the design-as-engineering approach, and illustrates the value of different perspectives is experience design.

3   The Challenge of Experience-Centred Design

Experience is becoming an increasingly important problem for HCI research and over the last two or three years much has been written about not only what 'user experience' is but also how to design for it. For some, the shift towards placing experience, 'felt-life', and technology at the centre of our theorizing and design practice has led to an exploration of quite radically interdisciplinary literature (E.g. [9, 13, 20]). As an example, our own approach takes its inspiration from the pragmatist philosophy of John Dewey [11] and also the philosophy and literary theory of Mikhail Bakhtin [21]. Briefly our account can be characterised by three themes:

1. A holistic approach to experience wherein the intellectual, sensual and emotional stand as equal partners in experience
2. Continuous engagement and sense making wherein the self is the centre of experience, is already engaged in experience and brings to a situation a history of meanings and anticipated futures in order to complete the experience through acts of sense making
3. A relational or dialogical approach wherein self, object and setting are actively constructed as multiple centres of value with multiple perspectives and where an action, utterance or thing is designed and produced but can never be finalised since the experience of it is always completed in dialogue with those other centres of value.

3.1   A Holistic Approach

Most approaches to experience recognize the need to consider, not only the cognitive, intellectual and rational but also, the emotional and the sensual as important aspects of our experience. Norman [23] for example, identifies visceral, behavioural and reflective levels of design that connect with these aspects of experience. In our approach we argue against the reductive tendency to see these as independent (albeit interacting) levels that can be treated separately. The separation of form and content, behaviour and emotion, aesthetics and function, feeling and knowing is not helpful to an analysis of experience since the quality of experience emerges as the interplay between these things.

3.2   Continuous Engagement and Sense Making

We argue that human experience is also constituted by continuous engagement with the world through acts of sense making at many levels. Continuous engagement involves an irreducible relationship between self and object, the concerned, feeling person acting with materials and tools. In our approach, everyday experience is primarily aesthetic since meaning emerges out of the dynamic relationship between sensual, emotional and intellectual levels of engagement at a particular time and place that bring about a particular quality of experience be it satisfying, enchanting, disappointing or frustrating. In a meaningful and satisfying experience each act relates coherently to the total action and is felt by the experiencer to have a unity or a wholeness that is fulfilling.

This continuous engagement implies that how an individual makes sense of a situation, interaction, episode or artefact is as much about what the individual brings to the experience as it is about what the designer puts there. If we take for example the everyday experience of watching a movie, different people may take away different things from watching the same movie. Even the same person watching a movie for a second time may have different feelings about it and understand it differently. Two people's experiences of the same movie will have some commonalities but there will also be differences because the two people bring different experiences to the movie. Not only different experiences of past films but also different experiences of the day they have just had. The quality of the felt experience of one person after a bad day in the office may be entirely different to that of another person after a relaxing day at home for example. Moreover, one person's feeling that they should really be at home preparing for what is likely to be another demanding day tomorrow brings an expectation of a future experience into the present one. But how we experience the movie isn't only about what we bring to it. The movie also brings something to us, it may temporarily dispel the troubles we bring or allow us see them in a different light. We can be totally engrossed by the narrative and spectacle, we can empathise with the characters. The movie also gives us a new experience, a new story that we can reflect on and recount to others. When we recount our own experiences to others, or other people's experiences are recounted to us, the connection between the individual experience the social and the cultural is made. This connection in turn affects how we reflect on and interpret our experiences. It changes the sense we make of them. It allows us to see how other people might be expecting us to experience the movie that may or may not be how we actually experience it. Either way, we learn something about other people as well as ourselves, the movie and the people that made it. These processes shape how we appropriate our experiences into our sense of self. They are what we refer to as dialogical.

3.3 A Dialogical View of Interaction

Our movie example above highlights the dialogical character of experience, in which self, and others, technology, and setting are actively constructed as multiple centres of value, emotions and feelings and the experience is completed simultaneously by self and others, not determined solely by one or the other. A dialogical relation involves at least two centres of meaning or two consciousnesses. In a dialogical account, the meaning of an action, utterance, communication or artefact, is open because its interaction with the other makes the meaning something else. For example an utterance once uttered remains open to parody, sarcasm, agreement, disagreement, empathy, disgust, etc. Thus the other brings something to an interaction and responds to the act, utterance or artefact in a way that is informed by their own unique position in the world. Since each other is unique, the meaning of the act utterance or artefact is multi-perspectival, open to change and ultimately unfinalisable.

But a dialogical understanding of meaning does not imply that a dialogue is a 'dialogue of the deaf' with neither side comprehending the terms of reference of the other. On the contrary because we can see what is uniquely our contribution and what is uniquely that of the other and what is shared between our selves and others, we can make sense of the other in relation to ourselves and vice versa. Empathy in the sense of being able to see something from one's own perspective and that of another is an essential foundation for dialogue. In the movie example above, if someone tells us that a movie is great and that we'll enjoy it, when we don't, we learn something about the other person, about how they see us, about ourselves, about how we see them and about the movie. This is the essence of a dialogical relation based on centres of value.

3.4 Experience and the Design-as-Craft Perspective

Our account of experience briefly described above stands as an example of the kinds of rich conceptions of experience that are emerging at this time. Such accounts offer serious challenges to design-as-engineering as the sole perspective on design in HCI. Recall that we characterized this approach as representing the user as a set of well defined tasks, an emphasis on methodology and an attempt to control the user's interaction through properties and features of the design. If design-as-engineering is the only perspective on design we have, then inevitably, the richness of the concept of experience will be reduced to properties of the interface and issues of control and prediction. Consider as an example Garrett's [14] idea of designing for experience taken from his recent book on web design:

> "The user experience development process is all about ensuring that no aspect
> of the user's experience with your site happens without your conscious, explicit
> intent. This means taking into account every possibility of every action the user
> is likely to take and understanding the user's expectations at every step of the
> way through that process… That neat, tidy experience actually results from a

whole set of decisions—some small, some large—about how the site looks, how it behaves, and what it allows you to do." (pp. 21–22)

This kind of description of user experience and its relation to design is deeply rooted in a design-as-engineering perspective. Note its emphasis on a development process, the designer's total control over the interaction and the emphasis on visual and behavioral properties of the interface. This approach to experience design does not fit well with the rich conception of experience outlined above. But there are different ways of looking at design that are more appropriate. For example, we have been working with digital jeweller Jayne Wallace [27] whose approach to designing for experience is based on a craft arts perspective. The design-as-craft approach is quite different to the design-as-engineering perspective described earlier. It is more like what Fallman [12] describes as the pragmatist and artistic accounts of design.

The design-as-craft perspective sees design as necessarily being an engagement with a particular world and particular materials, people and artifacts. The emphasis is on the process of making sense of a situation, where designers interpret the effects of their designs on the situation at hand and the effects of the situation at hand on their designs. It has been described as a reflective conversation with the materials of the design situation [26]. Pye [25] captures the difference between craft perspective and the engineering perspective with the terms 'workmanship of risk' and 'workmanship of certainty'. In a craft practice each piece is unique and the outcome to some extent, uncertain. In an engineering practice, methodology and proceduralisation help to reduce risk in favour of certain and reproducible outcomes.

Wallace [27] has created a collection of bespoke jewellery pieces that relate to the particular and personal significance of an individual client. The forms and digital function of the pieces refer to objects, memories, human connections and experiences, which are described as personally precious or meaningful to that client. For Wallace design is about engaging in dialogue with her participants and her materials. She works in a one-to-one relationship with her participants and engages them in dialogue around experiential moments shared through a set of 'stimuli' similar to the 'Probe' sets [15]. The probe stimuli, are not seen as requirements elicitation tools, nor are they simply sources of artistic inspiration removed from the client. Rather they are resources in a dialogue. The pieces she makes are bespoke and unique and create an environment where personally significant aspects of the person's life can be referenced and paid attention to. The finished pieces are not the final statement in the dialogue. Rather she is concerned to understand how the pieces come to be appropriated into each person's life and create new experiences [26].

For Wallace then, design-as-craft is about an emphasis on particular personhood and an empathetic stance in relation to both client and materials [27]. Elsewhere [29], we have also argued that designing for experience requires an empathetic relation between designer, materials, and user as separate centres of value. From a dialogical perspective, empathy is not simply about attempting to be another person in the sense of giving up one's own unique position and experience in order to become, or fuse with the other. Rather it is about understanding another's perspective and its sameness or difference to one's own. A person must understand what it feels like to be in another's position without giving up their own. This perspectivalism is necessary if something new is to be created out of the dialogical engagement between different centres of value. The craft-based approach seems to be much more in tune with this philosophy.

Viewing experience-centred design from the design-as-craft perspective seems to offer insights over and above the more familiar design-as-engineering perspective. However, our aim here is not to supplant one perspective on design with another. Our view is that having these co-existent perspectives enter into dialogue offers more potential for innovation in design and research. No one perspective alone is sufficient, HCI requires a radically interdisciplinary dialogue which crosses sciences and arts. In the case of Wallace's own work, this dialogue centres around the issues of how to deal with the power and range of wireless transmitters in relation to the size and weight and appearance of the wearable jewellery, and issues of how to develop appropriate soft-ware for the delivery of digital content.

4   HCI Design as Radically Interdisciplinary Dialogue

HCI has always been an interdisciplinary subject. In its early years the dialogue was between computer science and cognitive science and in particular, cognitive psychology. This was a natural and easy alliance since both disciplines shared a scientific worldview and a design-as-engineering perspective. Later the dominance of the cognitivist discourse was challenged by social scientists arguing against representationalist models of action in favour of practice theories. But here again the common philosophical foundation was a rationalist, scientific one. Only more recently, have these perspectives on HCI been complemented by perspectives from design disciplines. For example, Crampton Smith and Tabor [8] distinguish between the artist-designer and the engineer-designer. Artist-designers have training and skills areas such as graphic design, film-making, product design and architecture. Crampton Smith and Tabor argue that too often when design-as-engineering dominates, the artist-designer is lim-ited to providing cosmetic look and feel after the 'serious' design work is done. They argue that this is a consequence of artificial distinctions between content and form and between function and aesthetics that occur when design-as-engineering is made central.

Buchanan[7] also distinguishes between science and design in a number of interesting ways. Science is concerned with classification, understanding and explanation of the natural—of what exists. Its purpose is to observe, classify and model what exists objectively and without interfering or changing what they observe. The scientist's position is outside of the system being studied. In contrast, design is concerned with the conception and planning of the artificial—of what does not yet exist. Its purpose is to supplement, re-interpret, change and transform what exists. The designer's position is inside the system affecting and being affected by it. For Buchanan, while scientists often share an interest in the artificial and also need to engage in design thinking, they are also distinguished from designer by being master of a highly specialized body of subject matter knowledge and related methods such as is found in for example the disciplines of biology, physics, mathematics, psychology and so on. Design, however, has no specialized subject matter, it is, by definition, interdisciplinary—the problems addressed seldom fall within one disciplinary boundary.

For Buchanan then, design thinking is more than just the application of science (although it involves this), because it involves solving 'wicked' problems. Wicked problems are problems that are ill-formulated, potentially unbounded, open to alternative formulations with no obvious means of choice or stopping rule and are particular to a situation, setting or context. A wicked problem is open to a potentially universal set of solutions yet the designer must come up with a particular and concrete solution out of the particular and concrete materials that constitute the problem situation. As an example to illustrate this, consider designing a solution to the problem of elderly and disabled people who can't get out of their homes to buy groceries [3]. There is no subject-matter independent solution to this problem and the subject matter of this problem could be medical, social, technological, or economic. any one of a number of subject-matters is potentially relevant to a concrete solution. Design thinking is concerned with how a concrete solution might be forged out of these abstract subject matters. Thus, while design practice can be characterised in terms of a philosophy or set of principles and methods, heuristics etc., design thinking is fundamentally concerned with the particular solution, and this for Buchanan, is the fundamental difference between scientific thinking and design thinking, there can be no "science of the particular". A statistical analysis of the number of falls amongst the over 65s can, for example, produce information like the odds of a fall for a person in that age group, but it cannot tell you that your grandmother will break her leg on the way to the corner shop next week. For Buchanan and for Crampton Smith and Tabor, design is an integrative discipline in which engineering and art stand as equal partners in a dialogical process, separated by different subject matters, values and ways of looking, but united by a common problem and by design thinking. These are essential pre-requisites for innovation and creative understanding to occur, along with an empathetic relation between the individuals concerned. But the process of integration across disciplines is not always easy.

5   Resources for Interdisciplinary Dialogue

Dialogue across disciplines will always be difficult. A fundamental problem is having sufficient knowledge of another's language, practice, perspective and ways of looking to begin to engage empathetically in dialogue. A tendency in this situation is to reduce the other's perspective to one's own. That is to do a kind of translation process which can undermine the uniqueness of that perspective. Ultimately, we will argue that the way forward here is the kind of liberal arts education that we will discuss in the next section. But in addition dialogue can be fostered by a number of conceptual tools, philosophies and resources that help designers to see problems from another's perspective. For Buchanan [7], one of the most important of these conceptual tools is the 'doctrine of placements', a kind of conceptual re-positioning of the design problem. He contrasted placements with the more scientific notion of classification thus:

> "Understanding the difference between a category and placement is essential
> if design thinking is to be regarded as more that a series of creative accidents.
> Categories have fixed meanings that are accepted within the framework of a
> theory or a philosophy, and serve as a basis for analysing what already exists. Placements have boundaries to shape and constrain meaning but are not

rigidly fixed and determinate. The boundary of a placement gives a context or orientation to thinking, but the application to a specific situation can generate a new perception of that situation and, hence, a new possibility to be tested. Therefore, placements are sources of new ideas and possibilities when applied to problems in concrete circumstances." (pp. 10–11)

By moving a concrete design problem out of its habitual placement and placing it in some other disciplinary context or orientation, an innovative solution can occur. For example, instead of seeing a building as a physical space—its habitual placement, it could be viewed as an emotional space or information space. In a similar way we have tried to encourage theoretical insight about interactive system design by reframing technology as experience [20] and reframing design as novelistic authorship [29]. The doctrine of placements also has similarities to the process of defamiliarisation that ethnographers have described [2] and also to Agre's ideas on reversing centre and margin [1].

The doctrine of placements and these other techniques serve an important role in allowing disciplines with specialist subject matters to contribute to interdisciplinary dialogue. By using the doctrine of placements to generate a way of framing a problem and its solution, the designer establishes what Buchanan refers to as a 'principle of relevance' for knowledge from the arts and sciences. Placements help determine how a particular discipline's subject matter might be relevant to a design problem without reducing the problem to that discipline.

We have also argued elsewhere for the use of open representations, rich scenarios, cultural probes and prototyping as tools in dialogical design [29], and Fallman [12] and others have argued a central role for sketching in dialogical design. But is important to note that it is not any inherent property of these tools that facilitates a dialogical approach. Rather it is the way they are used in design in practice. So for example, Gaver [15] has argued that cultural probes when appropriated into a design-as-engineering perspective resemble a closed requirements elicitation technique rather than a stimulus to dialogue favoured by Gaver and typical of Wallace's use described earlier. When used in a dialogical way they support innovative design by helping to open up spaces and new ways of looking at the problem and solution in ways very similar to Buchanan's doctrine of placements.

Brown and Duguid [6], introduce the term genre (more commonly associated with literary theory and cultural and media studies) as a way of characterising how an object's placement in an unspoken context determines in part, how the object will be understood. Knowing for example, that you are reading a detective novel generates certain expectations and certain habitual ways of understanding what is written, pictured, or said. Many design disciplines have toolkits of resources and styles to encour-age this kind of implicit processes of framing. But Brown and Duguid argue that unlike classification systems of a more scientific provenance, genres offer more per-meable boundaries whose crossing stimulates innovation and move a discipline on. Crossing an unseen boundary brings the boundary to light and leads to a questioning that can give rise to a boundary re-definition. Good artists push the boundaries of a genre which leads to the response, "is this art?" and thereby define a tradition and a new way of thinking. Brown and Duguid, use the example of Jazz to show how innovation emerges at boundary crossings:

"In jazz, for instance, Miles Davies claimed that Wynton Marsalis was too respectful of old forms to go anywhere new. Other musicians, however criticized Davis for moving too far beyond the conventional forms to be understood. Almost every time that he moved across musical boundaries, Davis was charged with incoherence ... Before long, however, it became apparent that he had built a new audience for his work, and a new frontier for musicians—often led by Davis himself—to cross." (p.142)

In addition to showing how pushing genre boundaries stimulates innovation and progress, Brown and Duguid's example also describes a process of critical reflective practice [1, 26], in which practitioner's continually question assumptions and ways of interpreting. This kind of critical reflection is particularly well facilitated when arts and sciences meet in interdisciplinary dialogue. At these boundaries radically different perspectives on the same design problem offer significant surpluses for forging new frontiers. For instance Bolter and Gramola [4], who take a digital arts perspective as their starting point, critically question a number of assumptions that are fundamental to a the usability engineering perspective on interaction design. For example, they bring to light assumptions concerning the utility of transparency and invisibility as design goals and note the ways in which such principles can stifle innovation and research. In place of the metaphor of window they offer a metaphor of mirror and in place of transparency they discuss the value of reflectivity, and argue that in reality, interaction is an oscillation between moments of transparency and reflection. But Bolter and Gramola go further than this, and like many from an arts perspective use their critical reflective practice to challenge assumptions about the role of technology in society and culture.

6   Towards a Liberal Arts of HCI

HCI researchers having a long history of interdisciplinary dialogue, but despite the best of intentions and conceptual tools, it can sometimes seem like a 'dialogue of the deaf'. At times this is a result of participants not having a sufficiently empathetic stance towards each other, preferring to establish one design approach (e.g., design-as-engineering, design-as-art) as the dominant voice and translate the other's terms of reference into that voice. At other times it is plainly and simply the fact that the participants lack sufficient common ground with each other even to begin to identify surplus and relate their own expertise to that of others. As Kapor [18] argues, many people in HCI lack the technical grounding to be an effective participant in the dialogue. Programmers quickly lose respect for people who do not understand the technical limitations, and artists feel artificially fettered by technical limitations and lack respect for programmers who fail to grasp the importance of conceptual work.

From our own experience, we observe that artistic and engineering skills seldom reside in the same person, largely because there is too much subject matter knowledge and too much practical experience for most people trained at undergraduate level in one discipline to be 'converted' at postgraduate level to expertise in another. However, following Buchanan's consideration of design as a liberal art, there is more that could be done in higher education to provide the common ground necessary for radically interdisciplinary dialogue. A broader education in HCI as a design discipline would integrate skill sets and subject matters from the parent disciplines. Computer science, psychology, sociology, visual, literary and performing arts, TV film and thea-tre would all become applied subjects matters in a new liberal arts of HCI. Such an education would embrace not only an understanding of the skills of the software programmer, electronics engineer and network developer, but also the techniques of the artist-designer, including graphic design, sketching, the use of 3-D visualization tools, and the use of multimedia editing tools for scenario development. In addition, qualitative and quantitative research methods would provide a basis for understanding the process of empirical research and evaluation. There would be a strong practical, problem-based and team based ethos to the mode of study. But in addition such an education could offer foundation courses in science, technology and the design disciplines as well as the philosophical foundations of interaction design. In particular, the critical, reflective thinking of the humanities curriculum would have a valuable role to play in a critical technical practice of HCI design.

7   Conclusions

In this paper we have argued that since HCI has grown and developed to take more complex challenges beyond usability, there needs to be more emphasis on radical interdisciplinary research which crosses sciences and arts, we have argued that inter-disciplinary dialogue is essential to 'wicked problems' like designing for experience, and we have outlined some of the sensibilities, tools and training that may be required to make this possible. If nothing else, we are arguing that HCI might be best under-stood as a design discipline that integrates radically interdisciplinary research and practice. To us, this has a liberating feel to it. Shifting the focus to design and explor-ing what the term actually means in different subject matter disciplines has provided a positive energy to our research. This shift is also not without precedent. Papers at the ACM CHI conference (e.g. [12]) are exploring what a design-oriented HCI might mean and in the UK, research councils are beginning to seek to support collaborations across arts and sciences. But framing HCI as a design discipline is not without its risks.

The art and design education sector was severely criticized throughout the last decade. The 1995/6 HESA first destination study revealed that those students who studied creative Arts and Design were most likely to be unemployed (12%) one year after graduation. This crisis was relieved by the publication of a document called "The Creative Industries" by the Department of Culture, Media and Sport in 1998 [10]. This document expanded previous classifications of the cultural industries to include commercial arts such as advertising and interactive and leisure software. This new aggregate of sectors produced some startling figures: the creative industries were growing at twice the rate of the economy as a whole, they contributed more than four percent of the domestic economy, they employed around one and a half million people and generated over sixty billion pounds a year. Although the proportion of art and design graduates who went on to success in the creative industries might be small, their contribution to GDP, so the argument went, was disproportionately high. The design education sector then underwent something of a transformation. From justifying its existence in terms of how well it developed communication skills or teamwork it became a glittering example of the utility of higher education to the general economy.

HCI has long found gainful employment for ethnographers and ethnomethodologists who are probably as surprised as anyone that their sociological training should turn out to be useful to design. As HCI's scope expands still further, arts and humanities graduates may yet discover that their studies were not, as they probably thought, without immediate utility. Indeed HCI may yet become the last bastion of a liberal arts education. Subject disciplines like sociology, psychology and english literature may offer the best grounding in understanding the human in human computer interaction, and craft disciplines together with engineering science and visual and performance arts may offer the best grounding in designing and building interactive environments, products and services.

Acknowledgements

This paper was developed from the keynote address given by the first author at DSVIS 2005. Many thanks to the EPSRC for support in the form of the Leonardo (GR/T21042/01) and Affective Communication networks (GR/T21264/01) which have provided the opportunity of real radical interdisciplinary explorations and for support in the form of a visiting fellowship (GR/S18779/01) and a responsive mode grant (GR/S70326/01) that have allowed us to develop our theoretical and methodo-logical framework for experience-centred design.

References

1. P. Agre. *Computation and Human Experience*. Cambridge University Press, 1997.
2. G. Bell, M. Blythe, and P. Sengers. Making by making strange: Defamiliarisation and the design of domestic technologies. *Transactions on Computer-Human Interaction Special Issue on HCI and Social Issues*, (In press).
3. M. Blythe and A.F. Monk. Net neighbours: Adapting hci methods to cross the digital divide. *Interacting with Computers*, 17:35–56, 2005.
4. J.D. Bolter and D. Gramola. *Windows and Mirrors: Interaction Design, Digital Art, and the Myth of Transparency*. MIT Press, 2003.
5. J.D. Bolter and R. Grusin. *Remediation: Understanding New Media*. MIT Press, 2001.
6. J.S. Brown and P. Duguid. Keeping it simple. In T. Winograd, editor, *Bringing Design to Software*, pages 129–145. ACM Press, 1996.
7. R. Buchanan. Wicked problems in design thinking. In R. Buchanan and V. Margolin, editors, *The Idea of Design*, pages 3–20. MIT Press, 1995.
8. G. Crampton Smith and P. Tabor. The role of the artist designer. In T. Winograd, editor, *Bringing Design to Software*, pages 37–57. ACM Press, 1996.
9. Marc Davis. Theoretical foundations for experiential systems design. In *ETP '03: Proceedings of the 2003 ACM SIGMM Workshop on Experiential Telepresence*, pages 45–52. ACM Press, 2003.
10. Department of Culture, Media and Sport. Creative industries mapping document, 1998.
11. J. Dewey. *Art as Experience*. Pedigree, 1934.
12. D. Fallman. Design-oriented human-computer interaction. In *Proceedings of CHI 2003*, pages 225–232. ACM Press, 2003.
13. J. Forlizzi and S.Ford. The building blocks of experience: An early framework for interaction designers. In *Proceedings of Designing Interactive Systems (DIS 2000)*, pages 419–423. ACM Press, 2000.

14. J.J. Garrett. *The Elements of User Experience: User-Centred Design for the Web*. New Riders Publishers, 2002.
15. B. Gaver, A. Boucher, S. Pennington, and B. Walker. Cultural probes and the value of uncertainty. *Interactions*, XI, September–October 2004.
16. W.D. Gray, B.E. John, and M.E. Atwood. The précis of Project Ernestine or an overview of a validation of GOMS. In P. Bauersfeld, J. Bennet, and G. Lynch, editors, *Striking a Balance: Proceedings of the CHI'92 =Conference on Human Factors in Computing Systems*, pages 307–312. ACM Press, 1992.
17. M.D. Harrison and P. Barnard. Integrating cognitive and system models in human-computer interaction. In A. Sutcliffe and L. Macaulay, editors, *People and computers V*, pages 87–104. Cambridge University Press, 1989.
18. M. Kapor. A software design manifesto. In T. Winograd, editor, *Bringing Design to Software*, pages 1–9. ACM Press, 1996.
19. K.Y. Lim and J. Long. *The MUSE Method for Usability Engineering*. Cambridge University Press, 1994.
20. J. McCarthy and P. Wright. *Technology as Experience*. MIT Press, 2004.
21. G.S. Morson and C. Emerson. *Mikhael Bakhtin: Creation of a Prosaics*. Stanford University Press, 1990.
22. J. Nielsen. *Usability Engineering*. Academic Press, 1992.
23. D.A. Norman and S. Draper. *User Centered System Design: New perspectives on Human-Computer Interaction*. Lawrence Erlbaum Associates, 1986.
24. S. Pocock, M.D. Harrison, P. Wright, and P. Johnson. Thea: A technique for human error assessment early in design. In M. Hirose, editor, *Proceedings of INTERACT '01. IFIP TC.13 International Conference on Human-Computer Interaction*, 2001.
25. D. Pye. *The Nature and Art of Workmanship*. Herbert Press, 1968.
26. D. Schon. *The Reflective Practitioner*. Basic Books, 1983.
27. J. Wallace and M. Press. All this useless beauty: Craft practice in design for a digital age. *The Design Journal*, 7.2, 2004.
28. J. Whiteside, J. Bennett, and K. Holtzblatt. Usability engineering: Our experience and evolution. In M. Helander, editor, *Handbook of Human-Computer Interaction*, pages 791–817. Elsevier Science Publishers, 1988.
29. P.C. Wright and J. McCarthy. The value of the novel in understanding work for design. In A. Pirhonen, H. Isomki, C. Roast, and P. Saariluoma, editors, *Future Interaction Design*, pages 9–30. Springer, 2005.

Formalising Performative Interaction

Alan Dix[1], Jennifer G. Sheridan[1], Stuart Reeves[2], Steve Benford[2],
and Claire O'Malley[2]

[1] Computing Department, InfoLab 21, South Drive,
Lancaster University, Lancaster LA1 4WA
alan@hcibook.com, sheridaj@comp.lancs.ac.uk
[2] School of Computer Science and IT,
Nottingham University, Jubilee Campus,
Wollaton Road, Nottingham NG8 1BB
{str, sdb}@cs.nott.ac.uk,
com@psychology.nottingham.ac.uk

Abstract. In this paper we attempt to formalise some of the basic attributes of performative interaction against a background of sociological analysis in order to better understand how computer interfaces may support performance. We show how this generic formalisation can be used in the deconstruction, analysis and understanding of performative action and more broadly in live performance. Two examples of this form of analysis are shown: the installation piece *Deus Oculi*; and Stelarc's *Ping Body* performance piece. The analysis of these pieces renders visible the varied (re)mappings of the causal nature of interaction, direct and indirect effects, and how these are perceived and exploited by the various members of performance social groupings. Our aim, then, is to provide a model that can be used to explore the relationships that exist in performative activities across domains.

1   Introduction

Computing technology has come to be used increasingly in many forms of performance in order to augment and extend (human) agents' ability [1] for performative action. Although this may be seen as part of a wider trend in art to engage with sciences [10], computer technology in particular presents the artist with ways of breaking some essential physical restrictions (such as location, e.g., mobile phones), and obfuscating causal relations between actions. The very nature of this use of technology in art also breaks from the original emphasis in human-computer interaction (HCI) of efficiency, and as such we have few means for investigating these breaks. Our interest, then, is in defining a formal method for describing performative actions.

2   What Do We Mean by Performance?

While there are many, often conflicting, definitions of live performance, it is necessary that we point out that it is not our intent to create a new definition. However, to improve the clarity of this paper, we must discuss what we include in our definition of live

S.W. Gilroy and M.D. Harrison (Eds.): DSVIS 2005, LNCS 3941, pp. 15–25, 2006.

performance. The complex essense of performance may be viewed in many ways. For example, live performance may be seen as "tripartite interaction" [8], i.e., synchronous, real-time interaction that occurs between a number of agents (such as performers, participants in the performance, and "observers" of the performance). Some models, on the other hand, only draw a distinction between a performer and a spectator and their transitioning relationship as mediated by the interface [5]. For the purposes of this paper, our simplified view on the 'component' parts of performance follows a tripartite model, introducing the key notion of 'framings' (discussed shortly):

- *Performers* construct the 'frame' of the performance, and perform to an audience with a particular (typically premeditated) intent.
- *Participants* interpret the 'framing' of the performance, and are engaged in the intended performance through some witting or unwitting activity.
- *Bystanders* also interpret this performance framing and although their presence is integral to the performance, their performative actions are not. They may also interpret a framing either wittingly or unwittingly.

Note that we consider the performative actions themselves (i.e., those actions conducted by participants and performers) to be very much part of the performance, not just the effects that are produced as a result of them (as discussed in [6]). Other definitions deepen this action-to-effect mapping, including, for example, gestures around the interface [5], however this is beyond the scope of this paper.

The concept of a performance framing here is central to understanding the background sociological concepts inside which our formal method is placed. The "frame" is a term developed from sociologist Erving Goffman's work [3] broadly meaning a constructed context within the limits of which individual human agency and social interaction takes place. For example, a theatrical frame [3][pp. 124–155] involves the construction of a higher-level frame on top of a "primary framework," i.e., the reality in which the fantasy takes place. In this example, actors assume a character, audiences suspend disbelief and events have their meaning transformed (e.g., compare the use of a mobile phone in public with its use in a theatre). We note that although all social interaction may be seen from a dramaturgical perspective, meaning everyday social interaction becomes performance in some sense [2], we deliberately narrow our analysis to cover more stabilised 'established' forms of performance. What this means, then, is defining performance framings as an activity done within the intended frame "by an individual or group" who have some established knowledge about the frame, and are "in the presence of and for another individual or group" [7].

Also pertinent to this model is 'intent'; participants and bystanders may perceive the performance differently than the performer intended. However, in this paper we do not focus on intention since intention rests with the makers of the live performance (orchestrators, designers, technicians, etc.). We believe that intention is imperative to the understanding of HCI in live performance and yet this issue adds a layer of complexity that deserves its own careful analysis. Instead, then, we focus on the nature of observation and participation, and how technology changes bystander perception so that we may use this knowledge as an entry point for understanding the application of interactivity in this domain.

3   Overview

We begin with a generic model of activity and perception. This reflects the fact that much of performance is really about social action. We then go on to look at the beliefs (the reality of some being or phenomenon) that participants have about their actions and the effects of those actions. Together these enable us to produce (weak) definitions of witting and unwitting performative action based on beliefs about the effects of actions and the extent of the performative frame (that the being or phenomenon is part of the performance).

4   Actions

The key objects in performance are represented by two sets:

Agent

> The set of all (human, animal, machine, etc.) agents involved in the performance.

Phenomenon

> The set of all world phenomena that can be affected or sensed by agents. This includes real world physical things like cups, balls, etc., visual and aural things like the sound at a location of a room, and virtual things like the appearance of a web page. However, the directly perceivable phenomena are ultimately real world rather than virtual (e.g., the appearance of the screen on which the web page is shown).

At any moment and situation an agent has a set of actions available:

$$available\_actions : Agent \rightarrow set(Action)$$

This and the other relations below will change depending on the current context and time. However to avoid repeating '$Context \times Time$' as parameters for every function we will take these as read.

If an agent actually performs an action at a particular moment we write this as '$A[a]$'. Of course, this is only possible if the action is available:

$$A[a] \Rightarrow a \in available\_actions(A)$$

These actions act on phenomena:

$$effect : Action \rightarrow set(Phenomenon)$$

However, in general there are also indirect influences due to physical or digital causal effects, for example the sound of played music may be picked up by microphones that create lighting effects, or dropping a glass may make a crash!

$$causal\_link : Phenomenon \rightarrow set(Phenomenon)$$

Note that this *causal_link* will depend on the behaviour of technological and mechanical devices.

These causal links give rise to a set of phenomena that are indirectly influenced by a person's actions and hence may influence others:

$$indirect\_effect \quad : \quad Action \rightarrow set(Phenomenon)$$
$$indirect\_effect\,(a) = causal\_link(effect(a)) \cup effect(a)$$

We write $A[a] \searrow p$ to mean that agent A performs action a that potentially indirectly affects phenomena p:

$$A[a] \searrow p \iff A[a] \wedge p \in indirect\_effect(a)$$

5   Perception

Similarly each agent has a set of phenomena that can be perceived at any moment:

$$perceivable : Agent \rightarrow set(Phenomenon)$$

As with the case of actions, the causal links in the world mean that an agent may indirectly perceive phenomena not otherwise directly observable.

$$indirectly\_perceivable \quad : \quad Action \rightarrow set(Phenomenon)$$
$$indirectly\_perceivable\,(a) = causal\_link(perceivable(A)) \cup perceivable(A)$$

An agent may directly perceive the effects of another's actions if these sets interact. We write $p \nearrow A$ to mean that agent A may perceive phenomena p:

$$p \nearrow A \iff p \in indirectly\_perceivable(a)$$

6   Influences

If the indirect effect of one agent intersects with the perceivable phenomena of another, then the actions of one may influence the other. We will write $A \searrow B$ if agent A potentially influences agent B:

$$A \searrow B \iff \exists a, p \; s.t. \; A[a] \searrow p \nearrow B$$

Note that this is just representing that some action may give rise to a perceived effect. It does not necessarily mean that agent A necessarily performs the particular actions that may be indirectly perceived by agent B, nor that agent B actually notices the phenomena affected by agent A, nor even if the effects are perceived, that agent B realises that agent A is their cause. Figure 1 illustrates some combinations of influence and perception. We can consider a stronger conceptualisation of interaction by recognising that they can occur in two forms: actions by agent A that give rise to an effect perceivable by agent B; and actions that give rise to an effect that is actually noticed by agent B. This, however, does not distinguish effects on B that may be unconscious or not the focus of attention (e.g., peripheral awareness), or ones that may not be perceived as being in any way explicitly caused (e.g., small changes in temperature).

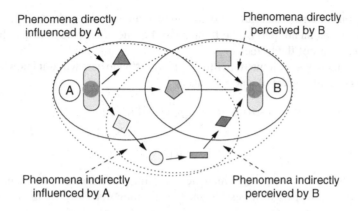

Phenomena directly
influenced by A

Phenomena directly
perceived by B

Phenomena indirectly
influenced by A

Phenomena indirectly
perceived by B

Fig. 1. Spheres of influence and perception

7   Knowledge, Frames and Performance

A key difference between someone who acts and is observed or perceived in some way by another and one who actively performs for another is one of knowledge. To perform for another one must know that the other person may perceive the effects of one's actions.

We will write '$\beta_A\{X\}$' to represent the current beliefs of A about the world (read '$\beta_A\{X\}$' as '*A believes X*'). If we perform for another then we must both act and believe that the other person will perceive our actions:

$$A\ performs\_to\ B \Rightarrow A[a] \wedge \beta_A\{A[a] \searrow B\}$$

This would include everything from speaking to someone to hitting a person on the head, but performances in the artistic sense require more. The participating agents have, in some way, to understand that their actions and effects are part of the performance. This is the role of the frame that was discussed earlier. Giving your friend a toffee during a play is not part of the performance, but an actor standing on stage and throwing the toffee probably is.

Each agent has different levels of experience in interpreting and making sense of framings. In this way performance framings are active and dynamic since they may be perceived differently by different people (e.g., a child and an adult). In the traditional theatrical context, it is commonly understood (although often also deliberately broken) as the time between the curtain rising and falling and the space on stage [3][p. 139]. In street theatre the physical and temporal boundaries are not so well defined. What is important is what people believe to be the frame.

As a simplification we will model the frame as a collection of phenomena (e.g., the things that happen on stage). Using this we can have a stronger definition of performance:

$$A\ performs\_to\ B \iff A[a] \wedge \exists p \in Phenomenon\ s.t.$$
$$\beta_A\{A[a] \searrow p\} \wedge \beta_A\{p \in Frame\} \wedge$$
$$\beta_A\{p \nearrow B\} \wedge \beta_A\{\beta_B\{p \in Frame\}\}$$

That is, we must believe that our actions influence another through some phenomena, that these phenomena are part of the frame, and that the other person also believes the phenomena are part of the frame.

We can contrast this with the 'unwitting performer' who acts without knowledge that their actions constitute part of a performance:

$$A \; unwittingly\_performs\_to \; B \iff \exists p \; s.t. \; A[a] \searrow p \diagup B \; \wedge$$
$$\neg(\beta_A\{A[a] \searrow p\} \wedge \beta_A\{p \in Frame\}) \; \wedge$$
$$\beta_B\{p \in Frame\}$$

Note that there are two ways in which the unwitting performer may fail to understand that their actions are part of a performance. They may not know of the existence or bounds of the frame:

$$\neg\beta_A\{p \in Frame\}$$

or may not know of the effects of their actions:

$$\neg\beta_A\{A[a] \searrow p\}$$

The latter may occur because the unwitting performer does not understand the causal connections between directly influenced and indirectly influenced phenomena.

8   The Effect of Technology

Adding technological interfaces will change the available phenomena that can be acted upon (e.g., knobs, dials) or perceived (e.g., screens, sound from speakers).

Furthermore, technological interfaces can affect the existing phenomena and create new causal connections. For example, adding a microphone and speaker will make a causal connection between the sound near the microphone and the sound near the speaker.

Technological manipulations may even remove or weaken existing causal connections. For example, bright lights or loud sounds may block other stimuli.

Whilst physical linkages are readily visible, technological ones may be invisible. This invisibility means that those implicated in a performance may not know whether their actions will affect particular phenomena and hence, as noted above, they as participants or bystanders may unwittingly place themselves within the performance frame.

The act of discovering or understanding these connections effectively shifts one's perception of the boundaries of the performance frame. This thus creates changes in the way in which those involved may view their roles in a performance and so also affect their behaviour. This is exactly what occurs in *Deus Oculi*, which we shall now examine.

9   Analysis of *Deus Oculi*

Deus Oculi was an interactive installation exhibited at the Chelsea International Crafts Fair in September 1999. This was a large renaissance-style painted scene featuring two figures whose faces were painted on small doors. Behind the doors were small CCTV

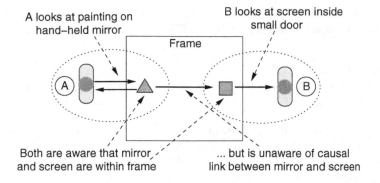

A looks at painting on hand-held mirror

B looks at screen inside small door

Frame

Both are aware that mirror and screen are within frame

... but is unaware of causal link between mirror and screen

Fig. 2. *Deus Oculi*

Table 1. Tableaux of beliefs during *Deus Oculi*

	actual situation	β_A (*A*'s beliefs)	β_B (*B*'s beliefs)
1. A and B come to the exhibit	$mirror \in Frame$ $screen \in Frame$ $mirror \seararrow screen$	$mirror \in Frame$ $screen \in Frame +$ knows B's beliefs	$mirror \in Frame$ $screen \in Frame +$ knows A's beliefs
2. A looks at mirror, B looks at screen	$mirror \nearrow A$ $screen \nearrow B$ $A \seararrow mirror$	$mirror \nearrow A$ $screen \nearrow B$ $A \seararrow mirror$	$mirror \nearrow A$ $screen \nearrow B$ $A \seararrow mirror$
3. B sees A in screen	$A \seararrow mirror \seararrow$ $screen \nearrow B$		
4. B infers relationships			$mirror \seararrow screen$
5. A looks at mirror, B looks at screen	$mirror \nearrow B \; B \seararrow$ $mirror \; mirror \seararrow$ $screen \; screen \nearrow B$	$screen \in Frame$	$B \seararrow mirror \seararrow$ $screen \nearrow A + $ knows A's beliefs

screens that were linked directly to two hand-held mirrors situated on either side of the painting. When a visitor, assuming the role of a performer, picked a mirror and looked into it, an image of their face was captured on a hidden video camera and then displayed on one of the screens in the painting. As a result, performers could not see the effects of their own manipulations resulting in highly engaging collaborative exchanges as the spectators pointed them out to the performers and/or bystanders [4].

Figure 2 shows the phenomena and frame in *Deus Oculi*. Two visitors, Alison (A) and Brian (B) visit the gallery and view the exhibit. The tableaux in Table 1 shows the various stages that they go through. Initially (step 1) they both realise that the mirror and screen are part of the frame. However, they are unaware that there is a causal link between the two.

At step 2, Alison looks in at the mirror and Brian looks at the screen however, the mirror and screen are linked by the hidden camera hence at step 3 Brian sees Alison's face.

At step 3 Alison is an unwitting participant. Looking back at our definition, the key phenomenon ('p' in the formula) is the screen. Brian believes the screen is part of the frame. Alison's action of looking at the mirror indirectly affects the screen, however Alison does not know that she is having this effect because she is ignorant of the causal link.

$$\left.\begin{array}{l} A[a] \searrow screen \nearrow B \wedge \\ \neg\beta_A\{A[a] \searrow screen\} \\ \wedge\beta_B\{screen \in Frame\} \end{array}\right\} \Longleftrightarrow A \; unwittingly\_performs\_to \; B$$

At this point however, Brian realises that there is some connection between mirror and screen and this is reflected in his changed beliefs at step 4. Brian does not share his new knowledge with Alison but knows that she does believe that the screen is part of the frame of the exhibit.

Now they swap positions. Brian looks in the mirror and makes silly faces whilst Alison looks at the screen. Similar to step 2 and 3, the hidden camera means that Brian's faces are visible to Alison. However, unlike Alison at step 3, Brian is aware of this link.

As he knows about the link it is not hard to work out that if he looks in the mirror Alison will see him.

$$\beta_B\{A[a] \searrow mirror\} \wedge \beta_B\{mirror \searrow screen\}$$
$$\Rightarrow \beta_B\{A[a] \searrow screen\}$$

Of course, even with perfect knowledge some technical interfaces may be such that with bounded rationality we are not able to work out all such relationships, or they may only become apparent after a long time. However, in this case Brian does know that his actions affect the screen that Alison is seeing and that both he and she regard this as part of the exhibit's frame.

This makes him a witting participant:

$$\left.\begin{array}{l} \beta_B\{B[look\_in\_mirror] \searrow screen\} \\ \wedge\beta_B\{screen \in Frame\} \\ \wedge\beta_B\{screen \nearrow A\} \\ \wedge\beta_B\{\beta_A\{screen \in Frame\}\} \end{array}\right\} \Rightarrow B \; performs\_to \; A$$

Brian's actions, whilst not specifically scripted into the exhibit are expected. In acquiring knowledge about the performance frame Brian transitions from an unwitting to witting participant which gives him the ability to perform to an audience.

Brian's performative actions with and around the interface are tethered in a relatively linear fashion to the resulting effects (e.g., his face on the screen). This causal mapping enables swift (and humorous) transitions from unwitting to witting participant. Next we shall examine how these causal mappings themselves have greater depth, using Stelarc's *Ping Body* as an example.

10 Analysis of *Ping Body*

Ping Body, in contrast to *Deus Oculi*, is explicitly framed as a performance, rather than as an installation that encourages performative action. Stelarc performs his work, Ping Body, to demonstrate not how the body can be actuated by other bodies in other places, but how the body can be actuated by internet activity itself thus producing an inversion of the usual interface of the body to the internet. Not only is Stelarc's performance an event, but the performative interaction is an event itself [6]. A fascinating concept in this piece, then, is how this inversion exposes the complex and obscure causal mappings that constitute routine Internet activity, (i.e., routine activity as would be experienced for the usual interface of the body to the Internet). In one performance Stelarc describes:

> "We also used the ping Internet protocol in a performance where the Body was moving through internet data. During the performance I would ping 40 global sites. The reverberating signals were measured in milliseconds mapped to the body muscles in a very crude way, but what was effectively happening was that the body was becoming a barometer of Internet activity. The Body moved according to the internet activity from that global site." [9]

Figure 3 illustrates the performative activity occurring in this performance.

Firstly we can decompose this in a similar way to *Deus Oculi*, drawing out the mechanics of unwitting and witting performance (unlike *Deus Oculi*, however, the participants in this case never know about their participation in the performance, and do not necessarily make the transition within the time span of the performance):

$$\beta_A \left\{ \begin{array}{l} R[a] \searrow N \wedge \\ N[a] \searrow B \wedge \\ B[a] \nearrow A \wedge \\ \neg\beta_R\{R[a] \searrow B\} \wedge \\ \left\{ \begin{array}{l} \{R \in Frame\} \wedge \\ \{\neg\beta_R\{R[a] \searrow B\} \wedge \\ \{N[a] \searrow B\} \end{array} \right\} \wedge \\ \beta_B \left\{ \begin{array}{l} \{R \in Frame\} \wedge \\ \{\neg\beta_R\{R[a] \searrow \\ B\} \\ \wedge\{N[a] \searrow B\} \end{array} \right\} \wedge \end{array} \right\} \Rightarrow R \; unwittingly\_performs\_to \; A$$

The causal links between these unwitting participants (R) and Stelarc's (B) body movements are aggregated, which becomes part of this process of inverting the interface. Figure 4 illustrates several examples of different sets of causal linkages.

We might think of *Deus Oculi* as exploiting a relatively linear causal link, i.e., $A \searrow$ *mirror* $\searrow$ *screen* $\nearrow$ B, Figure 4(a). Fig. 4(b), on the other hand, illustrates a more obfuscated, indirect chain of causal links, e.g., $A \searrow p_1 \searrow p_2 \searrow p_3 \searrow p_4 \nearrow B$. We can even imagine a tree of indirect causal links, Fig. 4(c). For *Ping Body*, however, these causal links are not only highly obfuscated causal links, but also aggregates of causal links such that (put crudely):

$$R_1[a] \cup R_2[b] \cup R_3[c] \cup \ldots R_n[z] \searrow p \nearrow B$$

In short, then, we are able to unpack some of the elementary details that lie behind these experiences by assuming a simple formalisation of the various interactions that take place in both examples, *Deus Oculi* and *Ping Body*.

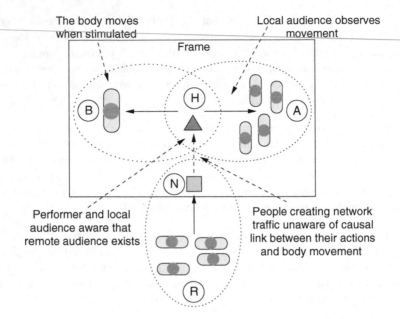

The body moves when stimulated

Local audience observes movement

Frame

Performer and local audience aware that remote audience exists

People creating network traffic unaware of causal link between their actions and body movement

Fig. 3. *Ping Body*

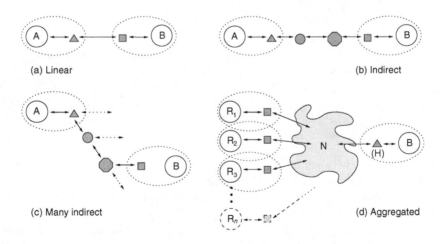

(a) Linear

(b) Indirect

(c) Many indirect

(d) Aggregated

Fig. 4. An analysis of the causal linkages

11   Conclusion

In this paper we have seen how performative acts may be formalised in order to understand how interaction with interfaces impacts performers, participants and bystanders, and how sociological aspects in turn impact this interaction itself. Some salient features of our formalisation are

- The direct and indirect effects of actions performed by a (human) agent
- Direct and indirect perception of those effects
- Influences as the combination of indirect effects and indirect perception
- Causal links that bind these together and their varyingly complex structures
- Wittingness and its relationship to the frame of performance

Through our two examples, we demonstrated how this model may be applied in order to reveal the detail of interactions that may occur by virtue of the interface's configuration within a given setting.

The main application for such decomposition would be to direct the design of interfaces in order to craft certain experiences both for the performer of that system and, as we have also considered here, the resulting experience for participants and bystanders. Future work will be concerned with analysing further examples of live performance as well as applying this model as a design tool, in particular how it may be exploited and subverted in implementations of interfaces designed for performance.

References

1. J Clarke. pros + thesis. In Adrian Heathfield, editor, *Live: Art and Performance*, pages 208–209. Tate, London, 2004.
2. Erving Goffman. *The Presentation of the Self in Everyday Life*. Doubleday, New York, 1959.
3. Erving Goffman. *Frame Analysis: An Essay on the Organization of Experience*. Harper & Row, 1974.
4. Christian Heath and Jon Hindmarsh. Analysing interaction: Video, ethnography and situated conduct. In T. May, editor, *Qualitative Research in Practice*, pages 99–121. Sage, 2002.
5. Stuart Reeves, Steve Benford, Claire O'Malley, and Mike Fraser. Designing the spectator experience. In *Proceedings of SIGCHI Conference on Human Factors in Computing Systems (CHI)*, pages 741–750, April 2005.
6. D Saltz. The art of interaction: Interactivity, performativity and computers. *Journal of Aesthetics and Art Criticism*, 55(2):117–127, 1997.
7. R Schechner. *Performance Theory*. Routledge, London, 1977.
8. Jennifer Sheridan, Alan Dix, Simon Lock, and Alice Bayliss. Understanding interaction in ubiquitous guerrilla performances in playful arenas. In *Proceedings of British HCI Conference*, September 2004.
9. Stelarc. The body. *Switch Journal (online)*, 2004. Verified 4/3/05.
10. Stephen Wilson. *Information Arts: Intersections of art, science and technology*. The MIT Press, 2002.

DiCoT: A Methodology for Applying Distributed Cognition to the Design of Teamworking Systems

Ann Blandford and Dominic Furniss

UCL Interaction Centre, University College London,
Remax House, 31-32 Alfred Place, WC1E 7DP, UK
{A.Blandford, D.Furniss}@cs.ucl.ac.uk

Abstract. Distributed Cognition is growing in popularity as a way of reasoning about group working and the design of artefacts within work systems. DiCoT (Distributed Cognition for Teamwork) is a methodology and representational system we are developing to support distributed cognition analysis of small team working. It draws on ideas from Contextual Design, but re-orients them towards the principles that are central to Distributed Cognition. When used to reason about possible changes to the design of a system, it also draws on Claims Analysis to reason about the likely effects of changes from a Distributed Cognition perspective. The approach has been developed and tested within a large, busy ambulance control centre. It supports reasoning about both existing system design and possible future designs.

1 Introduction

Most interactive systems do not consist of a single user with a single desktop computer. Yet most of the established methods for reasoning about the design and use of systems are still best suited for such single-user–single-device systems. Mobile, pervasive and distributed systems bring new sets of design challenges, and correspondingly new approaches are needed for reasoning about such systems. Distributed Cognition (DC) is an approach to reasoning about the interaction of multiple people and artefacts who share a common purpose. Within the system of people and artefacts, it considers the coordination of knowledge and goals, and the flow of information. It has been widely promoted as a method for reasoning about the design of distributed systems involving multiple people and interactive devices. However, despite the relevance of DC to HCI, it has lacked visibility in the HCI community [12,13] and, to the best of our knowledge, there has been no concerted attempt to develop or test a methodology for applying the ideas of DC in a structured way for distributed work. In this paper, we present DiCoT (Distributed Cognition for Teamwork), a structured approach to analysing a work system in terms of the central ideas of Distributed Cognition as presented in the DC literature.

1.1 The Approach

The approach taken was to start with a systematic study of the DC literature. From this literature, a set of core principles for DC were derived and classified according to

S.W. Gilroy and M.D. Harrison (Eds.): DSVIS 2005, LNCS 3941, pp. 26–38, 2006.

primary theme. Five themes emerged; for the three main themes, appropriate representations were developed to support reasoning about that aspect of the distributed system. For this, we drew extensively on the early stages of Contextual Design [2]. These representations and the associated reasoning process form the core of DiCoT.

The representations were developed and tested by applying them to a case study involving team working in ambulance control. Two visits, each of half a day, were made to the case study organisation (London Ambulance Service, LAS); each involved both focused observation work and Contextual Inquiry interviews [2]. Data was gathered from call takers (who are seated in a group separately from the main control area), and from representatives of the three main control roles: telephone dispatchers, radio operators and allocators (who lead the teams and are responsible for planning, co-ordination and decision making). Data gathered during these visits was represented and analysed using DiCoT. The core DC principles were used to support reasoning about qualities of the design of the current system. In order to test the utility of DiCoT for reasoning about new designs, two re-designs of the system were proposed. DiCoT was applied to reasoning about these re-designs. Since these re-designs have not been implemented, it is not possible to validate the conclusions drawn, but this exercise has been a 'proof of concept' to show that the method can be applied to both existing and proposed designs.

Before presenting the detailed literature analysis and the case study, we briefly review related work on DC.

1.2 Background: Distributed Cognition

Various team-working contexts have been analysed in terms of DC. Hutchins [9] analysed the team working behaviours of, and the designs of the artefacts used by, the navigation team on a large naval vessel. Hutchins and others [7,8] have conducted similar analyses of team working and the design of systems in an aircraft cockpit. Fields, Wright, Marti and Palmonari [5] apply DC to an air traffic control (ATC) room to assess the representations and their distribution, manipulation and propagation through the ATC system. They recognise that a potential criticism of their work is the lack of method that takes them from analysis to design. This is one of the issues that our work on DiCoT addresses.

Artman and Waern [1] analyse work in an emergency control room from a Distributed Cognition perspective. Their work contrasts with that reported here in that they focus primarily on the dialogue between participants and how understanding is shared through the verbal channel, whereas the work reported here also considers the artefacts in the environment and how their design and spatial arrangements support or hinder group working.

Wright, Fields and Harrison [13] have made DC more accessible to the HCI community by developing a Resources Model which clarifies how abstract resource structures can be coordinated in strategies to produce behaviour. Wright *et al* [13] intentionally address a single-user–single-device system to show how DC can be applied to traditional software design. However, they acknowledge that there is more work to be done to extend DC to collaborative settings.

2 From the Literature to DiCoT

Hutchins [9] presents DC as a view on how information is transformed and propagated around a system. The DC approach can be distinguished from other theoretical methods by its commitment to two related principles [6]:

1. The unit of analysis is expanded so that the "cognitive process is delimited by the functional relationships among the elements that participate in it, rather than by the spatial collocation of the elements".
2. The analysis looks for a range of mechanisms that can partake in the cognitive system rather than restricting itself to symbol manipulation and computation (e.g., the interplay between human memory, external representations and the manipulation of objects).

Hollan et al. [6, p.176] argue that many of the concepts and vocabulary familiar to classical information processing cognitive science can be retained, but that the unit of analysis needs to be expanded from the individual to the wider system. They suggest three ways in which cognition may be distributed:

1. "Cognitive processes may be distributed across the members of a social group."
2. "Cognitive processes may involve coordination between internal and external (material or environmental) structure."
3. "Processes may be distributed through time in such a way that the products of earlier events can transform the nature of later events."

This gives some indication of the sorts of observations and phenomena that a DC analysis might highlight; we have expanded on these by reference to the broader DC literature to present a set of principles of DC. The three themes that have been the focus of the work to date are: physical layout; information flow; and the design and use of artifacts. Two further themes—evolution over time and the role of social structures in coordinating activity—have not to date formed a focus for analysis, and are therefore omitted from the current account.

For each of the three primary themes, there are three components to DiCoT. The first is the set of principles that pertain to that theme; the second is a set of diagrammatic representations that illustrate structure and flow from the relevant perspective; the third is a set of tabular representations that present a summary of the system, details, further observations and issues that emerge, all from the viewpoint of the theme. This tabular representation focuses on narrative, and on highlighting features of the system in relation to the relevant principles.

2.1 Physical Layout

The physical model describes those factors that influence the performance of the system, and of its components, at a physical level. This description is important from a distributed cognition perspective as those things that can be physically heard, seen and accessed by individuals have a direct impact on their cognitive space and hence will shape, empower and limit the calculations that individuals perform.

Thus, the first set of principles relate to the physical organisation of work— whether concerning the large-scale structures or the details.

Principle 1: Space and Cognition. Hollan et al. [6] discuss the role of space in supporting cognition. They present examples of the use of space such as supporting choice and problem solving. For example, in the work presented here, we found that ambulance controllers lay information out on their desks in ways that support their planning (e.g., by grouping the 'tickets' that correspond to future jobs by time).

Principle 2: Perceptual Principle. Norman [11, p.72] argues that spatial representations provide more support for cognition than non-spatial ones provided that there is a clear mapping between the spatial layout of the representation and that which it represents. An example from the ambulance control domain is that calls are displayed on the allocator's screen in order of priority.

Principle 3: Naturalness Principle. Similarly, Norman [11, p.72] argues that cognition is aided when the form of the representation matches the properties of what it represents; in these cases what is experienced is closer to the actual thing, so the necessary mental transformations to make use of the representation are reduced. This is referred to elsewhere as 'stimulus–response compatibility'.

Principle 4: Subtle Bodily Supports. In interacting with the environment, an individual may use their body to support their cognitive processes; for example, pointing at a place in a book whilst responding to an interruption is part of the mechanism of remembering where we are (Hutchins, 1995a, p.236).

Principle 5: Situation Awareness. One of the key aspects of shared tasks is that people need to be kept informed of what is going on, what has happened and what is planned (Norman, 1995). The quality of this situation awareness can be influenced by how accessible the work of the team is. This can also be influenced by the proximity of the person, involving both observation and overhearing conversation. Situation awareness in ambulance control has been studied by Blandford and Wong [3].

Principle 6: Horizon of Observation. The horizon of observation is what can be seen or heard by a person [9, p.268]. For each person in an environment, this depends on their physical location, the activities they are close to, what they can see, and the manner in which activities take place. The horizon of observation of a person plays a large role in influencing their situation awareness.

Principle 7: Arrangement of Equipment. From a DC perspective, the physical layout of equipment affects access to information, and hence the possibilities for computation. This applies to the different levels of access to people, their conversations and their work as well as to physical representations and artefacts [9, p.197]. For example, in each ambulance control team, the allocator and radio operator share access to certain items.

As we move from the principles towards modelling, there are a number of different levels which we might choose to model. We may take the environment of the individual, the team, the wider working unit or the organisation; the focus should be on sensible units of interest rather than pre-determined physical spaces. For ambulance control, we chose to focus on the structure of the sector desks (i.e., the main unit in which a team works) and the layout of the room (the environment within which teams coordinate their activities).

In considering the effect of the physical layout of the system we focus on the component parts of the system and ask ourselves questions about the proximity of, and access to, devices and people: what can be seen in an individual's horizon of observation and what can be heard in an individual's zone of normal hearing? The answers to these questions affect the information processing ability of an individual and the information flow in the system.

For each level of description, we generate a summary, then details, then add further observations and highlight issues that arise. Details cover two important aspects: support for communication and access to artefacts. We illustrate this briefly with extracts from the room level model.

The room level model describes the physical layout of the Central Ambulance Control room, both graphically (Fig. 1) and in text. The description focuses on overall layout and the location of important shared artefacts such as call status boards. The summary and edited highlights from the additional detail sections are presented in Table 1.

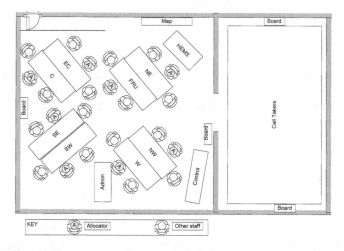

Fig. 1. Room layout (most sector desks are labelled with a region of the city; HEMS = helicopter control, FRU = fast responder units)

This description is produced iteratively. First, the diagram is checked to ensure that it includes all important artefacts and features. Second, the table is refined, pulling out issues relating the design of the system to the principles (identifying both positive and negative features). Space does not permit a full illustration of this process, but Table 1 provides a snapshot of the kind of reasoning involved.

Table 1. Physical model: Extracts from the room level description

SUMMARY There are seven sector desks in the London Ambulance Service control room, each of which has the responsibility of allocating ambulances to incidents in an area of London. Although these sectors provide operational boundaries, where different allocators are responsible for certain areas, it is their collective responsibility to provide the best service for the whole of London; this entails cross boundary working. This is achieved by allocators communicating with each other across the room.
DETAILS *Communication (Access to Actors)* The sector desks are organised roughly geographically, so sectors that border each other are close by for communication (*Principle 5*). When an allocator identifies the ambulance closest to an incident, it may be from a neighbouring sector. Permission to allocate ambulances from different sectors has to be obtained from that sector allocator. Hence, ease of communication between allocators is important for cross boundary working. Depending on where allocators are seated in the room, people will generally raise their voices to get their attention and communicate with them. If this is not possible then the telephone will be used. [...] *Access to Artefacts* The most prominent shared artefacts, at room level, are the boards which indicate the status of incoming calls: how many call takers are free and the percentage of calls that have been answered within an allocated time period. These boards are located high on the wall so that they are accessible by everyone. This information gives an indication of how busy the call takers are, which indirectly indicates overall workload. [...]
FURTHER NOTES – Call takers are situated in a different area from the sector desks. The floor to the call taker's area is at a lower level. This adds a further degree of distinction between the two and could help reduce sound travelling. – The control desk is raised to provide an overview of the room (*Principle 6*). [...]
ISSUES – The allocators are not always within easy reach of each other. This may be important where an incident requires multiple crews from different sectors. – The display giving the status of the call takers' work load and performance does not directly impact on the allocators' work load.

2.2   Information Flow

The physical structure partly determines how information flows and is transformed within a work setting. The second theme for analysis focuses on information flow more specifically. This turns the focus of the analysis to the communication between the participating members, what their roles are and the sequences of events, which define the mechanics of the system. We start by outlining the principles derived from the literature relating to how information flows and is transformed.

Principle 8: Information Movement. Information moves around the system. This can be achieved in a number of different ways which have different functional consequences for information processing. These ways differ in their representation and their physical realisation. Different mechanisms include: passing physical artefacts; text; graphical representation; verbal; facial expression; telephone; electronic mail; and alarms. Even inaction might communicate information [9].

Principle 9: Information Transformation. Information can be represented in different forms; transformations occur when the representation of information changes. This can happen through artefacts and communications between people. Appropriate representations support reasoning and problem solving [9]. One important transformation is filtering, in which information is gathered, sifted and structured. In ambulance control, filtering is a central activity of call takers, who solicit and structure information from callers for onward transmission to the relevant sector desk.

Principle 10: Information Hubs. Information hubs can be considered as a central focus where different information channels meet, and where different information sources are processed together (e.g., where decisions are made on various sources of information [3]). Busy information hubs can be accompanied by buffers that control the information to the hub, to keep it working effectively.

Principle 11: Buffering. As information propagates around a system, there may be times when the arrival of new information interferes with important ongoing activity. This can create conflict and increase the chances of an error occurring, either because the new information gets lost or distorted or because the interruption provokes a mistake within the ongoing activity [9, p.195]. Buffering allows the new information to be held up until an appropriate time, when it can be introduced. In the case of ambulance control, radio operators frequently buffer information for their sector allocators.

Principle 12: Communication Bandwidth. Face-to-face communications typically impart more information than those conducted by other means, including computer mediated communication, radio and telephone [9, p.232]. This richness needs to be recognised when technologies are redesigned.

Principle 13: Informal Communication. Informal communication can play an important functional role in the system, including the propagation of important information about the state of the system and the transfer of knowledge through stories, which can have important consequences for learning how the system behaves [9].

Principle 14: Behavioural Trigger Factors. It is possible for a group of individuals to operate without an overall plan as each member only needs to know what to do in response to certain local factors. These can be dubbed 'trigger factors' because of their property of triggering behaviour [9].

Three separate viewpoints on information flow have been developed to capture different aspects of the way information is transferred around a system:

1. A high level view focuses on the overall input, transformation and output of the system.
2. An agent-based view focuses on the principal agents within the system and the flows between them. The properties of each of the main communication channels are identified. In this case study, we chose to focus on the human agents, and not to consider the interactions between a human and their computer systems: that was left for the artefact model. This decision was made because there is little computer-mediated communication in the current system design.
3. The third view is an adaptation of the second, focusing on how information is buffered, filtered and transformed within the system (referring specifically to the principles for information flow presented above).

For the second and third views, we have adopted the same structure as the physical model described above, of presenting a summary, detail, further notes and issues. For illustrative purposes in this paper, we present just the diagrammatic representation of the enhanced information flow model (item 3 in the list above). This is shown in Figure 2, and expanded on in Table 2, which includes an outline of the key properties of each information channel and node.

The issues that emerge from this representation include the importance of buffers for helping the allocator perform effectively under high workload conditions, and the

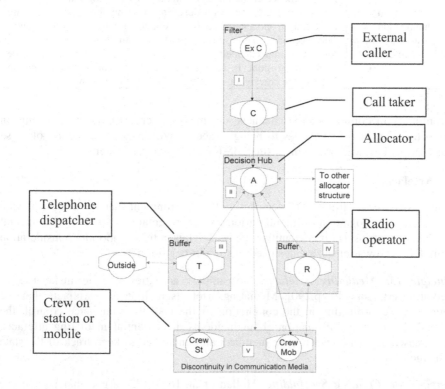

Fig. 2. Overview of information flow, focusing on buffers, hubs and filters (see also Table 2)

Table 2. Description of the main flow properties shown in Fig. 2

Process	Summary
I Filtering of External Caller Information	Call takers receive calls from external callers who help in filtering out the required information so that the system can perform effectively. When appropriate, they will also negotiate times that hospital transfers need to be made with doctors, which has an impact on the management of resources in the rest of the system.
II Allocator at the Decision Hub	In focusing on the process of allocating ambulances to incidents, the allocator can be seen as the central person that makes the decision of what ambulance should go where and when.
III The Buffer of the Telephone Dispatcher	The telephone dispatcher supports the allocator by dealing with incoming telephone calls and contacting outside parties as required through the business of allocating. This provides an extended arm of communication for the allocator and protection against a potential barrage of incoming calls.
IV The Buffer of the Radio Operator	The radio operator supports the allocator by dealing with incoming radio communications from mobile crews and contacting them whilst away from the station. This provides an extended arm of communication for the allocator and protection against a potential barrage of incoming requests and queries.
V Discontinuity in Communication Media used by the Ambulance Crews	The ambulance crews have two mains forms of communication that they use to talk to the sector desk: they use the phone when they are at the station and away from their vehicle; and use the radio when in their vehicle. This discontinuity is amplified as the two communication channels are dealt with by different people at the LAS control room. In addition, the allocator can send information direct to the crew when mobile via their mobile data terminal.

discontinuity in communication channels and media as crews move from being on station to being in their vehicles to being at scene. We discuss the second of these issues further below in proposing a small design change to the system.

2.3 Artefacts

As discussed above, from a DC perspective the environment that we inhabit plays a central role in cognition, bringing artefacts, representations, and environmental affordances centre stage in a cognitive analysis. Thus, a third important consideration within DC is how artefacts are designed to support cognition.

Principle 15: Mediating Artefacts. To support activities, people make use of 'mediating artefacts' [9, p.290]. Mediating artefacts include any artefacts that are brought into coordination in the completion of the task. In ambulance control, the 'tickets' that contain information about incidents are essential mediating artefacts, being passed around between team members and annotated to keep track of the state of the incident.

Principle 16: Creating Scaffolding. Hollan et al. [6, p.192] argue that people use their environment constantly by creating "external scaffolding to simplify our cognitive tasks". For example, we may create reminders of where we are in a task.

Principle 17: Representation–Goal Parity. One way in which external artefacts can aid cognition is by providing an explicit representation of the relationship between the current state and a goal state [9]. The closer the representation is to the cognitive need or goal of the user, the more powerful that representation will be. In the case of ambulance control, the allocator's goal is often to obtain a clear screen – one with no outstanding jobs.

Principle 18: Coordination of Resources. Abstract information structures, or 'resources', can be internally and externally coordinated to aid action and cognition. The six resources Wright et al [13] describe in their Resources Model are: plans, goals, affordance, history, action-effect, and current state.

The artefact model considers the detailed design of individual artefacts that support the work of the team. In our case study, we focused attention on those artefacts and representations considered central to the performance of the system—i.e., the computer system, a supporting paper ticket system and a communal status board.

At an individual artefact level, we want to ask questions about how its design impacts on shaping, structuring and empowering cognition at either team or individual level. By building up a model of the artefact, and the system in which it operates, we aim to understand how it contributes to system performance. To this end we can use the Resources Model [13] to inform how resources are internally and externally represented in the system. The better the understanding we have of how information propagates around the current system, the better our chances of identifying design issues that should be attended to in any system redesign.

Diagrammatic representations of artefacts include both physical structures (e.g., the layout of a computer display) and how artefacts move around the systems (e.g., the ways ambulance control tickets are passed between team members and the significance of each transaction in terms of communication and coordination). These representations and related structures help identify strengths and limitations of the current artefact designs; for instance, as the ambulance service considers replacing paper tickets by a computer-based representation, the model helps identify the important roles and features of paper tickets that need to be preserved in any computer based implementation of this functionality.

3   Reasoning About Re-design

As a brief example of the use of DiCoT to reason about re-design, we consider changing the flow of communication between allocator and crews. As shown in Figure 2, and discussed above, there is a discontinuity in the ways Central Ambulance Control communicate with crews. We could propose changes in the information flow structure. More flexible communication channels could be added (e.g., personal radio or other mobile device) so that the crew could be contacted regardless of whether they are at a station or mobile. Also, the allocation of a crew at a station could be more automated; for example, an allocator could allocate a station, a data terminal would then alert all crews of the details at the station, and one crew would accept the call, which would then be forwarded to their vehicle. Both of these communication changes would reduce the need for a telephone dispatcher. An alert for station data terminals could even be incorporated on the new communication devices; e.g. it could operate something like a pager.

The merits and disadvantages of this modification can be considered by comparing a DC analysis of the new information flow with that of the old. Claims Analysis, described by Carroll and Rosson [4] as a form of "cognitive design rationale", has been chosen to represent this comparison. Such a design rationale is illustrated in Table 3. Since this analysis is being conducted from a DC perspective, considerations such as costs of set-up and maintenance of alternative communications devices have been omitted, but would clearly be important in a full consideration of design changes.

This example is necessarily brief. It serves simply to illustrate one possible approach to using DiCoT to support reasoning about the design of systems that have not yet been implemented. The consideration of this design option has led to the identification of potential design issues that need to be considered if the system is to be reorganised (see Table 3 for example). In practice, those design ideas that appear to have the best chance of improving the current system were not found to be big structural changes, but incremental modifications such as reviewing the communication channels between the sector desks and crews, and improving cross-boundary working through the computer system.

Table 3. Claims Analysis of more flexible communications to crews

Design Feature	Hypothesized Pros (+) or Cons (-) of the Feature
Have a one-stop communication channel with crews	+ allows greater flexibility in contacting crew + could open potential for telephone dispatcher and radio operator to job share + can improve communications between crew and external party
Further automate allocating crews at a station	+ telephone dispatcher's call to station is automated, freeing them for other tasks + allocator can treat allocating a call to a station in much the same manner as to a mobile vehicle - automation will need further equipment and the addition of activities performed by the crew - reducing verbal communication between LAS staff and crews might have negative social consequences

4 Discussion

The aim of this paper has been to develop a structured method of analysis for DC, iteratively developing an approach based on existing research and practice, using a case study to focus development. This case study approach ensured that we took account of practical limitations, complexities and constraints, and made it possible to constantly evaluate what was done well, what was not, and what needed to be included to make the method work practically.

The method took explicit account of most of the DC principles that had been identified in the literature, both in devising the representations to be developed (which also drew on the Contextual Design approach [2]), and in the subsequent analysis approach. The DC principles that have been downplayed in the approach are those that relate to the evolution of the design—a factor that is more central to Activity Theory [10] than DC— and to social factors. These would ideally be considered in an extended DC method, but were outside the scope of this study.

As well as developing a preliminary methodology for conducting a DC analysis, this study has also yielded useful insights into the design of an ambulance control system. Although the study has highlighted a few areas where the design of systems and work spaces could be improved, it has also highlighted why so many aspects of the current design work well. For example, it has shown why the positioning of the radio operator to the side of the allocator (so that many artefacts can be shared and good situation awareness maintained, and so that the radio operator can buffer information for the allocator at times of high workload) is effective.

The conception of how DC can be used as a design tool should be viewed as one possible approach to developing DC rather than a complete account. The possibility of such a use for DC has been alluded to elsewhere but, to the best of our knowledge, has not previously been described. The use of such an approach in this context seems like a suitable way to proceed given that large complex systems (e.g., control rooms) cannot simply be physically built and tested. Claims analysis [4] has been used as an approach to aid design reasoning, and appears to be promising.

In the work reported here, we have aimed to address claims that DC lacks visibility within the HCI community, although it is relevant for analysis and design [13], and that DC cannot currently be used as an 'off the shelf' methodology [12]. By making the theory more accessible to understand and apply, it is hoped that practitioners and researchers will be in a better position to engage with it through practice, criticism and development.

Acknowledgements

This work is supported by EPSRC grant GR/S67494. We are grateful to the management and staff of London Ambulance Service who supported us in this study.

References

1. Artman, H. & Waern, Y. (1999) Distributed Cognition in an Emergency Co-ordination Center. *Cognition, Technology and Work.* 1. 237-246.
2. Beyer, H., Holtzblatt, K.: *Contextual Design*. San Francisco : Morgan Kaufmann. (1998).
3. Blandford, A. & Wong, W. (2004) Situation Awareness in Emergency Medical Dispatch. *International Journal of Human–Computer Studies.* 61(4). 421-452.
4. Carroll, J. M. & Rosson, M. B. (1992) Getting around the task-artifact cycle: how to make claims and design by scenario. *ACM Transactions on Information Systems*, 10(2), 181-21.
5. Fields, R., Wright, P., Marti, P. & Palmonari, M. (1998). Air Traffic Control as a Distributed Cognitive System: a study of external representation. In Green, T., Bannon, L., Warren, C. & Buckley, J. (eds) *ECCE9: Proceedings of the Ninth European Conference on Cognitive Ergonomics.* pp 85-90.

6. Hollan, J. D., Hutchins, E. L. & Kirsh, D. (2000) Distributed cognition: toward a new foundation for human-computer interaction research. *ACM Transactions on CHI, 7.2*, 174-196.

7. Hutchins, E. & Klausen, T. (1991) Distributed Cognition in and Airline Cockpit. in Y. Engeström and D. Middleton, Eds. *Cognition and Communication at Work,* Cambridge: Cambridge University Press.

8. Hutchins, E. (1995) How a Cockpit Remembers Its Speed. *Cogntiive Science,* 19, 265-288

9. Hutchins, E. (1995a) *Cognition In The Wild*. MIT Press, Cambridge, MA.

10. Nardi, B. (1996a). Studying Context: A comparison of activity theory, situated action models, and distributed cognition. In Nardi, B. (ed) *Context and Consciousness: Activity theory and human-computer interaction*. pp 69-102. MIT Press.

11. Norman, D. (1995). *Things that Make Us Smart*. Addison Wesley.

12. Rogers, Y. & Scaife, M. (1997). Distributed Cognition. Retrieved 12/08/04, from www-sv.cict.fr/cotcos/pjs/TheoreticalApproaches/DistributedCog/DistCognitionpaperRogers.htm

13. Wright, P. C., Fields, R. E. & Harrison, M. D. (2000) Analysing Human–Computer Interaction as Distributed Cognition: The Resources Model. *HCI Journal*. 15.1. 1-41.

Towards Model Checking Stochastic Aspects
of the thinkteam User Interface*

Maurice H. ter Beek, Mieke Massink, and Diego Latella

CNR/ISTI – 'A. Faedo', Via G. Moruzzi 1, 56124 Pisa, Italy
{m.terbeek, m.massink, d.latella}@isti.cnr.it

Abstract. Stochastic model checking is a recent extension of traditional model-checking techniques for the integrated analysis of both qualitative and *quantitative* system properties. In this paper we show how stochastic model checking can be conveniently used to address a number of usability concerns that involve quantitative aspects of a user interface for the industrial groupware system thinkteam. thinkteam is a ready-to-use Product Data Management application developed by think3. It allows enterprises to capture, organise, automate, and share engineering product information and it is an example of an asynchronous and dispersed groupware system. Several aspects of the functional correctness, such as concurrency aspects and awareness aspects, of the groupware protocol underlying thinkteam and of its planned publish/subscribe notification service have been addressed in previous work by means of a traditional model-checking approach. In this paper we investigate the trade-off between two different design options for granting users access to files in the database: a retrial approach and a waiting-list approach and show how stochastic model checking can be used for such analyses.

1 Introduction

Computer Supported Cooperative Work (CSCW) is an interdisciplinary research field that deals with the understanding of how people work together, and the ways in which computer technology can assist. This technology mostly consists of multi-user computer systems called groupware [16]. Groupware is often classified according to the time-space taxonomy given by Ellis [16], (i.e., whether its users: (1) work together at the same (synchronous) or at different (asynchronous) times and (2) work together in the same (co-located) or in different (dispersed) places). In this paper we deal with thinkteam, which is an asynchronous and dispersed groupware system, as is email.

Recently there has been an increasing interest in using model checking for formal verification of (properties of) groupware [6, 26, 27]. Some properties of interest are related to important groupware design issues like user awareness and concurrency control. In [7, 8] we have used a traditional model-checking approach, using the model checker SPIN [22], to formalise and verify some properties specifically of interest for the correctness of general groupware protocols (i.e., not limited to thinkteam's context).

---

* This work has been partially funded by the EU project AGILE (IST-2001-32747). For further details, the reader is referred to the technical report of this paper [5].

S.W. Gilroy and M.D. Harrison (Eds.): DSVIS 2005, LNCS 3941, pp. 39–50, 2006.

Many interesting properties of groupware protocols and their interfaces can be analysed *a priori* (i.e., before implementation) by means of a model-based approach and model-checking techniques. There are, however, usability issues that are influenced by the *performance* of the groupware system rather than by its functional behaviour. One such issue was raised by the analysis of thinkteam with a traditional model-checking approach in [7, 8]. It was shown that the system could exclude a user from obtaining a file simply because other users competing for the same file were more 'lucky' in their attempts to obtain the file. Such behaviour was explained by the fact that users were only provided with a file-access mechanism based on a retrial principle. While analysis with traditional model checking can be used to show that such a problem exists, it cannot be used to quantify the effect that it has on the user. In other words, it cannot be used to find out how often, in the average, a user needs to perform a retry in order to get a single file. Of course, the number of retries a user has to perform before obtaining a file is an important ingredient for measuring the usability of the system.

In this paper we address the retrial problem by means of stochastic model checking. This is a relatively new extension of traditional model checking that allows also for the analysis of *quantitative* properties of systems such as those related to performance and dependability issues [10, 20, 24]. Other work on the use of stochastic modelling for usability analysis has been performed in [11], where it has been shown that Markov models and traditional Markov-chain analysis can be used to obtain measures that give an indication of how hard it is for a user to use certain interactive devices. In [14], stochastic modelling has been used to analyse the finger-tracking interface of a whiteboard with augmented reality. The analysis was based on stochastic process algebra models with general (i.e., not necessarily exponential) distributions and discrete event simulation. The main purpose of this paper is to show that stochastic model checking can be a convenient model-based analysis technique to address usability issues that involve quantitative measures. We will explain *how* such analysis can be performed in the context of a simple but relevant industrial case study. In a further study we plan to collect more detailed statistical information on typical use of thinkteam in practice in order to calibrate the models for the analysis of specific situations. The current paper shows the formal specification of users and the system and their interactions, the formalisation of relevant quantitative properties and a number of numerical results.

2   thinkteam

In this section we present a brief overview of thinkteam. For more information we refer the reader to [5, 7, 8] and http://www.think3.com/products/tt.htm.

thinkteam is think3's Product Data Management (PDM) application catering to the document management needs of design processes in the manufacturing industry. Controlled storage and retrieval of documents in PDM applications is called vaulting, the vault being a file-system-like repository. Next to providing a secure and controlled storage environment, vaulting must prevent inconsistent changes to the document base while still allowing maximal access compatible with the business rules. This is implemented in thinkteam's underlying groupware protocol by a standard set of operations:

get – extract a read-only copy of a document from the vault,
import – insert an external document into the vault,
checkOut – extract a copy of a document from the vault with the intent to modify it,
unCheckOut – cancel the effects of a previous checkout,
checkIn – replace an edited document in the vault, and
checkInOut – replace an edited document in the vault, but retaining it checked out.

It is important to note that access to documents (via a *checkOut*) is based on the 'retrial' principle: currently there is no queue or reservation system handling the requests for editing rights on a document. thinkteam typically handles some 100,000 documents for 20–100 users. A user rarely checks out more than 10 documents a day, but she can keep a document checked out from anywhere between 5 minutes and a few days.

To maximize concurrency, a *checkOut* in thinkteam creates an exclusive lock for write access. An automatic solution of the write access conflict is not easy, as it is critically related to the type, nature, and scope of the changes performed on the document. Moreover, standard but harsh solutions—like maintaining a dependency relation between documents and use it to simply lock all documents depending on the document being checked out—are out of the question for think3, as they would cause these documents to be unavailable for too long. For thinkteam, the preferred solution is thus to leave it to the users to resolve such conflicts. However, a publish/subscribe notification service would provide the means to supply the clients with adequate information by: (1) informing clients checking out a document of existing outstanding copies and (2) notifying the copy holders upon *checkOut* and *checkIn* of the document.

In [7, 8] we studied the addition of a lightweight and easy-to-use publish/subscribe notification service to thinkteam and we verified several correctness properties. These properties addressed issues like concurrency control, awareness, and denial of service. Most properties were found to hold, with the exception of one concurrency-control and a denial-of-service property. The problem with the concurrency-control property arises when a user simply 'forever' forgets to *checkIn* the file it has checked out, which means that the lock on this file is never released. In thinkteam, such a situation is resolved by the intervention of a system administrator.

The problem with the denial-of-service property is that it may be the case that one of the users can never get its turn to, *e.g.*, perform a *checkOut*, because the system is continuously kept busy by the other users, while this user did express its desire to perform a *checkOut*. Such behaviour forms an integral part of the thinkteam protocol. This is because access to documents is based on the 'retrial' principle: thinkteam currently has no queue or reservation system handling simultaneous requests for a document. Before simply extending thinkteam with a reservation system, it would be useful to know: (1) how often, in the average, users have to express their requests before they are satisfied and (2) under which system conditions (number of users, file processing time, etc.) such a reservation system would really improve usability. We come back to this later.

3   Stochastic Analysis

Traditionally, functional analysis of systems (i.e., analysis concerning their functional correctness) and performance analysis have been two distinct and separate areas of research and practice. Recent developments in model checking, in particular its extension to address also performance and dependability aspects of systems, have given rise to a renewed interest in the integration of functional and quantitative analysis techniques.

A widely used model-based technique for performance analysis is based on Continuous Time Markov Chains (CTMCs). CTMCs provide a modelling framework, proved to be extremely useful for practical analysis of quantitative aspects of system behaviour. Moreover, in recent years proper stochastic extensions of temporal logics have been proposed and efficient algorithms for checking the satisfiability of formulae of such logics on CTMCs (i.e., stochastic model checkers) have been implemented [10, 20, 24].

The basis for the definition of CTMCs are exponential distributions of random variables. The parameter which completely characterises an exponentially distributed random variable is its *rate* λ, which is a positive real number. A real-valued random variable X is exponentially distributed with rate λ—written $EXP(\lambda)$—if the probability of X being at most t, *i.e.* $\mathrm{Prob}(X \leq t)$, is $1 - e^{-\lambda t}$ if $t \geq 0$ and is 0 otherwise, where t is a real number. The expected value of X is λ^{-1}. Exponentially distributed random variables enjoy the so called *memoryless property* (i.e., $\mathrm{Prob}(X > t + t' \mid X > t) = \mathrm{Prob}(X > t')$, for $t, t' \geq 0$).

CTMCs have been extensively studied in the literature (a comprehensive treatment can be found in [23]; we suggest [19] for a gentle introduction). For the purposes of the present paper it suffices to recall that a CTMC $\mathcal{M}$ is a pair $(\mathcal{S}, \mathbf{R})$ where $\mathcal{S}$ is a finite set of *states* and $\mathbf{R} : \mathcal{S} \times \mathcal{S} \to \mathbb{R}_{\geq 0}$ is the *rate matrix*. The rate matrix characterises the transitions between the states of $\mathcal{M}$. If $\mathbf{R}(s, s') \neq 0$, then it is possible that a transition from state s to state s' takes place, and the probability of such a transition to take place within time t, is $1 - e^{-\mathbf{R}(s,s') \cdot t}$. If $\mathbf{R}(s, s') = 0$, then no such a transition can take place.[1] We would like to point out that the traditional definition of CTMCs does not include self-loops, (i.e., transitions from a state to itself). On the other hand, the presence of such self-loops does not alter standard analysis techniques (e.g., transient and steady-state analyses) and self-loops moreover turn out to be useful when model checking CTMCs [4]. Therefore we will allow them in this paper.

Usually CTMCs are not obtained in a direct way, due to the increasing complexity of the analysed systems, but instead generated automatically from higher-level specifications given in languages such as *e.g.* stochastic Petri nets, stochastic process algebras or stochastic activity nets [9, 25]. Our approach is no different. We specify our model of thinkteam's underlying groupware protocol in the stochastic process algebra PEPA (Performance Evaluation Process Algebra) [21]. This specification is consequently read into a stochastic model checker, which then automatically builds a CTMC from it.

4   Stochastic Model Checking

In the model-checking approach to performance and dependability analysis a *model* of the system under consideration is required together with a desired *property* or *performance/dependability measure*. In case of stochastic modelling, such models are

---

[1] This intuitive interpretation is correct only if there is only one transition originating from s. If this is not the case, then a *race condition* arises among all transitions originating from s.

typically CTMCs or high-level specification languages to generate them, while properties are usually expressed in some form of extended temporal logic. Here we use Continuous Stochastic Logic (CSL) [2, 3], a stochastic variant of the well-known Computational Tree Logic (CTL) [12]. CTL allows to state properties over *states* as well as over *paths*.

CSL extends CTL by two probabilistic operators that refer to the steady-state and transient behaviour of the system under study. The steady-state operator refers to the probability of residing in a particular state or set of *states* (specified by a state formula) in the long run. The transient operator allows us to refer to the probability mass of the set of *paths* in the CTMC that satisfy a given (path) property. To express the time span of a certain path, the path operators until ($\mathcal{U}$) and next (X) are extended with a parameter that specifies a time interval. Let I be an interval on the real line, p a probability value and $\bowtie$ a comparison operator, (i.e., $\bowtie \in \{<, \leq, \geq, >\}$). The syntax of CSL is:

State formulae: $\Phi ::= a \mid \neg\Phi \mid \Phi \vee \Phi \mid \mathcal{S}_{\bowtie p}(\Phi) \mid \mathcal{P}_{\bowtie p}(\varphi)$

$\mathcal{S}_{\bowtie p}(\Phi)$: probability that Φ holds in steady state $\bowtie p$

$\mathcal{P}_{\bowtie p}(\varphi)$: probability that a path fulfills $\varphi \bowtie p$

Path formulae: $\varphi ::= X^I \Phi \mid \Phi \mathcal{U}^I \Phi$

$X^I \Phi$: next state is reached at time $t \in I$ and fulfills Φ

$\Phi \mathcal{U}^I \Psi$: Φ holds along path until Ψ holds at $t \in I$

The meaning of atomic propositions (a), negation ($\neg$) and disjunction ($\vee$) is standard. Using these operators, other boolean operators like conjunction ($\wedge$), implication ($\Rightarrow$), true (TRUE) and false (FALSE), and so forth, can be defined in the usual way. The state formula $\mathcal{S}_{\bowtie p}(\Phi)$ asserts that the steady-state probability for the set of states satisfying Φ, the Φ-states, meets the bound $\bowtie p$. $\mathcal{P}_{\bowtie p}(\varphi)$ asserts that the probability measure of the set of paths satisfying φ meets the bound $\bowtie p$. The operator $\mathcal{P}_{\bowtie p}(.)$ replaces the usual CTL path quantifiers $\exists$ and $\forall$. In CSL, the formula $\mathcal{P}_{\geq 1}(\varphi)$ holds if *almost all* paths satisfy φ. Moreover, clearly $\exists \varphi$ holds whenever $\mathcal{P}_{>0}(\varphi)$ holds.

The formula $\Phi \mathcal{U}^I \Psi$ is satisfied by a path if Ψ holds at time $t \in I$ and at every preceding state on the path, if any, Φ holds. In CSL, temporal operators like $\Diamond$, $\Box$ and their real-time variants $\Diamond^I$ or $\Box^I$ can be derived, *e.g.*, $\mathcal{P}_{\bowtie p}(\Diamond^I \Phi) = \mathcal{P}_{\bowtie p}(\text{TRUE } \mathcal{U}^I \Phi)$ and $\mathcal{P}_{\geq p}(\Box^I \Phi) = \mathcal{P}_{\leq 1-p}(\Diamond^I \neg\Phi)$. The untimed next and until operators are obtained by $X \Phi = X^I \Phi$ and $\Phi_1 \mathcal{U} \Phi_2 = \Phi_1 \mathcal{U}^I \Phi_2$ for $I = [0, \infty)$. In a variant of CSL the probability p can be replaced by '?', denoting that one is looking for the value of the probability rather than verifying whether the obtained probability respects certain bounds.

The model checker PRISM [24] is a prototype tool that supports, among others, the verification of CSL properties over CTMCs. It checks the validity of CSL properties for given states in the model and provides feedback on the calculated probabilities of such states where appropriate. It uses symbolic data structures (i.e., variants of Binary Decision Diagrams). PRISM accepts system descriptions in different specification languages, among which the process algebra PEPA and the PRISM language—a simple state-based language based on the Reactive Modules formalism of Alur and Henzinger [1]. An example of an alternative model checker for CSL is ETMCC [20].

5   Stochastic Model of thinkteam—The Retrial Approach

In this section we describe the stochastic model of thinkteam for the retrial approach, after which we perform several analyses on this model. We use the stochastic process algebra PEPA to specify our model. In PEPA, systems can be described as interactions of *components* that may engage in *activities* in much the same way as in other process algebras. Components reflect the behaviour of relevant parts of the system, while activities capture the actions that the components perform. A component may itself be composed of components. The specification of a PEPA activity consists of a pair *(action type, rate)* in which *action type* symbolically denotes the type of the action, while *rate* characterises the *exponential* distribution of the activity duration. Before explaining our model, we briefly describe the PEPA language constructs that we will use. For a more detailed description of these constructs we refer the reader to [21].

The basic mechanism for constructing behaviour expressions is by means of prefixing. The component $(\alpha, r).P$ carries out activity (α, r), with action type α and duration Δt determined by rate r. The component subsequently behaves as component P.

The component $P + Q$ represents a system which may behave either as component P or as component Q. The continuous nature of the probability distributions ensures that the probability of P and Q both completing an activity at the same time is zero. The choice operator represents a competition (the race condition) between components.

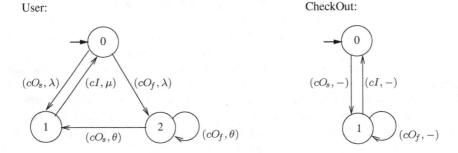

Fig. 1. The retrial approach: automata of the User and the CheckOut components

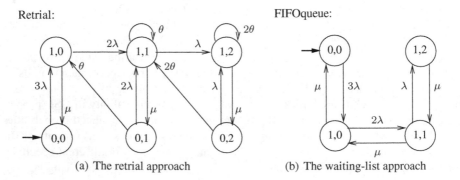

(a) The retrial approach   (b) The waiting-list approach

Fig. 2. (a)-(b) The CTMCs in case of 3 users for the two approaches of this paper

The cooperation operator $P \bowtie_L Q$ defines the set of action types L on which components P and Q must synchronise or *cooperate*. Both components proceed independently with any activities that do not occur in L. In particular, when $L = \varnothing$ then $P \bowtie_L Q$ thus denotes *parallel composition* and the shorthand notation $P \parallel Q$ is used. The expected duration of a cooperation where activities are shared (i.e., $L \neq \varnothing$) will be greater than or equal to the expected durations of the corresponding activities in the cooperating components. A special case is the situation in which one component is *passive* (i.e., has the special rate $-$) wrt the other component. In this case the total rate is determined by that of the *active* component only.

We are now ready to explain our model in detail. In Fig. 1 the models of the User and CheckOut components are drawn as automata for reasons of readability.

We consider the case that there is only one file, the (exclusive) access to which is handled by the CheckOut component. A user can express interest in checking out the file by performing a *checkOut*. This operation can either result in the user being granted access to the file or in the user being denied access because the file is currently already checked out by another user. In Fig. 1, the successful execution of a *checkOut* is modelled by activity (cO_s, λ), while a failed *checkOut* is modelled by (cO_f, λ). The exponential rate λ is also called the *request* rate. If the user does not obtain the file, then she may retry to check out the file, modelled by activity (cO_s, θ) in case of a successful retry and by (cO_f, θ) in case the *checkOut* failed. The exponential rate θ is also called the *retrial* rate. The *checkIn* operation, finally, is modelled by activity (cI, μ) and the exponential rate μ is also called the *file processing* rate. The CheckOut component takes care that only one user at a time can have the file in her possession. To this aim, it simply keeps track of whether the file is checked out (state $\langle 1 \rangle$) or not (state $\langle 0 \rangle$). When a User tries to obtain the file via the *checkOut* activity, then she is denied the file if it is currently checked out by another user while she might obtain the file if it is available.

The formal PEPA specifications of the User and the CheckOut component, and the composed model for three User components and the CheckOut component

$$(\text{User} \parallel \text{User} \parallel \text{User}) \bowtie_{\{cO_s, cO_f, cI\}} \text{CheckOut}$$

is given in [5]. These specifications are accepted as input by PRISM and then translated into the PRISM language. The resulting specification is given in [5]. From such a specification PRISM automatically generates a CTMC with 19 states and 54 transitions that can be shown behaviourally equivalent for the purpose of transient and steady-state analysis (strongly equivalent in [21]) to the much simpler CTMC given in Fig. 2(a).[2]

The states of this CTMC are tuples $\langle x, y \rangle$ with x denoting whether the file is checked out ($x = 1$) or not ($x = 0$) and $y \in \{0, 1, 2\}$ denoting the number of users currently retrying to perform a *checkOut*. Note, however, that when a user inserts the file she has checked out back into the Vault via a *checkIn* activity, the CheckOut component does allow another user to *checkOut* the file but this need not be a user that has tried before to obtain the file. In fact, a race condition occurs between the request and retrial rates associated to the *checkOut* activity (*cf.* states $\langle 0, 1 \rangle$ and $\langle 0, 2 \rangle$). Note also that once

---

[2] Moreover, the CTMC obtained by removing the self-loops from that of Fig. 2(a) is frequently used in the theory of *retrial queues* [17, 18, 23].

the file is checked in, it is *not* immediately granted to another user, even if there are users that have expressed their interest in obtaining the file. In such a situation, the file will remain unused for a period of time which is exponentially distributed with rate $\theta + \lambda$.

We use the stochastic model and the stochastic logic to formalise and analyse various usability issues concerning the retrial approach used in thinkteam. In this context it is important to fix the time units one considers. We choose hours as our time unit. For instance, if $\mu = 5$ this means that a typical user keeps the file in its possession for $60/5 = 12$ minutes on the average.

5.1   Analyses of Performance Properties

We first analyse the probability that a user that has requested the file and is now in 'retry mode' (state $\langle 2 \rangle$ of the User component), obtains the requested file within the next five hours. This measure can be formalised in CSL as (in a pseudo PRISM notation):[3]

$$\mathcal{P}_{=?}([\text{ TRUE } \mathcal{U}^{\leq 5}\ (\text{User\_STATE} = 1)\ \{\text{User\_STATE} = 2\}\ ]),$$

which must be read as follows: "what is the probability that path formula TRUE $\mathcal{U}^{\leq 5}$ (User_STATE = 1) is satisfied for state User_STATE = 2?".

The results for this measure are presented in Fig. 3(a) for request rate $\lambda = 1$ (*i.e.* a user requests the file once an hour on average), retrial rate θ taking values 1, 5 and 10 (i.e., in one hour a user averagely retries one, five or ten times to obtain the file), file processing rate $\mu = 1$ (i.e., a user on average keeps the file checked out for one hour) and for different numbers of users ranging from 1 to 10.

Clearly, with an increasing number of users the probability that a user gets her file within the time interval is decreasing. On the other hand, with an increasing retrial rate and a constant file processing rate the probability for a user to obtain the requested file within the time interval is increasing. Further results could easily be obtained by model checking for different rate parameters that may characterise different profiles of use of the same system. In particular, this measure could be used to evaluate under which circumstances (e.g., when it is known that only a few users will compete for the same file) a retrial approach would give satisfactory results from a usability point of view.

A slightly more complicated measure can be obtained with some additional calculations involving steady-state analysis (by means of model checking). Fig. 3(c) shows the average number of retrials per file request for request rate $\lambda = 1$, retrial rate θ taking values 5 and 10, file processing rate μ ranging from 1 to 10 and for 10 users. The measure has been computed as the average number of retries that take place over a certain system observation period of time T divided by the average number of re-quests during T. To compute the average number of retries (requests, resp.) we pro-ceeded as follows. We first computed the steady-state probability p (q, resp.) of the user being in 'retry mode' ('request mode', resp.), *i.e.* $p \stackrel{\text{def}}{=} \mathcal{S}_{=?}(\text{User\_STATE} = 2)$ ($q \stackrel{\text{def}}{=} \mathcal{S}_{=?}(\text{User\_STATE} = 0)$, resp.). The fraction of time the user is in 'retry mode' ('request mode', resp.) is then given by $T \times p$ ($T \times q$, resp.). The average number of

---

[3] Here and in the sequel, User_STATE always refers to one specific user.

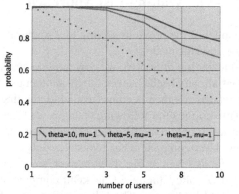

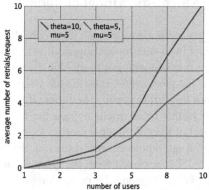

(a) Probability for users in 'retry mode' to *checkOut* requested file within next 5 hrs

(b) Average number of retrials per file request for a varying number of users

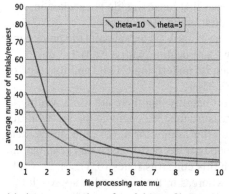

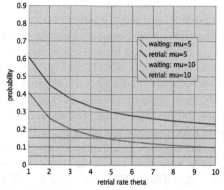

(c) Average number of retrials per file request in case of 10 users

(d) The retrial approach *vs.* the waiting-list approach

Fig. 3. (a)-(d) Results of the analyses performed for this paper

retries (requests, resp.) is then $\theta \times T \times p$ ($\lambda \times T \times q$, resp.). Hence the measure of interest is $(\theta \times p)/(\lambda \times q)$.

It is easy to observe in Fig. 3(c) that the number of retrials decreases considerably when the file processing rate is increased (i.e., when the users update, by means of a *checkIn*, a file they had checked out after a shorter time). We also note that a relatively high file processing rate is needed for obtaining an acceptably low number of retrials in the case of 10 users that regularly compete for the same file.

The effect on the average number of retries is even better illustrated in Fig. 3(b), where with a similar approach as outlined above the average number of retrials per file request is presented for request rate $\lambda = 1$, retrial rate θ taking values 5 and 10, fixed file processing rate $\mu = 5$ and various numbers of users. Clearly, the average number of retrials per file request increases sharply when the number of users increases.

6 Stochastic Model of thinkteam—The Waiting-List Approach

In this section we compare the stochastic model of the previous section to a stochastic model for a waiting-list approach, which we describe next.

In contrast with our model for the retrial approach of Sect. 5, we now assume that a user's request to *checkOut* the file when it has already been checked out by another user is put in a FIFO queue. The moment in which the file then becomes available, the first user in this FIFO queue obtains the file. This implies the following changes w.r.t. the model of Sect. 5. Since a user no longer retries to obtain the file after her initial unsuccessful attempt to *checkOut* the file, the new User component has two states only, viz. state $\langle 2 \rangle$ is removed from the User component as given in Fig. 1. Moreover, since the CheckOut component now implements a FIFO policy, the new CheckOut component must keep track of the number of users in the FIFO queue. The full specifications of the new User and CheckOut components can be found in [5]. Here we directly use the strongly-equivalent CTMC for three users given in Fig. 2(b).

The state tuples of this CTMC have the same meaning as before, but states $\langle 0, 1 \rangle$ and $\langle 0, 2 \rangle$ no longer occur. This is due to the fact that, once the file is checked in, it is immediately granted to another user (viz., the first in the FIFO queue).

The fact that we consider an exponential request rate λ, an exponential file processing rate μ, one file, and three users means that we are dealing with a M|M|1|3 *queueing system* [19, 23]. The CTMC of Fig. 2(b) is then its underlying CTMC and this type of CTMC is also called a *birth-death process* [19, 23].

We now compare the two models wrt the probability that there are users waiting to obtain the file after a *checkOut* request. To measure this, we compute the probabilities for at least one user not being granted the file after asking for it, (i.e., the steady-state probability p to be in a state in which at least one user has performed a *checkOut* but did not obtain the file yet). In the retrial approach this concerns states $\langle 0, 1 \rangle$, $\langle 0, 2 \rangle$, $\langle 1, 1 \rangle$ and $\langle 1, 2 \rangle$ of the CTMC Retrial in Fig. 2(a), whereas in the waiting-list approach this concerns states $\langle 1, 1 \rangle$ and $\langle 1, 2 \rangle$ of the CTMC FIFOqueue in Fig. 2(b). Hence this can be expressed (again, in a pseudo PRISM notation) as the CSL steady-state formula

$$p \stackrel{\text{def}}{=} \mathcal{S}_{=?}([\ (\text{Retrial\_STATE} = \langle 0, 1 \rangle)\ |\ (\text{Retrial\_STATE} = \langle 0, 2 \rangle)\ |$$
$$(\text{Retrial\_STATE} = \langle 1, 1 \rangle)\ |\ (\text{Retrial\_STATE} = \langle 1, 2 \rangle)\ ])$$

in the retrial approach, while in the waiting-list approach the formula is

$$p \stackrel{\text{def}}{=} \mathcal{S}_{=?}([\ (\text{FIFOqueue\_STATE} = \langle 1, 1 \rangle)\ |\ (\text{FIFOqueue\_STATE} = \langle 1, 2 \rangle)\ ])$$

The results of our comparison are presented in Fig. 3(d) for request rate $\lambda = 1$, retrial rate θ (only in the retrial approach of course) ranging from 1 to 10, file processing rate μ taking values 5 and 10 and, as said before, 3 users.

It is easy to see that, as expected, the waiting-list approach outperforms the retrial approach in all the cases we considered: The probability to be in one of the states $\langle 1, 1 \rangle$ or $\langle 1, 2 \rangle$ of the CTMC FIFOqueue of the waiting-list approach is always lower than the probability of the CTMC Retrial of the retrial approach to be in one of the states $\langle 0, 1 \rangle$, $\langle 0, 2 \rangle$, $\langle 1, 1 \rangle$ or $\langle 1, 2 \rangle$. Note that for large θ the probability in case of the retrial approach is asymptotically approaching that of the waiting-list approach, of course given the same values for λ and μ. While we did verify this for values of θ upto 10^9, it is of course extremely unrealistic to assume that a user performs 10^9 retries per hour. We thus conclude that the time that a user has to wait 'in the long run' for the file after it has performed a *checkOut* is always less in the waiting-list approach than in the retrial approach. Furthermore, while increasing the retrial rate (i.e., reducing the time inbetween retries) does bring the results for the retrial approach close to those for the waiting-list approach, it takes highly unrealistic retrial rates to reach a difference between the two approaches that is insignificantly small.

7   Conclusions and Further Work

In this paper we have addressed the formal analysis of a number of quantitative usability measures of a small, but relevant industrial case study concerning an existing groupware system for PDM, thinkteam. We have shown how the quantitative aspects of the interaction between users and the system can be modelled in a process-algebraic way by means of the stochastic process algebra PEPA. The model has been used to obtain quantitative information on two different approaches for users to obtain files from a central database; one based on retrial and one based on a reservation system implemented via a FIFO waiting list. The quantitative measures addressed the expected time that users are required to wait before they obtain a requested file and the average number of retries per file, for various assumptions on the parameters of the model. These measures have been formalised as formulae of the stochastic temporal logic CSL and analysed by means of the stochastic model checker PRISM.

The results show that, from a user perspective, the retrial approach is less convenient than the waiting-list approach. Moreover, it can be shown that the situation for the retrial approach rapidly deteriorates with an increasing number of users that compete for the same file. The use of stochastic model checking allowed for a convenient modular and compositional specification of the system and the automatic generation of the underlying CTMCs on which performance analysis is based. Furthermore, the combination of compositional specification of models and logic characterisation of measures of interest provides a promising technique for *a priori formal* model-based usability analysis where quantitative aspects as well as qualitative ones are involved.

We plan to apply the developed models and measures for the analysis of different user profiles of the actual thinkteam system in collaboration with think3. Such *a priori* performance evaluation is addressed also in [25], where stochastic Petri nets are the model that is used to discuss usability aspects of users interacting with a non-groupware system. In a further extension we also plan to deal with the quantitative effects of the addition of a publish/subscribe notification service to thinkteam.

Acknowledgements

We would like to thank Alessandro Forghieri and Maurizio Sebastianis of think3 for providing the thinkteam case study and related information and for discussions on the thinkteam user interface.

References

1. R. Alur & T. Henzinger, Reactive modules. *Formal Methods in System Design* 15 (1999), 7-48.
2. A. Aziz, K. Sanwal, V. Singhal & R. Brayton, Model checking continuous time Markov chains. *ACM Transactions on Computational Logic* 1, 1 (2000), 162-170.
3. C. Baier, J.-P. Katoen & H. Hermanns, Approximate symbolic model checking of continuous-time Markov chains. In *Concurrency Theory, LNCS* 1664, 1999, 146-162.
4. C. Baier, B. Haverkort, H. Hermanns & J.-P. Katoen, Automated performance and dependability evaluation using model checking. In *Performance'02, LNCS* 2459, 2002, 261-289.
5. M.H. ter Beek, M. Massink & D. Latella, Towards Model Checking Stochastic Aspects of the thinkteam User Interface—FULL VERSION. Technical Report 2005-TR-18, CNR/ISTI, 2005. URL: http://fmt.isti.cnr.it/WEBPAPER/TRdsvis.pdf.
6. M.H. ter Beek, M. Massink, D. Latella & S. Gnesi, Model checking groupware protocols. In *Cooperative Systems Design*, IOS Press, 2004, 179-194.
7. M.H. ter Beek, M. Massink, D. Latella, S. Gnesi, A. Forghieri & M. Sebastianis, Model checking publish/subscribe notification for thinkteam, Technical Report 2004-TR-20, CNR/ISTI, 2004. URL: http://fmt.isti.cnr.it/WEBPAPER/TRTT.ps.
8. M.H. ter Beek, M. Massink, D. Latella, S. Gnesi, A. Forghieri & M. Sebastianis, Model checking publish/subscribe notification for thinkteam. In *Proc. FMICS'04. ENTCS* 133, 2005, 275-294.
9. E. Brinksma, H. Hermanns & J.-P. Katoen (Eds.), *Lectures on Formal Methods and Performance Analysis, LNCS* 2090, 2001.
10. P. Buchholz, J.-P. Katoen, P. Kemper & C. Tepper, Model-checking large structured Markov chains. *Journal of Logic and Algebraic Programming* 56 (2003), 69-96.
11. P. Cairns, M. Jones & H. Thimbleby, Reusable usability analysis with Markov models. *ACM Transactions on Computer Human Interaction* 8, 2 (2001), 99-132.
12. E. Clarke, E. Emerson & A. Sistla, Automatic verification of finite-state concurrent systems using temporal logic specifications. *ACM Transactions on Programming Languages and Systems* 8 (1986), 244-263.
13. E.M. Clarke Jr., O. Grumberg & D.A. Peled, *Model Checking*. MIT Press, 1999.
14. G. Doherty, M. Massink & G.P. Faconti, Reasoning about interactive systems with stochastic models. In *Revised Papers of DSV-IS'01, LNCS* 2220, 2001, 144-163.
15. P. Dourish & V. Bellotti, Awareness and coordination in shared workspaces. In *Proc. CSCW'92*, ACM Press, 1992, 107-114.
16. C.A. Ellis, S.J. Gibbs & G.L. Rein, Groupware—Some issues and experiences. *Communications of the ACM* 34, 1 (1991), 38-58.
17. G.I. Falin, A survey of retrial queues. *Queueing Systems* 7 (1990), 127-168.
18. G.I. Falin & J.G.C. Templeton, *Retrial Queues*. Chapman & Hall, 1997.
19. B. Haverkort, Markovian models for performance and dependability evaluation. In [9], 38-83.
20. H. Hermanns, J-P. Katoen, J. Meyer-Kayser & M. Siegle, A tool for model-checking Markov chains. *Int. Journal on Software Tools for Technology Transfer* 4 (2003), 153-172.
21. J. Hillston, *A Compositional Approach to Performance Modelling*. CU Press, 1996.
22. G.J. Holzmann, *The SPIN Model Checker*. Addison Wesley, 2003.
23. V. Kulkarni. *Modeling and Analysis of Stochastic Systems*. Chapman & Hall, 1995.
24. M. Kwiatkowska, G. Norman & D. Parker, Probabilistic symbolic model checking with PRISM: A hybrid approach. In *Proc. TACAS'02, LNCS* 2280, 2002, 52-66.
25. X. Lacaze, Ph. Palanque, D. Navarre & R. Bastide, Performance Evaluation as a Tool for Quantitative Assessment of Complexity of Interactive Systems. In *Revised Papers of DSV-IS'02, LNCS* 2545, 2002, 208-222.
26. C. Papadopoulos, An extended temporal logic for CSCW. *Comp. Journal* 45 (2002), 453-472.
27. T. Urnes, *Efficiently Implementing Synchronous Groupware*. Ph.D. thesis, Department of Computer Science, York University, Toronto, 1998.

Incident and Accident Investigation Techniques to Inform Model-Based Design of Safety-Critical Interactive Systems

Sandra Basnyat[1], Nick Chozos[2], Chris Johnson[2], and Philippe Palanque[1]

[1] LIIHS – IRIT, University Paul Sabatier,
118 route de Narbonne, 31062 Toulouse, Cedex 4
{Basnyat, Palanque}@irit.fr
http://liihs.irit.fr/{basnyat, palanque}
[2] Dept. of Computing Science, University of Glasgow,
Glasgow, G12 8QQ, Scotland
{Nick, Johnson}@dcs.gla.ac.uk
http://www.dcs.gla.ac.uk/~{Nick, Johnson}

Abstract. The quality of the design of an interactive safety-critical system can be enhanced by embedding data and knowledge from past experiences. Traditionally, this involves applying scenarios, usability analysis, or the use of metrics for risk analysis. In this paper, we present an approach that uses the information from incident investigations to inform the development of safety-cases that can, in turn, be used to inform a formal system model, represented using Petri nets and the ICO formalism. The foundations of the approach are first detailed and then exemplified using a fatal mining accident case study.

1 Introduction

Due to their safety-critical nature, the design of interactive safety-critical systems (S-CIS) must be grounded on concrete data. Typically, data used for such a design stems from requirements gathering phase, task analysis, extant system analysis, etc. Before a system is implemented, formal model-based approaches allow designers to apply techniques to validate their models and verify properties. This is particularly important for a safety-critical system as design flaws may have catastrophic impact and put human life at stake. Such techniques include model checking, formal verification and performance evaluation.

A complementary way to enhance a system's safety is to take into account information from previous real life cases. One such usually available and particularly pertinent source is the outcome of an incident or accident investigation. Designs of any nature can be improved by taking into account previous experiences, both positive and negative. However, for a safety-critical system, previous incidents and accidents are interesting factors as they are clearly what we wish to avoid. In this paper we present an approach exploiting incident and accident investigation techniques to support the design of a safety-critical system.

Recent accidents in domains ranging from aviation to healthcare have highlighted a growing concern for the role human 'error' has in causing incidents and accidents.

S.W. Gilroy and M.D. Harrison (Eds.): DSVIS 2005, LNCS 3941, pp. 51–66, 2006.

We can consider the main causes for incidents and accidents to stem from human 'errors', system 'failures' and managerial issues. In practice, most accidents stem from complex combinations of each of these different types of cause. If we can begin to understand why these causes occur and take them into account in safety-critical systems design then we can head towards safer, safety-critical interactive systems.

To date, input to a safety-critical interactive system (S-CIS) design from an incident or accident investigation has not been considered in a systematic way. There are some notable exceptions [3]. One reason for this lack of integration is that systems design and incident investigations are usually performed by experts with different backgrounds and belonging to different organizations. In this paper we propose investigation analysts to apply analysis techniques to an accident investigation report and provide systems designers with extracted information and show how such information can support the design of safer S-CIS.

To be more concrete, we have devised an approach that allows a system to be formally modelled and then formally analyzed to prove that the sequence of events described in the accident report is not able to be triggered again in that model. On the incident and accident investigation side, safety cases provide an important link between the events that are identified in the aftermath of an accident and higher-level arguments about the future safety of an interactive system. This is important because the individual events that lead to an accident often provide evidence of deeper-seated and more systematic flaws in the assumptions that underpin a design. On the system modelling side, Interactive cooperative Objects [1] are used to model the system. We have implemented this approach on a fatal mining accident case study.

The following section introduces the case study so that the reader can understand the models provided later. Section 2 presents an overview of the case study. In Sect. 3 we present our approach for informing interactive safety-critical systems design using safety cases and accident investigation techniques. We present an overview of safety cases and briefly introduce the Interactive Cooperation Objects (ICO) formalism. This formal specification technique has been designed to address specific problems raised by the specification of interactive systems. We then present the application of the approach on the given case study which includes system modelling, safety cases, system re-modelling and finally we discuss possible simulation of a scenario on the interface part of the system to test that the accident cannot be triggered again on the newly informed system.

2 Case Study

The case study we have chosen to illustrate the proposed approach is a fatal US mining accident [16]. A Quarry and Plant system is designed to produce cement. However, the part we are interested in is the delivery of waste fuel used to heat the plant kilns. We successively detail the plant layout and its operation and then the accident.

The Waste Fuel Delivery System is comprised of two separate liquid fuel delivery systems, the north and the south. Each system delivers fuel to the three plant kilns independently and cannot operate at the same time. See Fig. 1 for a layout diagram. This particular application was chosen because it relies upon the operation of a complex, embedded command and control system. The design of these applications continues to pose considerable challenges that are often neglected by more traditional research into Human Computer Interaction, although they form the focus of wider studies within the field of Human Factors and Ergonomics. Each delivery system contains the following components (presented here in the order of fuel flow): A fuel storage tank (right of the diagram); Two different sets of pumps, known as G and S, including motors and valves; A grinder, including motor and a ¾″ ball valve.

In order to understand the events leading to the accident, we must first describe the interaction between the command and control system and the north Waste Fuel Delivery System. If the north fuel storage tank is open, fuel flows from the storage tank to north pump-S. The north pump-S motor pumps the fuel to the north grinder. The fuel is grinded and passes to north pump-G. The north pump-G motor then pumps the fuel into the three kilns. The waste fuel delivery systems also contain sensors located in different areas. Each delivery system has at least one temperature sensor and one fuel line pressure sensor.

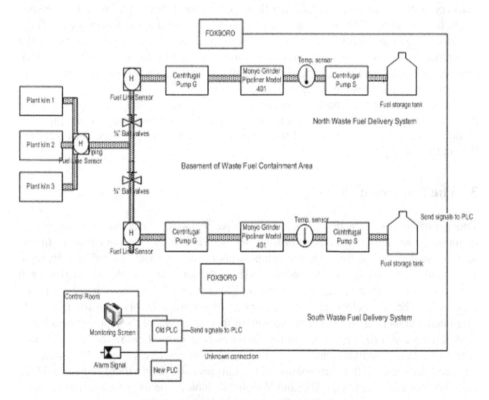

Fig. 1. Simplified waste fuel delivery plant

There is also a pressure sensor in the plant kiln area where the north and south fuel lines join. They are represented by the following symbol in the diagram:

The sensors detect a number of abnormal conditions that will generate warning alarms in the control room. The command and control system will also automatically intervene to increase or decrease the speed of the pump motors when pressure is too low or too high. The fuel line pressure sensors also send information directly to the pump-S and G motors to maintain the correct pressure of fuel to the three plant kilns via the automatic step increase program.

The waste fuel delivery system has two independent but interconnected electronic systems for monitoring and controlling both the north and the south fuel delivery systems. The 'F' system receives signals from sensors located on fuel lines. The data is transmitted to a PLC, which raises audible and visible alarms in the control room and can also update more detailed process information on the monitoring screen.

2.1 Events Leading to the Accident

A seal on the north grinder overheated. The kiln control operator and supervisor decided to switch waste fuel delivery systems from north to south. The worker switched delivery systems; however fuel did not flow to the plant kilns as planned. The personnel believed the problem was due to air being trapped in the south fuel pipes. They, therefore, bled the valves of the south system while the motors were running. In the meantime, due to the low pressure being sensed in the fuel lines, the automatic step increase program was increasing the speed of the motors on the south pumps in an attempt to increase pressure in the fuel line.

These various factors combined to create a 'fuel hammer effect' in the pipe feeding the south pump. The hammer effect is caused by rebound waves created in a pipe full of liquid when the valve is closed too quickly. The waves of pressure converged on the south grinder.

3 The Approach

The approach has been designed to show how incident and accident investigation techniques can support the design of safety-critical interactive systems design. In this section we decompose the principle components of the approach, notably the incident and accident investigation side and the system design side, and detail the role each part has in the method. Fig. 2 represents an illustration of the phases involved in the approach. The key below describes the types of activities involved in the approach. The black numbering highlights the section in this paper where the phase is detailed.

Although a significant amount of research has been carried out in the fields of incident and accident analysis and system modelling of interactive systems, little research has been dedicated to the combination of techniques used within these domains. There are some notable exceptions. Hill and Wright [6] look at the use of Petri nets (as well as Accident Fault Trees and Why-Because-Graphs) to graphically represent incident and accident reports to improve safety in safety-critical systems by learning from accidents. Although this aim is the same as ours, we are not implying that incident and accident investigators should learn to use techniques generally uncommon to their domain. Instead we wish incident and accident investigators to continue using techniques that they are experienced with. We are also not suggesting the combination of

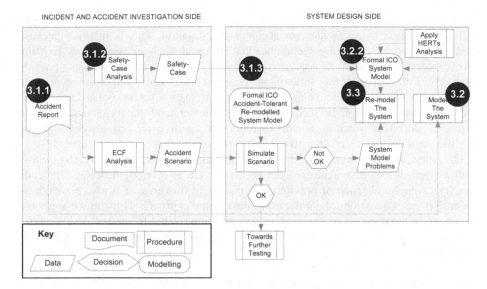

Fig. 2. Key phases in the approach

incident and accident investigation techniques with system modelling techniques to reduce the complexity and improve the understanding of accident reports. We aim for the results of accident investigation to be used to inform the systems engineers in two ways. Firstly, by informing the modelling the system and secondly, by taking into account hazardous events identified using the investigation techniques.

Johnson [3] has also used Petri-nets to reconstruct general systems failures that characterise safety-critical incidents, where places can be considered as human behaviour, conditions, environmental attributes etc., and transitions can be considered as events that trigger a mishap. However, the purpose of method is not to identify ways in which the mishap could have been avoided but to show that the notation was able to represent all the relevant information provided in a report. In this paper, we do not aim to use Petri nets to model the accident. By modelling hazardous events identified using the accident investigation techniques, we are able to use formal analysis with to indicate ways in which the accident place modelled by a Petri net can be blocked from being marked with a token.

3.1 Incident and Accident Investigation

Previous editions of the DSVIS workshop series have presented many different ways in which specification and verification techniques can be used to support the design of novel interactive systems. The assumption is usually that a period of requirements elicitation helps to drive the design, then implementation and finally evaluation of an interactive system. Usually these different activities merge and are conducted in an iterative fashion. In contrast, this paper focuses on the aftermath of an adverse event. In such circumstances, there is a pressing need to ensure proposed designs do not propagate previous weaknesses into future systems.

Incident and Accident Investigation Techniques. As mentioned, our analysis begins with the products of an incident or accident investigation. This is justified because there are no recognized design techniques that start with such an assumption. Existing investigatory tools, such as Ladkin and Loer's Why Because Analysis, provide relatively little support for subsequent redesign [8]. They focus more on the identification of root causes in an objective and systematic manner. Other approaches, such as Leveson's STAMP technique, help to understand the organizational and systemic context in which an accident occurs but, again, offer few insights into the specific steps that can be taken to avoid any future repetitions of adverse events [9].

Of course, our decision to begin with the products of an accident investigation is both a strength and a weakness of our technique. It is a strength because it lends novelty given the absence of previous approaches in this area. It is also a weakness because it raises questions about the usefulness of the approach. How do we apply the technique in the absence of an accident investigation? What happens if risk analysis identifies a potential problem with an existing design but no accident has happened yet and there is no formal investigation yet?

In order to address these issues, we have chosen to use a safety case notation to represent the insights from an accident investigation. Techniques such as the Goal Structuring Notation, illustrated below, help to identify the key arguments that can be used to demonstrate the relative safety of a complex system. Accidents often reveal the flaws in these arguments. Hence, we can represent the insights obtained in the aftermath of an adverse event in terms of the consequent changes that must be made to a safety case. Of course, this is not the only way in which we might trigger revisions to such arguments. Near-miss incident reports or revised hazard and risk assessments can also be used to further inform the safety cases that justify a complex system [3].

Safety Cases. A safety case is "a documented body of evidence that provides a convincing and valid argument that a system is adequately safe for a given application in a given environment" [7]. Safety cases comprise of safety requirements and objectives, the safety argument, and the supporting evidence. Goal Structuring Notation (GSN) [7] is a graphical argumentation notation, which represents the components of a safety argument, and their relationships.

Fig. 3 depicts a safety case using GSN. The safety requirement G1 in this example would be to assure that the 'Monitoring of Pressure in the South Waste Delivery System' is as safe as possible. In order to argue that G1 is valid, two strategies have been deployed (S1.1 and S1.2). The argument is continued with new safety sub-goals, until they can not be broken down any more. At this stage, evidence proving proof that the safety requirement is met is required (E1.2). For arguments that need further elaboration, GSN uses the diamond symbol to index to related elements of a safety case.

Safety Cases are interesting and useful because they present the whole view and strategy towards achieving safety. When applied in an accident the way proposed in this paper, we can therefore discuss not only technical or human failures, but understand more about the deeper problems that led to these failures taking place, organizational and so on. An example safety case using the Goal Structuring Notation is presented in Fig. 3. Although based on our hypothetical views about the system, we can assume that in order to assure safety of the command and control system of our case study, claims like the ones in Fig 5 would have been made.

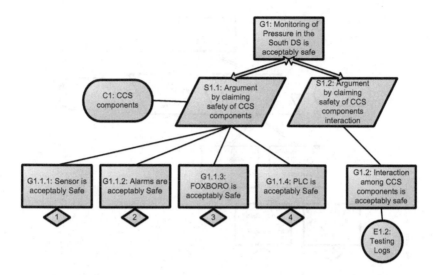

Fig. 3. Safety case using the Goal Structuring Notation

This safety case argues that, in order to achieve safety of the 'Monitoring of Pressure in the South Waste Delivery System', all components of the monitoring system should be functioning properly, and that their interaction is non- hazardous. In order to establish this claim, the safety of each component would then be elaborated in a new safety case, and so on, until a safety goal cannot be broken down to any other sub-goals.

Analyzing the Accident. Accident reports can be an unreliable source of information; they may be incomplete and can be subject to bias. This would create potential problems for any approach that uses the results of these investigations to inform future redevelopment. It is, therefore, important that potential omissions, inconsistencies and bias are identified prior to the analysis described in this paper, for instance, using the types of systematic analysis advocated in Johnson (2003). In contrast, our use of GSN focuses on establishing an argument for redesign rather than on the identification of weaknesses within a mishap report. There are two dimensions of this accident. Firstly, the workers interfered with the pump in a manner against manufacturer's guidelines, setting off the chain of events that led to the 'water-hammer effect' occurring and thus the accident. The second dimension is the failure of the monitoring system to identify the pressure increase in the piping of the system, and initiating the control mechanisms that would have probably prevented the accident from happening. In this section we will discuss how and what assumptions about safety regarding these two aspects were false, and what implications they have about system design, by constructing safety cases about them.

Water-Hammer Effect. First of all, the 'water- hammer effect' refers to the generation of a pressure peak to a pipe. This is caused by a sudden fluctuation on pressure. It is a known phenomenon that can damage equipment and engineers have suggested a number of approaches to prevent it from occurring at times where pressure is rising

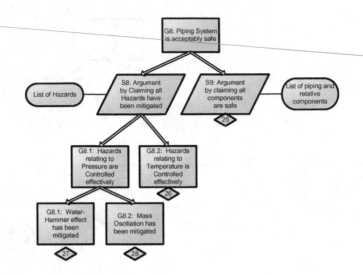

Fig. 4. Considering all hazards that can arise from High-Pressure

dangerously [5]. During the design of the fuel handling system we are investigating, the water-hammer effect was probably not taken into account. Although it is a result of high pressure, which is monitored by the command and control system, applications such as 'pressure intensifiers' [5] have been suggested as barriers against the water-hammer effect. In any case, we can assume that when considering all possible hazards that could reach the piping, the water-hammer effect, along with other phenomena such as 'mass oscillation' could have been taken into account [15] (Fig. 4).

Failure of the Command and Control System. As mentioned, safety cases consist of claims that are based on design and use of the system. For instance, in order to argue that a component of the system is 'acceptably safe', claims about training practices regarding the use of the specific component, as well as maintenance adhering to manufacturer's guidelines would also have to be incorporated in the argumentation (Fig. 5). In this way, we can visualize how technical, human and organizational aspects are interconnected in order to assure safety. On the other hand, we can also see at a high level how these issues relate to each other in a failure.

Regarding monitoring activities of manual handling (Fig. 5), the two workers involved in the accident were been watched by the control operator in the control room, and had radio contact. However, their training did not include the manufacturer's guidelines not to bleed air from the pumps while they are operating, nor were they aware of the automatic shutdown process the system initiated on its own. Therefore, when discussing the role of human error in this case, it should be taken into account the workers were not trained accordingly. In fact, other workers had performed the exact same activities, ignoring manufacturer's guidelines in the past.

The safety case in Fig. 6 argues the safety of the PLC, the component of the Command and Control System that was identified in the accident report as a major cause of the accident. Although this can be viewed as a technical failure, it also has

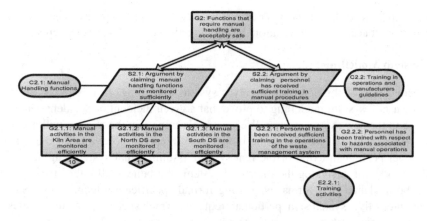

Fig. 5. Safety of manual activities

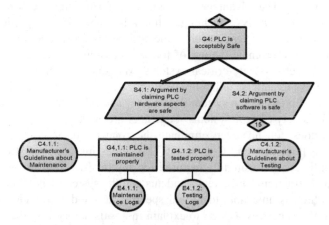

Fig. 6. Arguing the safety of the PLC

organizational implications: Maintenance and testing were not carried out as they were supposed to be. This allowed for the technical failure to occur, as the PLC was not connected for a period of three months.

The previous section has extended the application of GSN from safety case generation to provide a very high level framework for the analysis of accidents and incidents. It can be used to identify any underlying problems in the arguments that were intended to demonstrate the safety of a complex system. It also encourages analysts to think beyond the specific events in an accident to consider whether they are symptomatic of wider failures. For instance, a failure to maintain key components in a programmable system might indicate the need to look for similar failures in other areas of an application by looking for similar maintenance arguments to G4.1.1. in other areas of the GSN.

Unfortunately, the level of analysis supported by the GSN is not detailed enough to work out the specifics of any subsequent redesign. It is for this reason that we have recruited the assistance of the DSVIS community to identify specific ways of using the products of accident investigation during the redesign of complex systems.

3.2   System Modelling Side

The second side of the approach involves system modelling. In this paper, we promote the use of system modelling to prove that a given incident or accident cannot be triggered in the new system design. We are not claiming that the mishap will not recur in the real system, but merely in the model describing the behaviour of the system. This model is an abstraction of the real system assuming that system engineers will use that model for designing the improved system. We believe all interactive systems should be modelled in a formal way using formal specification techniques. Safety-critical interactive systems in particular require formal specification techniques as they provide non-ambiguous, complete and concise notations. This ensures that the description of the system model is precise and that the model allows accurate reasoning about the system. The advantages of using such formalisms are widened if they are provided by formal analysis techniques that allow checking properties about the design, thus giving an early verification to the designer before the application is actually implemented. We promote the use of formal notations so that we can verify the properties of interactive safety-critical systems. Without such notations there is no means for designers to address reliability. Even for a system that is not safety-critical, it is still necessary to ensure the system's efficiency and reliability but these issues are more salient for safety-critical systems. Petri nets are widely used in systems engineering. This does not, however, eliminate the concern that a complementary approach based on Petri nets and Concurrent Task Trees may impose strong expectations on the skill sets that would be required for any investigation. It is also hard to make the right abstractions of the real accidents and the system behaviour involved in the accident, which is amenable to formal specification and automatic analysis and still reflects all the necessary aspects to explain in a satisfactory way the causes of an accident. Equally, a range of recent initiatives have begun to recognize the importance of explicit and detailed training if accident investigation agencies are to cope with the increasing complexity of many safety-critical application processes. For example, the NTSB recently opened its Academy for investigators in Virginia. Brevity prevents a detailed introduction to the Petri net notation however interested readers can look at [14].

Informal presentation of the ICO formalism. This section recalls the main features of the ICO formalism that we use for the system modelling of the case study in Sec. 0. The Interactive Cooperative Objects (ICOs) formalism is a formal description technique dedicated to the specification of interactive systems [2]. It uses concepts borrowed from the object-oriented approach (dynamic instantiation, classification, encapsulation, inheritance, client/server relationship) to describe the structural or static aspects of systems, and uses high-level Petri nets [4] to describe their dynamic or behavioural aspects.

ICOs are used to provide a formal description of the dynamic behaviour of an interactive application. An ICO specification fully describes the potential interactions that users may have with the application. The specification encompasses both the "input" aspects of the interaction (i.e. how user actions impact on the inner state of the application, and which actions are enabled at any given time) and its "output" aspects (i.e. when and how the application displays information relevant to the user). An ICO specification is fully executable, which gives the possibility to prototype and test an application before it is fully implemented [12]. The specification can also be validated using analysis and proof tools developed within the Petri nets community and extended in order to take into account the specificities of the Petri net dialect used in the ICO formal description technique.

Modelling using ICOs. The waste fuel delivery system has been modelled using the ICO notation to deliver a relatively high level of detail of the behaviour of the system. In this section, we present one Petri net model (Fig. 7) representing the north pump-s and its motor to provide an overview of modelling using Petri nets. We later present a model of the entire waste fuel delivery system which is composed of a number of smaller Petri nets representing each component of the plant. In the following analysis, we use the following symbols:

- States are represented by the distribution of tokens into places.
- Actions triggered in an autonomous way by the system are called transitions and are represented as arrows.
- Actions triggered by users are represented by half bordered transition.

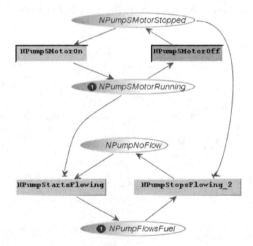

Fig. 7. Example of a Petri net modelling a north pump-s and its motor

The models presented in this section are based on the authors' interpretation of information provided in the accident report and also from data further obtained after researching for particular plant components on the internet. Each pump in the waste fuel delivery system consists of a motor to pump the fuel through the pipes and a valve (Fig. 7 does not include the valve). The motor can be 'on' or 'off' and the valve can be 'open' or 'closed' for the purpose of bleeding air. The Petri net model describing the behaviour of the pump motor (Fig. 7) is composed of two connected parts, the motor and the corresponding fuel flow, i.e. when the motor is running, the fuel flows provided the tank is open. This condition is not modelled in this Petri net as we are currently describing the independent behaviour of north pump component. The global Petri net, provided later in this section, models the interconnection of components and is dedicated to make explicit the description of such conditions. The north pump motors are set by default to 'on' to allow the fuel to flow to the kilns. Thus there is a token in place *NPumpSMotorRunning* and in place *NPumpFlowsFuel*. If the NPumpSMotorOff user action transition is fired, a token is placed in *NPumpSMotorStopped* and the fuel therefore stops flowing and a token is set in place *NPumpNoFlow*. The system model has been built based on the schematic diagram (see Fig. 1) of the waste fuel delivery system and reflects the same topology. Due to space constraints, we are not able to describe the behaviour of each part of the north system in terms of a Petri net and its functionality within the plant.

Fig. 8 below represents the entire plant as a Petri net based on several smaller nets (corresponding to the various components of the plant, such as that shown in Fig. 7) that have been connected to create the complete system model. The connections are based on fuel flow. Fuel can either stop flowing if its corresponding motor is not running or fuel from the previous component is not flowing. For example, fuel cannot flow from a grinder into a pump G, even if the grinder motor is running and the correct fuel storage tank is open, if the fuel is not flowing from the previous pump S.

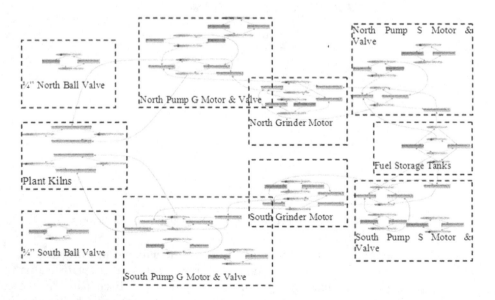

Fig. 8. Complete system model

3.3 Re-modelling Exploiting the Safety Cases

One of our aims for including data from incident and accident investigations in safety-critical interactive systems design is to ensure that the same incident or accident analyzed will not occur again in the re-modelled system. That is, that an accident place within the network will be blocked from containing a token. To this end, we extend the system model presented in Fig. 8 to include hazardous states identified in the safety-cases presented above. It is important to stress that the hazards shown in table 1 are not explicitly represented in the high-level safety-case shown in previous sections. They do, however, appear at more detailed levels of our analysis. Each hazard is explicitly represented in its own GSN diagram hence brevity prevents the inclusion of all of these individual diagrams.

The work on system modelling presented in this paper differs from what we have previously done. Indeed, previous work dealt with the design of new command and control systems and thus the design process was at first related to task analysis and modelling and then the construction of a system (through system modelling) compliant with the task models resulting from the task analysis phase. In this section, we present how this approach can be extended to take into account the hazards highlighted in the safety-cases. The system model for this case study has been extended to explicitly represent hazardous system states and actions identified from the safety cases. The aim is not to model every possible problematic situation that can occur in the system model. It is highly reasonable that not all of the information provided in a safety-case can be applied to a system model, for example information regarding personnel and training. However, we aim to show how the behaviour of the system can be influenced by hazardous events (such as a water hammer effect) and also lead to hazardous states.

Table 1. Summary of hazardous states identified from incident and accident investigation

	Hazard Name	Brief Description	Type of Dimension
1.	Water Hammer Effect	Caused by rebound waves created in a pipe full of liquid when a valve is closed too quickly.	System
2.	PLC Not Connected	The new PLC was not connected to the F-System.	Interactive
3.	Valves Bled While System in Operation	The valves should not be bled while the system is in operation	Interactive
4.	Motors Running Dry	Occurs when motors are turned on but fuel is not in pipes	Interactive
5.	Fuel Spreading	Occurs when the valves are bled while motors and fuel are running	Interactive
6.	Gathering Air	Air can gather in a pump if the valve was not bled before start-up of the system.	Interactive

The Petri Net in Fig. 9 shows the extended model for the north pump-S motor and valve components. The extensions include three possible hazards (4, 5 and 6) from Table 1. While incorporating potential hazards into the system model makes the Petri Net more complex.

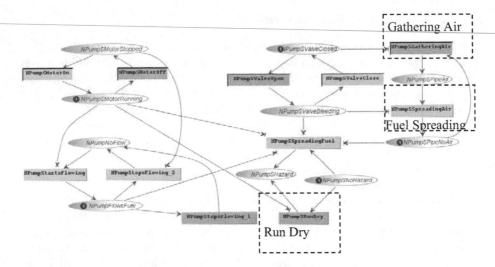

Fig. 9. North pump-S motor & valve including three hazards

However, these models can be easily manipulated thanks to the executability characteristics of the ICO formalism and its related environment PetShop [11]. Due to space constraints we only informally present this capability in next section.

3.4 Incident Scenario to Support New System Validation

Briefly, an ICO specification can be executed to provide a prototype User Interface (UI) of the application under design. It is then possible to proceed with validation of the system by applying techniques such as user testing.

However, in this paper, we are concerned with the application of a scenario that has been extracted using incident and accident investigation techniques in order to prove that the informed system design does not allow the same sequence of events to occur and thus not re-trigger the accident. By applying such development techniques, the validation of the safety-critical system appears earlier in the design process than in more classic techniques. A formal validation occurs through the use of verification techniques and analysis tools. This validation is possible due to the algebraic foundation of the Petri nets.

4   Conclusion

This paper has provided the first steps towards the use of accident investigations to inform system modelling and verification. We deliberately chose to integrate approaches that are pitched at different levels of abstraction. The accident analysis focused on a novel application of the GSN technique for the development of Safety Cases. This decision was deliberate because GSN provides means of representing the implicit assumptions that are often difficult to capture in formal models of interactive systems. For instance, previous diagrams have represented assumptions about maintenance intervals and the adequacy of training for particular system operators.

The decision to use GSN in the preliminary stages of this work creates numerous problems. It would have been far easier to use an event based reconstruction technique such as Events and Causal Factors analysis, promoted by the US Dept of Energy. There would then be a relatively automatic translation from this analysis into the places and transitions of the systems models. We chose not to do this because we believe that the higher-level analysis provided by GSN complements the more detailed systems modelling promoted in previous DSVIS workshops. However, there is no automatic translation from the insights provided by the application of GSN to the properties that we might want to verify using the ICO models. This is the subject of current research where, for example, task analysis has been used as a stepping-stone towards the identification of theorems to assert against particular system models [9]. We can take high-level safety goals from the GSN, such as the need to ensure effective maintenance. These can be broken into a large number of different sub-tasks. We can then analyze the systems support that is available for each of these subtasks. However, it is unlikely that we will ever be able to automate the process of deriving putative theorems from the often highly contextual and situated observations of accident investigations.

The second stage of our approach relies upon system modelling using the underlying Petri Net formalism embedded within the ICO approach. This offers numerous benefits. Firstly, the process of translating high-level observations from the safety case analysis helps to ensure that the meta-level arguments about system failures can be instantiated in terms of specific subsystems. In other words, the construction of the systems model helps to validate technical assumptions in the accident report. If we cannot develop a coherent system model then there may well be important details that have been omitted from the account of an accident. Secondly, the development of the system model provides an abstract representation that is amenable both to animation and various forms of proof. This enables us to go beyond the specific scenarios of an individual accident. We can begin to experiment with new designs to ensure that they would not suffer from the same problems as previous designs. In other words we can conduct various forms of reachability analysis to determine whether a new or revised system might reach the same unsafe state. This style of analysis offers other benefits because we can begin to look for other transitions that were not observed in the particular accident being analyzed but that might lead to the same undesired outcomes in future accidents.

Acknowledgements

This work was supported by the EU funded ADVISES Research Training Network, GR/N 006R02527. http://www.cs.york.ac.uk/hci/ADVISES/

References

1. Bastide R., Palanque P., Le Duc H., and Munoz J. Integrating Rendering Specifications into a Formalism for the Design of Interactive Systems. Proceedings Design, Specification and Verification of Interactive Systems DSV-IS'98, pp. 171–191, 1998. Springer Verlag
2. Bastide, Rémi; Sy, Ousmane; Palanque, Philippe, and Navarre, David. Formal specification of CORBA services: experience and lessons learned. ACM Conference on Object-Oriented Programming, Systems, Languages, and Applications (OOPSLA'2000), pp. 105–117. ACM Press; 2000.

3. C.W. Johnson, Handbook of Accident and Incident Reporting, Glasgow University Press, 2003.
4. Genrich, H.J. Predicate/Transitions Nets. High-Levels Petri-Nets: Theory and Application. K Jensen and G Rozenberg (Eds) Berlin: Springer Verlag (1991) pp 3-43
5. Haiko, S., Lehto, E. and Virvaldo, T. Modelling of Water Hammer Phenomenon- Based Pressure Intensifier. [http://www.callisto.si.usherb.ca/~fluo2000/PDF/Fl_078.pdf] Last accessed 23/2/05
6. Hill, J. C. & Wright, P. C. (1997) From text to Petri-Nets: The difficulties of describing accident scenarios formally. Design, Specification and Verification of Interactive Systems (DSVIS '97), pp. 161–176, Granada, Spain, Springer-Verlag
7. Kelly, T. and Rob Weaver. The Goal Structuring Notation: A Safety Argument Notation. Proceedings of the Dependable Systems and Networks 2004 Workshop on Assurance Cases, 2004
8. Ladkin, P and Loer, K, Why Because Analysis: Formal Reasoning About Incidents, Technical Report RVS-BK-98-01, University of Bielefeld, Germany, 1998.
9. Leveson N A New Accident Model for Engineering Safer Systems. Safety Science, 42 (2004): 237 – 270.
10. Navarre, D., Palanque, P. and Bastide, R. A Formal Description Technique for the Behavioural Description of Interactive Applications Compliant with ARINC 661 Specification. HCI-Aero'04 Toulouse, France, 29 September-1st October 2004
11. Navarre, D., Palanque, P., Bastide, R., 2003, A Tool-Supported Design Framework for Safety Critical Interactive Systems in Interacting with computers, Elsevier, Vol. 15/3, pp 309-328. 2003
12. Navarre, D., Palanque, P., Bastide, R., and Sy, O. Structuring Interactive Systems Specifications for Executability and Prototypability. 7th Ergonomics Workshop on Design, Specification and Verification of Interactive Systems. DSV-IS'2000, Limerick, Ireland. Lecture Notes in Computer Science, no. 1946. Springer (2000), 97-109
13. Palanque, P and Basnyat, S., 2004, Task Patterns for taking into account in an efficient and systematic way both standard and erroneous user behaviours. HESSD 2004 6th International Working Conference on Human Error, Safety and System Development, pp. 109–130, Toulouse, France.
14. Petri, C. A. Kommunikation mit automaten. Technical University Darmstadt; 1962
15. Thorley, A. R.D. Fluid Transients in Pipeline Systems, Co-published by Professional Engineering Publishing, UK, and ASME Press. 2004
16. United States Department Of Labor Mine Safety And Health Administration Report Of Investigation Surface Area Of Underground Coal Mine Fatal Exploding Pressure Vessel Accident January 28, 2002 At Island Creek Coal Company Vp 8 (I.D. 44-03795) Mavisdale, Buchanan County, Virginia Accident Investigator Arnold D. Carico Mining Engineer Originating Office Mine Safety And Health Administration District 5 P.O. Box 560, Wise County Plaza, Norton, Virginia 24273 Ray Mckinney, District Manager Release Date: June 20, 2002

Natural Modelling of Interactive Applications

Fabio Paternò and Marco Volpe

ISTI-CNR, Via G.Moruzzi,
1 56126 Pisa, Italy
fabio.paterno@isti.cnr.it
http://giove.isti.cnr.it/

Abstract. This paper presents an approach, and the associated environment, aiming to support designers to intuitively model interactive applications. The goal is to make modelling activity more natural. The approach is based on a transformation able to convert hand-drawn visual model sketches on boards into task-model specifications that are further editable and analysable through automatic visual tools. A first test of the environment has been carried out and has provided useful suggestions about how to improve it.

1 Introduction

Design and development of interactive software systems still require considerable effort. In natural interaction the goal is to ease the user interaction by providing techniques that make the interaction with a system similar to how humans usually interact. This has raised further interest in new interaction modalities and multi-modal interfaces in general. This natural interaction paradigm can also be applied to the design and development cycle in order to ease building interactive software systems. Some work has already been dedicated to obtaining natural programming [12], which aims to support programming through languages understandable by people without specific programming skills. On the one hand, natural development implies that people should be able to work through familiar and immediately understandable representations that allow them to easily express relevant concepts, and thereby create or modify applications. On the other hand, since a software artefact needs to be precisely specified in order to be implemented, there will still be the need for environments supporting transformations from intuitive and familiar representations into precise—but more difficult to develop—descriptions.

Thus, integrating informal and structured specifications is a key issue. The usability of development environments can benefit from using multiple representations with various levels of formality. In fact, at the beginning of the design process many things are vague and unclear, so it is hard to develop precise specifications from scratch, especially because a clear understanding of the user requirements is a non-trivial activity. The main issue is how to exploit personal intuition, familiar metaphors and concepts to obtain/modify a software artefact. Examples of informal input for more structured representations are textual scenarios [15] and sketches on boards [8]. For example, non-programmer users feel comfortable

S.W. Gilroy and M.D. Harrison (Eds.): DSVIS 2005, LNCS 3941, pp. 67–77, 2006.

with sketch-based systems that allow them to concentrate on concepts by exploiting natural interactions, instead of being distracted by cumbersome low-level details required by rigid symbolisms. Such systems are generally able to recognise graphical elements and convert them into formats that can be edited and analysed by other software tools.

The use of hand-drawn sketches for supporting the design cycle has already been considered in several works but, to our knowledge, it has not been considered for supporting the development of HCI models, such as task models. Software Design Board [17] has addressed the issue of supporting a variety of collaboration styles but in creating UML diagrams. SketchiXML [4] is a tool that allows the creation of sketches representing how the user interface should appear and convert them into logical concrete descriptions of the user interface that can then be manipulated for further processing through other tools. The Calì library [5] has been used to develop JavaSketchIt, a tool able to recognise user-drawn sketches representing user interfaces and generate the corresponding Java implementation.

Our work has a different goal: to provide an environment that makes it possible to interpret informal sketches and translate them into the associated task model descriptions that can be used for various purposes, including development of ubiquitous interfaces. In particular, one of the main contributions is in supporting a transformation able to recognise the semantic and syntactical structure of a ConcurTaskTrees task model [14] starting with some basic symbols recognised from hand-drawn sketches. This is part of a more general effort aiming to support end user development, which can be defined as a set of methods, techniques, and tools that allow users of software systems, including non-professional software developers, at some point to create, modify or extend a software artefact. In particular, our ultimate goal is to create environments that allow people with different backgrounds to easily create task models of ubiquitous interfaces, which can be used for prototyping the corresponding interfaces for the various devices supporting them. Indeed, a tool (TERESA [11]) already exists that is able to support a number of transformations to generate user interfaces adapted to different interaction platforms and modalities starting with logical descriptions of task models. The transformation from task descriptions to the user interface for a given platform exploits intermediate conceptual user interface descriptions and takes into account the interaction resources of the target platform. One advantage of this approach is that it allows designers to focus on the conceptual aspects without having to deal with a plethora of low-level implementation details of the potential devices. Thus, designers can be people without programming skills.

In this area the introduction of visual modeller tools represented an important step forward in the adoption of model-based approaches but it is not enough because many people still find this activity difficult and tedious, even when supported by such visual tools. Thus, research has started aiming to provide further support. Possible solutions have considered the use of textual scenarios where names are automatically associated with objects and verbs with tasks [16], or the use of vocal interfaces supported by some natural language processing [2]. In other cases the use of reverse engineering techniques applied to either user interface implementations [3, 13] or logs of user interactions [7] has been considered.

In this paper we present a novel solution based on the analysis of hand-drawn sketches. In particular, we first introduce the overall architecture of the proposed environment, and then we discuss how the sketches are interpreted and how the result of the first low-level recognition is used to obtain the task model specification. The results of a first test are reported along with some useful suggestions for improvements that have emerged. Lastly, conclusions and indications for future work are presented.

2   The Architecture of the Environment

A good deal of work has been dedicated to developing tools able to convert hand-written sketches into digital formats or to support hand-written sketches of user interfaces and then convert them into corresponding specifications or implementations. However, so far no work has been dedicated to the development of environments able to recognise task models from hand-written sketches on board. This is an important goal because often the modelling work is time-consuming and a bit tedious, and such support can ease this phase. In addition, often the modelling work is the result of an interdisciplinary discussion carried out with the support of boards, where the involved actors can easily draw, modify, and cancel the elements composing the model. In designing our environment we have considered two previously available tools: the Mimio board [9] and the CTTE (ConcurTaskTrees Environment) tool [10]. The former is a device able to detect the strokes drawn with special pens on the board using ultrasound signals. It uses a high-resolution ultrasonic position capture system consisting of a capture bar, colour-coded marker sleeves and an electronic eraser. The capture bar is an ultrasonic tracking array positioned along the upper left edge of the whiteboard. The capture bar connects to a personal computer. The electronic marker sleeves transmit an ultrasonic signal to the capture bar, which triangulates the pen's position on the board as the user writes. The only change users must make is to be sure they use the electronic eraser to make corrections, since Mimio cannot capture changes made with a standard eraser or with one's fingers. The Mimio system captures each move of a marker or stylus on the whiteboard surface as digital data that expresses vector strokes over time. The information detected can be stored in various electronic formats, including SVG, the language for vectorial graphical representations in Web environments. The CTTE environment is a publicly available tool that supports the possibility of editing and analysing task models specified in the ConcurTaskTrees notation. The features supporting editing are multi-fold (direct manipulation of the model structure, layout improvement, lining up of tasks at the same level, etc.) as well as those supporting analysis (interactive simulator, metrics calculation, comparison of models, etc.). The tool can import/export specifications in an XML-based description. Consequently, as shown in Fig. 1 (rectangles represent processes and hexagons represent their outputs), the new environment that we have designed has to support the transformation from the SVG description of the hand-written diagram into a XML specification of the task model that can be imported in the tool supporting further editing and analysis.

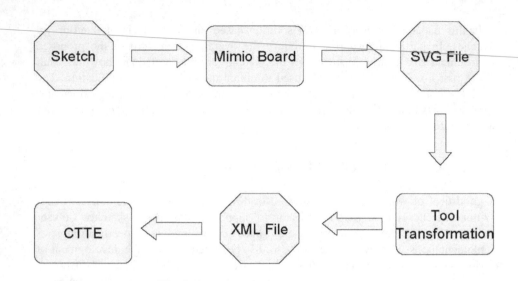

Fig. 1. The Architecture of the environment

Thus, one main component of our environment is a transformation able to take as input the low-level descriptions of the hand-drawn sketches and build the logical and syntactical structure of the corresponding task model. In next sections we discuss the solution that has been identified for this purpose.

3   Recognizing Hand-Written Sketches

As we have introduced in the foregoing, our environment has to provide a transformation able to take the description of a hand-written sketch and convert it into a specification of the task model that can be imported in a tool for further editing or analysis or used for development. To this end, we have not implemented the transformation able to take the elementary drawings and identify the corresponding symbols because a number of tools have already been developed for this purpose. Rather, we have designed a transformation able to take the set of elementary symbols associated with users strokes, recognise the corresponding elements of the task model and identify the associated structure in order to obtain a specification that can be imported in the task modelling environment. In particular, in order to recognise the basic symbols we have analysed two possible solutions: the Rubine [15] and Calì [5] libraries. Both of them have advantages and disadvantages. In Rubine's approach the set of basic graphical symbols recognisable is modifiable but it is only able to recognise graphic symbols drawn through a single stroke. In Cali it is possible to recognise graphical symbols that are drawn through multiple strokes but the set of recognisable gestures is fixed and it also requires information regarding when each stroke has been drawn. Thus, we have decided to use the Rubine's algorithm because it does not put any limitation in terms of graphical symbols that can be recognised and does not require temporal information regarding the various gestures (our electronic

Fig. 2. An example of use of the proposed environment

board does not provide such temporal information). Figure 2 shows an example of use of the electronic board for drawing a task model. It allows designers to freely draw and modify sketches of the visual specification.

4   The Transformation from Sketches to Models

The main visual elements in ConcurTaskTrees are the task names, the graphical symbols indicating how task performance is allocated, the symbols associated with temporal operators and the lines indicating task decomposition and task siblings. Figure 3 shows the user interface of the CTTE environment with an example of task model specification. One feature of the notation is to have different icons to represent task allocation: user (only internal cognitive activities), system (automatically performed), interaction, abstract (higher level tasks whose subtasks are allocated differently). Such icons can be represented in the tool in two ways selectable by the user: either images conveying the type of allocation or geometrical shapes that are useful when people draw task models on paper or board. The model in Fig. 3 uses icons in the latter representation. In the new environment, we have simply changed the representation of abstract tasks from dotted ovals to triangles, which are easier to draw.

In order to perform the transformation, we have first carefully identified the set of basic symbols that should be recognised (they are represented in Fig. 4). They are the graphical shapes representing task allocation, the lines connecting tasks, the symbols representing the temporal operators and the letters used for the task identifiers. In

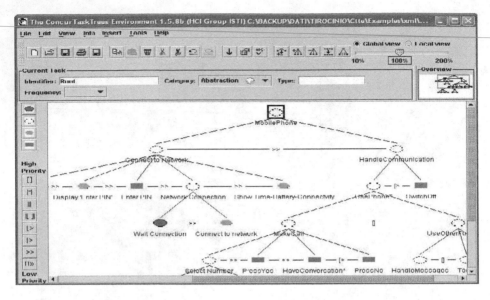

Fig. 3. An example of CTTE representation of the task model

Fig. 4. The set of basic symbols recognised

particular, the temporal operators are represented by composing five elementary symbols ("[", "]", ">", "l", "="). Regarding the lines for representing the structure of the tree we have considered four types of lines: vertical lines, two types of oblique lines, and horizontal lines. For each elementary graphical symbol only one method for drawing has been defined. For example, in the case of a triangle, the user has to start with the vertex located at the top and then draw in the anticlockwise direction.

In order to apply the transformation there is first a training phase during which at least ten examples of each basic graphical symbol to be recognised are provided and

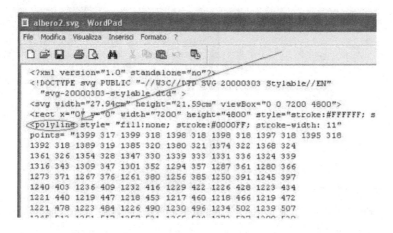

Fig. 5. An excerpt of a SVG specification generated by the Mimio software

analysed through the Rubine algorithm. We have used a Java implementation of this algorithm, which has been made publicly available by the GUIR group at University of Berkeley [6]. This algorithm is limited to the recognition of the basic symbols associated with each stroke type. To this end, the algorithm associates mathematical representations to the main geometrical features of the symbol, then it applies a function to identify which of the possible symbols is closest to the one currently considered.

The SVG file generated by the Mimio board is rather simple. Even if SVG supports various constructs, the files generated mainly contain only various polyline instances. Each polyline is associated with one stroke representing a single graphical element. The Rubine algorithm identifies the element associated with the graphic symbol detected by analysing the previously provided example set of each possible element and evaluating what the most similar is. Then, our algorithm performs a number of further processing steps necessary to recognise the elements of the task model and its structure. Task names are identified by analysing the positions of the characters recognised and grouping those which are located closest to each other. A similar process is followed to recognise the representations of temporal operators. A task is associated with each symbol instance representing task allocation, and the closest name recognised is associated to this instance.

Then, our algorithm first identifies the root task in the hierarchical structure, which is that positioned in the highest part of the board. In order to recognise the structure of the model we divide the lines between those useful to identify parent/child relations (vertical and oblique ones) and those for identifying sibling nodes (horizontal lines). Once a vertical or oblique line has been recognised, our algorithm looks for the task closest to the top and the bottom, which will be the parent and the child task, respectively. Likewise, two sibling tasks are identified when a horizontal line is recognised. Once the model has been built, it is coded into the corresponding XML-based specification, which can be imported into the CTTE environment.

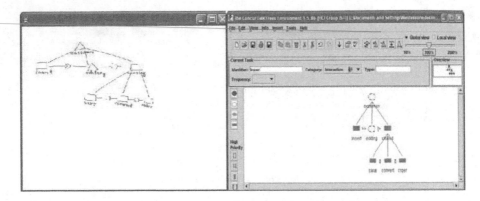

Fig. 6. SVG representation of hand-drawn model and its transformation

In order to perform its processing our tool takes as input the SVG file created by the electronic board and its software. It also supports previewing of the hand-drawn representation represented through SVG. Then, it asks for the set of examples to use to identify the main features of each basic symbol to recognise. Such input is used to calculate the task model structure. Figure 6 shows an example of the SVG representation and the corresponding task model imported in the CTTE environment.

5   A First Test

Once we had designed and created a first prototype, we tested it in order to assess the level of reliability and correctness of the transformation supported. In practice, we performed two types of test: one aiming at revealing whether the tool provides correct results if it uses a set of examples provided by another user; the other one to highlight the level of reliability in recognising the task model. Overall, the test involved 14 users recruited in the Institute or among friends.

In the first test different people created a set of hand-written examples for each symbol. Then, they had to create one task model and the tool was applied using the different sets of examples available in order to understand whether the recognition ability was affected by the person who drew the examples used by the algorithm. Thus, we compared the results when the set was provided by the same person who provided the examples or a different one. The test showed that when the task model was drawn by the same person almost everything was correctly recognised, whereas some problems came up in the case of a different person. In particular, there were some errors in recognising some characters (this was deemed a minor issue since if a character is not correct in a task name it can be easily correct later on), sometimes hexagons were replaced with triangles and some problems were detected in recognising horizontal lines.

In the other test, the 14 users had to draw a predefined task model on the board. Due to time constraints, before the exercise they received little information regarding the type of board used and how they had to draw the basic symbols in a single stroke.

They were asked to exploit all the space available in the board by distributing all the elements of the visual model. The results were then analysed at three levels:

1. If the XML specification was generated. This would not have been possible in the event that some tasks were not recognised or were confused with other elements or in the event there was confusion between horizontal and vertical or oblique lines.
2. If the hierarchical structure was recognised (mainly the parent/children relations).
3. If the temporal relations were recognised, this implied recognising the horizontal lines and the temporal operators.

While the first two levels were completely correct in the large majority of the cases (75% and 62%), some serious issues were detected in the third level. The problem was due to a lack of reliability in the recognition of horizontal lines, whereas the symbols representing temporal operators were recognised in the majority of cases. However, this issue can be addressed in various ways and solved. First of all, the subjects were requested to draw temporal relations by also drawing two segments indicating to what tasks they were associated, thus obtaining a representation identical to that supported in the CTTE tool. Some modellers pointed out that when they draw task models on the board or on paper they do not actually draw such lines, they just put the temporal operator symbol and its position clearly indicates to what tasks it refers to. In addition, if we still want to keep the horizontal lines, then it would be sufficient to add pre-processing to identify first the various types of lines (vertical, horizontal, and oblique) using a solution similar to that supported by the CALÌ environment.

6   Conclusions and Future Work

Modelling, as well as various phases in the design cycle, is sometimes a tedious activity. The introduction of visual tools has made the work of designers more efficient than when only pencil-and-paper is used but they still require considerable effort. There is a need for environments able to capture more immediately the representations resulting from a discussion or analysis of a possible design solution, such as those drawn on whiteboards.

The application of the natural interaction paradigm to modelling can provide useful results. While tools for providing recognition of low-level graphical symbols from hand-drawn sketches already exist, so far no proposal has addressed the conversion of these representations into task models able to support design of interactive systems.

In this paper we have presented a solution able to convert hand-drawn task models on an electronic board into an XML-based ConcurTaskTrees specification. A first prototype has been implemented and tested with a number of users. The results are encouraging and show the feasibility of the approach. Solutions for further improving the reliability of the recognition process have already been identified. Since there are tools (TERESA) able to support generation of ubiquitous interfaces starting with task model descriptions, this solution opens up the possibility of obtaining environments in which even people without programming skills can more easily design such interfaces.

Future work will be dedicated to supporting real-time transformation of hand-drawn sketches on board into desktop visual representation and extending the possibility of the environment in such a way as to capture both hand-written sketches and vocal description in various multi-modal combinations as input for creating the corresponding task model.

Acknowledgements

This work has partially been supported by the SIMILAR Network of Excellence on MultiModal User Interfaces (http://www.similar.cc).

References

1. Berti, S., Paternò, F., Santoro C., "Natural Development of Ubiquitous Interfaces", Communications of the ACM, September 2004, pp.63-64, ACM Press.
2. Berti, S., Paternò, F., Santoro C., Natural Development of Nomadic Interfaces based on Logical Descriptions, in End User Development, Springer Verlag, H.Lieberman, F.Paternò, W.Wulf (eds.), forthcoming.
3. Bouillon, L., Vanderdonckt, J. and Souchon, N., 2002. "Recovering Alternative Presentation Models of a Web Page with VAQUITA", Proceedings of CADUI'02, Valenciennes, pp.311-322, Kluwer.
4. Coyette, A., Faulkner, S., Kolp, M., Limbourg, Q., Vanderdonckt, J., SketchiXML: Towards a Multi-Agent Design Tool for Sketching User Interfaces Based on UsiXML, Proc. of 3rd Int. Workshop on Task Models and Diagrams for user interface design TAMODIA'2004 (Prague, November 15-16, 2004), pp. 75-82.
5. Fonseca, M.J., Jorge, J.A.. Using Fuzzy Logic to Recognize Geometric Shapes Interactively. Proceedings of the 9th Int. Conference on Fuzzy Systems (FUZZ-IEEE 2000). San Antonio, USA, May 2000 Available from: http://immi.inesc.pt/projects/cali/publications.html
6. GUIRlib, available at http://guir.berkeley.edu/projects/guirlib/
7. Hudson S., John B., Knudsen K., Byrne M., 1999. A Tool for Creating Predictive Performance Models from User Interface Demonstrations, *Proceedings UIST'99*, pp.93-102.
8. Landay J. and Myers B., "Sketching Interfaces: Toward More Human Interface Design." In IEEE Computer, 34(3), March 2001, pp. 56-64.
9. Mimio Board, http://www.mimio.com
10. Mori, G., Paternò, F., Santoro, C., (2002), "CTTE: Support for Developing and Analysing Task Models for Interactive System Design", IEEE Transactions on Software Engineering, pp.797-813, August 2002 (Vol. 28, No. 8), IEEE Press.
11. Mori, G., Paternò, F., Santoro, C., Design and Development of Multi-Device User Interfaces through Multiple Logical Descriptions, IEEE Transactions on Software Engineering, August 2004, Vol.30, N.8, pp.507-520, IEEE Press.
12. Pane J. and Myers B. (1996), "Usability Issues in the Design of Novice Programming Systems" TR# CMU-CS-96-132. Aug, 1996. http://www.cs.cmu.edu/~pane/cmu-cs-96-132.html
13. Paganelli, L., Paternò,F., 2003. A Tool for Creating Design Models from Web Site Code, International Journal of Software Engineering and Knowledge Engineering, World Scientific Publishing 13(2), pp. 169-189.

14. Paternò, F., Model-based Design and Evaluation of Interactive Applications, Springer Verlag, ISBN 1-85233-155-0, 1999.
15. Rubine D., Specifying Gestures by Example. Computer Graphics, vol. 25, no. 4, pp. 329–337,Luglio 1991.
16. Tam, R.C.-M., Maulsby, D., and Puerta, A., "U-TEL: A Tool for Eliciting User Task Models from Domain Experts", *Proceedings Intelligent User Interfaces'98*, pp. 77–80, ACM Press, 1998
17. Wu J., Graham, N., The Software Design Board: A Tool Supporting Workstyle Transitions in Collaborative Software Design, in *Proceedings of Engineering for Human-Computer Interaction and Design, Specification and Verification of Interactive Systems,* LNCS 2844, Springer Verlag, 92-106, 2004.

Task Model Simulation Using Interaction Templates

David Paquette and Kevin A. Schneider

Department of Computer Science,
University of Saskatchewan, Saskatoon SK S7N 5C9, Canada

Abstract. Interaction Templates were previously introduced as a method to help ease the construction of ConcurTaskTrees. In this paper, a language for defining Interaction Templates, the Interaction Template Definition Language, is introduced. This paper also demonstrates how Interaction Templates can be used to enhance task model simulation, allowing users to interact with concrete user interface components while simulating task models. A prototype task model simulator illustrates how Interaction Templates can be used in task model simulation.

1 Introduction

Model based approaches to interactive system design are based on the specification and evaluation of interactive systems using high-level models [9]. Using high-level models to specify interactive systems can help designers to focus on specifying the requirements and the behaviour of the system rather than immediately being hindered by implementation details. High-level models can be evaluated, often with simulation tool support, before implementation has begun, allowing for a refinement of the system specification with fewer resources than if source code were involved in the change. Task models focus on describing interactive systems in terms of user goals and the tasks required to reach those goals. Many model based approaches, such as ADEPT[13], SUIDT[5], and U-TEL/MOBI[12], acknowledge the importance of task models.

Interaction Templates [7] are a template based approach to task modelling. We will show how Interaction Templates can be used to promote re-use and consistency in task models, aiding in the building and understanding of task models. We will also show how concrete user interface components can be used with Interaction Templates to enhance the task model simulation process.

2 Background and Related Work

2.1 ConcurTaskTrees

ConcurTaskTrees (CTT) is a graphical notation used to describe interactive systems [10]. With CTT, tasks are arranged hierarchically, with more complex tasks broken down into simpler sub-tasks. CTT includes a rich set of temporal operators that are used to describe the relationship between tasks, as well as unary operators to identify optional and iterative tasks. A summary of the CTT notation can be seen in Figure 1.

S.W. Gilroy and M.D. Harrison (Eds.): DSVIS 2005, LNCS 3941, pp. 78–89, 2006.

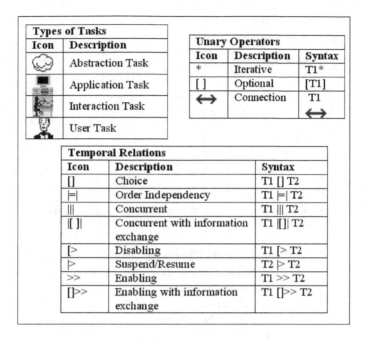

Types of Tasks	
Icon	Description
	Abstraction Task
	Application Task
	Interaction Task
	User Task

Unary Operators		
Icon	Description	Syntax
*	Iterative	T1*
[ ]	Optional	[T1]
↔	Connection	T1 ↔

Temporal Relations		
Icon	Description	Syntax
[]	Choice	T1 [] T2
|=|	Order Independency	T1 |=| T2
|||	Concurrent	T1 ||| T2
|[ ]|	Concurrent with information exchange	T1 |[]| T2
[>	Disabling	T1 [> T2
▷	Suspend/Resume	T2 ▷ T2
>>	Enabling	T1 >> T2
[]>>	Enabling with information exchange	T1 []>> T2

Fig. 1. Summary of the ConcurTaskTrees notation

2.2 ConcurTaskTree Simulation

One of the powerful features of CTT is the ability to simulate task models at an early stage in the development process, allowing for a simulation of the system before implementation has started. Simulation can help to ensure the system that is built will match the user's conceptual model as well as help to evaluate the usability of a system at a very early stage. Several task model simulators have been built for ConcurTaskTrees. First, we will discuss the process involved in simulating ConcurTaskTrees. Next, an overview of two specific task model simulators will be given.

The Simulation Process. ConcurTaskTree simulation involves, in some way, the simulated performance of specific tasks in order to reach a pre-defined goal. In a ConcurTaskTree, tasks are related to each other according to their temporal relations and hierarchical breakdown. Depending on what tasks have been performed, some tasks are enabled and others are disabled. The first step in ConcurTaskTree simulation is to identify the sets of tasks that are logically enabled at the same time. A set of tasks that are logically enabled at the same point in time is called an enabled task set (ETS) [9]. Enabled tasks sets are identified according to the rules laid out in [9]. The set of all enabled task sets for a specific task model is referred to as an enabled task collection (ETC).

Having identified the enabled task collection for a task model, the next step is to identify the effects of performing each task in each ETS. The result of this analysis is a state transition network (STN). In this state transition network, each ETS is a state, and

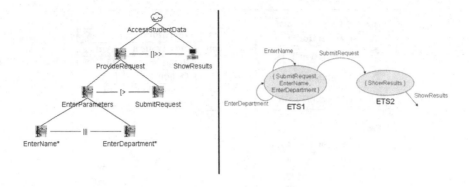

Fig. 2. A CTT (left) and its State Transition Network (right)

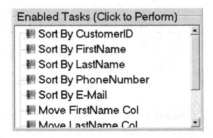

Fig. 3. A simple ConcurTaskTrees task model simulator

transitions between enabled task sets occur when tasks are performed. The final preparation step for simulation is to calculate the initial state. A simple example illustrating a ConcurTaskTree and its STN is shown in Fig. 2. A command-line tool called TaskLib [3] can be used to extract the ETC, STN, and initial state from a CTT. The details of TaskLib's implementation can be found in [4].

Once the ETC, STN, and initial state have all been identified, simulation can begin. This initial process is common to all ConcurTaskTree simulators. The actual simulation involves the user navigating through the STN by simulating the performance of tasks. As will be discussed shortly, how tasks are performed differs between simulation tools.

Simulation Tools

Basic Simulators. The most basic simulators, such as the one shown in Fig. 3, simply display the currently enabled tasks in a list. In these simple simulators, double-clicking on a task simulates the performance of that task. When a task is performed, the enabled tasks are updated accordingly. A basic task model simulator can be found in ConcurTaskTreesEnvironment (CTTE) [8], a tool for both building and simulating task models.

Dialogue Graph Editor. The Dialogue Graph Editor[2], a tool developed at the University of Rostock, provides a more complex simulation than the basic simulator found in

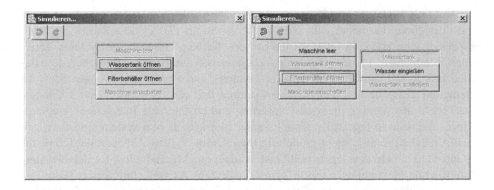

Fig. 4. Simulator included in Dialogue Graph Editor

CTTE. The Dialogue Graph Editor makes use of an extension to CTT that allows for the definition of finite sets of concurrent instances of actions. The Dialogue Graph Editor allows designers to create views and assign tasks from a task model to those views. The views can later be used to simulate the task model as shown in Fig. 4. When simulating the task model, views are represented as windows, elements (as well as tasks) inside the windows are represented by buttons, and transitions between states are represented by navigation between windows. Views become visible when they are enabled, and invisible when they are disabled. Likewise, buttons become enabled and disabled when their associated tasks are enabled or disabled. Users can simulate the task model by clicking buttons to perform tasks and navigate through windows to select between available tasks.

The windows and buttons generated by Dialogue Graph Editor for simulation purposes are considered to be abstract interface prototypes. However, clicking buttons to perform tasks does not seem to provide much of an advantage over the basic simulators, and at times might be more confusing. For example, clicking a button to simulate an interaction task that does not normally involve a button widget may seem strange to end users that may be involved in the simulation. The key advantage in Dialogue Graph Editor is the ability to organize tasks into a dialog. This requires an additional dialog model as well as a mapping between the dialog model and task model.

PetShop. PetShop[6] provides a different approach for simulating an interactive system. ConcurTaskTrees are mapped to a Petrie net based notation. They argue that detailed design is more appropriately specified with a model notation other than ConcurTask-Trees. We intend task notation to provide a more seamless transition when simulating the software for the end-user.

3   Interaction Templates

Task modelling has been shown to be useful when designing interactive systems [10]. Unfortunately, the task modelling process can become tedious and models can become very large when modelling non-trivial systems. Previous research has shown that while building task models to specify information systems, there are often subtrees that repeat throughout the model with only slight variations [7]. These subtrees are often associated with common interface interactions found in information systems. Interaction Templates [7] model these common interface interactions. They include a detailed task model, an execution path (i.e., dialog), and a presentation component. An Interaction Template is a parameterized subtree that can be inserted into a ConcurTaskTree at any point in the model. Inserting and customizing Interaction Templates reduces the need to repeatedly model similar interactions in a system, and thus, can greatly reduce the time spent modelling information systems. Interaction Templates are intended to help developers build task models quickly, and allow for detailed simulation while maintaining a useful system overview. As well, Interaction Templates can be designed and tested to ensure their usability in reaching user's goals. Interaction Templates are intended to provide abstract user interface plasticity as discussed in [11].

3.1   Defining Interaction Templates

Figures 5 and 6 outline how Interaction Templates are structured. An Interaction Template includes a set of parameters, some data, and a definition of how the template behaves depending on the data and parameters it is provided. Figure 5 shows a small portion of an Interaction Template that models a data table interaction. The data provided to this template is a schema defining the data that will be shown in the table. No parameters are needed for this portion of the data table Interaction Template. The Sort By 'Column' task is repeated for each column in the supplied data. Given the Interaction Template definition and the data, the template can be transformed into the expanded template shown in the figure.

Figure 6 displays the behaviour of an Interaction Template that models a selection task. This template includes some data in the form of a list specifying the options that are available to the user. This template also includes a parameter specifying whether or not the user is permitted to select multiple options. The template is expanded differently depending on the value of the MultiSelect parameter.

The above two examples have shown the types of transformations that are needed to define Interaction Templates. The remainder of this subsection will show an example of how we can define Interaction Templates that are capable of adapting their behaviour as shown in the above examples. Interaction Templates are described using a custom markup language, called the Interaction Template Definition Language (ITDL). The ITDL is embedded inside an XML description of a ConcurTaskTree. The *it:* namespace is used to denote elements that describe the options and behaviour of Interaction Templates. The XML language used here to describe ConcurTaskTrees is a modification of the language used by the ConcurTaskTreesEnvironment (CTTE) [8].

Figure 7 shows an Interaction Template defined using the ITDL. The root task of an Interaction Template is surrounded by an identifying *it:template* tag. The *it:template* tag contains a single *name* attribute specifying the name of the template. The first element found inside the *it:template* element is the empty *it:options* element. The *it:options* element contains attributes specifying all the options for the current template. The name of

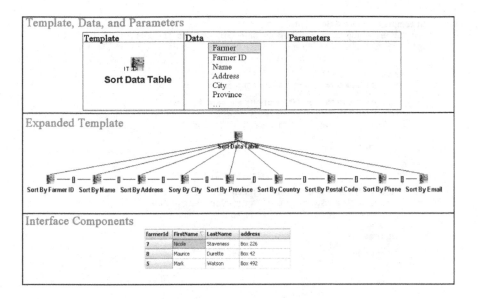

Fig. 5. A portion of the Data Table Interaction Template. This template shows how subtasks can be repeated for each field in a data element.

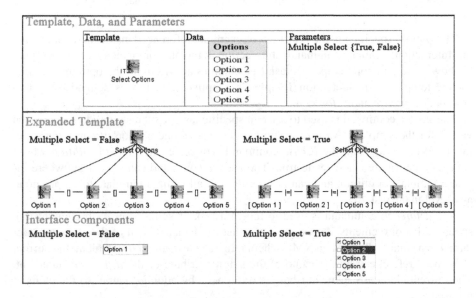

Fig. 6. An Interaction Template for selection from a list of options. This template gives the option to select a single option, or to select multiple options.

the attribute identifies the name of the option, while the value of the attribute identifies the option's type. Option types include boolean values, numbers, strings, or file paths to XML documents such as schemas or different types of sample data.

```
<it:template name="Select Options">
 <it:options MultipleSelect="Boolean" SelectableOptions="ListData"/>
 <Task Id="Select Options" Category="Interaction" Iterative="False" Optional="False">
  <SubTask>

   <it:case>
    <it:condition expression="$MultipleSelect=False">

     <it:foreach col="$SelectableOptions.element">
      <Task Id="Select $col" Category="Abstraction" Iterative="False" Optional="False">
       <TemporalOperator>Choice</TemporalOperator>
      </Task>
     </it:foreach>

    </it:condition>
    <it:condition expression="$MultipleSelect=True">

     <it:foreach col="$SelectableOptions.element">
      <Task Id="Select $col" Category="Abstraction" Iterative="False" Optional="True">
       <TemporalOperator>Concurrent</TemporalOperator>
      </Task>
     </it:foreach>

    </it:condtion>
   </it:case>

  </SubTask>
 </Task>
</it:template>
```

Fig. 7. An ITDL definition of an Interaction Template for selecting options from a list

The options specified in the *it:options* element are referenced inside the template using Interaction Template commands. Interaction Template commands are used to specify how an Interaction Template's task tree changes according to the options specified for the template. An Interaction Template's adaptive behaviour is defined using two commands: *it:case* and *it:foreach*.

The *it:case* command is used to select a specific task or subtask based on the option values for the template. An *it:case* command contains one or more *it:condition* statements. When evaluated, the *it:case* command will select the first *it:condition* whose expression attribute evaluates to true. The *it:case* command can appear anywhere inside a template definition and can also be nested, allowing a template to be plastic at any level in the task tree.

The *it:foreach* command is used to repeat a task or subtask for each element in a specified list of elements. An example of a list of elements is all of the elements contained in a complexType of an XML schema. Inside the *it:foreach* statement, the current element is referenced by the name of the single attribute of the *it:foreach* statement. The current element's name attribute is referenced by adding '.name' to the element reference.

When an Interaction Template is inserted into a ConcurTaskTree, and the required options have been set, the tree is expanded according to the *it:case* and *it:foreach* commands. References to options and the *it:foreach* attribute, identified by $optionName or $attributeName, are replaced by the option or attribute's value respectively.

A prototype of an Interaction Template Definition Language interpreter that recognizes and expands *it:foreach* commands has been implemented using TXL, a rule-based tree transformation language [1]. The prototype is fairly simple, consisting of only 5 rules implemented in just over 100 lines of TXL code.

3.2   Using Interaction Templates

After an Interaction Template has been defined using the ITDL as described above, using an Interaction Template is simply a matter of inserting the template into a CTT and setting values for the template's options. Once the options have been set, the Interaction Template is expanded using an ITDL interpreter. It is always possible to edit the expanded Interaction Template to customize the template to a specific use. It is also possible to change the options for a template and have the Interaction Template re-interpreted to reflect those changes. Edits to an expanded Interaction Template are recorded and re-applied to the re-interpreted Interaction Template if possible. Currently, no tool support exists for building task models using Interaction Templates.

4   Simulation with Interaction Templates

This section will show how partial user interface prototypes can be created from task models that are built using Interaction Templates. These partial prototypes can be used to enhance the task model simulation process, allowing users to interact with concrete user interface components to simulate portions of task models.

4.1   Enhanced Task Model Simulator

While Interaction Templates model common interface interactions found in information systems, there also exist concrete user interface components that implement many of those interactions. In interface builders such as Borland's Delphi, interfaces are composed using sets of pre-built components. If an Interaction Template models a common interface interaction and there exists an interface component that implements that common interface interaction, then that interface component can be used to simulate the Interaction Template. For example, the Data Table Interaction Template can be simulated using a data table interface component that is included with Delphi.

The Enhanced Task Model Simulator (ETMS), shown in Fig. 8, was built to show how concrete user interface components can be used to simulate the sections of a task model where Interaction Templates are used. The ETMS was built using Borland Delphi 6, and contains a traditional task model simulator based on the Enabled Task Sets and State Transition Networks derived using TaskLib [3]. The ETMS contains three views: the model view, the simulator view, and the prototype view. The model view shows a simple tree view of the entire task model. The simulator view, titled 'Task Model Simulator', contains a basic task model simulator as well as a list displaying the activity state. In the simulator view, tasks can be performed by double-clicking on them. When a task is performed, it is added to the bottom of the current activity state. The activity state shows a history of the interactions that have occurred in a simulation session. The prototype view shows the currently enabled Interaction Template prototypes. The Interaction Template prototypes allow the user to interact with a concrete user interface component to simulate a portion of the task model. When the tasks from an Interaction Template

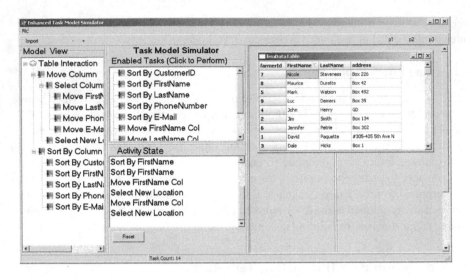

Fig. 8. A prototype of the Enhanced Task Model Simulator. Users can interact with the data table, shown on the right of the screen, to control the task model simulator.

become enabled in a simulation session, a prototype consisting of a concrete interface component corresponding to that Interaction Template is shown in the prototype view. When those tasks are disabled, the prototype is hidden. In the current implementation of the ETMS, creation, enabling, and disabling of prototype instances are done manually.

Interaction Template prototypes are manually built once, then instantiated and customized dynamically during simulation sessions. A new Delphi form containing the appropriate interface component is created for each type of Interaction Template. Each new prototype inherits from the generic *TfrmPrototype* object, which contains the functionality that is common with all Interaction Template prototypes. Common functionality between prototypes includes the ability to communicate with the simulator, as well as the ability to show and hide itself as controlled by the simulator.

Each specific prototype component implements its own adaptation logic. When a prototype object is created, it reads the *it:options* tag that contains the options for the current use of the Interaction Template. The prototype object adapts itself to the options specified in the *it:options* tag. With the Data Table Interaction Template for example, the data table prototype reads in the schema file to set the column headers and reads in the sample data to fill in the rows. Most other Interaction Template options have a one-to-one mapping to the attributes for the interface component that is used to simulate the Interaction Template. For example, the Data Table Interaction Template contains a boolean option called 'allowsort', which has a direct mapping to the boolean 'showsort' attribute of the data table component used in its prototype. Adaptation logic for those options is simply a matter setting the attribute values of the interface component. Finally, each specific prototype implements a mapping between events and task occurrences in the task model. Since communication between the prototype and the simulator is already implemented, this is simply a matter of specifying the name of the task that is performed when an event is triggered.

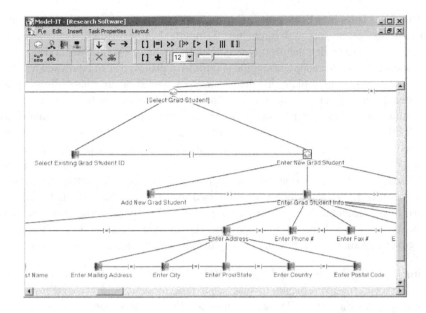

Fig. 9. Model-IT: An Interaction Template based task modelling tool

While other task model simulators use abstract interface objects to simulate tasks, concrete user interface components can be used to simulate tasks when Interaction Templates have been inserted into ConcurTaskTrees. Using the Enhanced Task Model Simulator, users can interact with concrete interfaces to simulate portions of a larger task model. The Interaction Template prototypes can also be populated with sample data, making the simulation less abstract and potentially easier for users to understand.

5   Conclusions and Future Work

This paper has further explored Interaction Templates as a tool to help in building and simulating Task Models using ConcurTaskTrees. A language for defining Interaction Templates has been introduced. The Enhanced Task Model Simulator has shown how concrete user interface components can be used to simulate task models using Interaction Templates. This paper concludes with a discussion of the current state of our research and plans for future work.

Tool Support.   Tool support is needed both for defining Interaction Templates and for building task models using Interaction Templates. A tool for building task models using Interaction Templates must include an interpreter for the Interaction Template Definition Language described earlier in order to interpret an Interaction Template and expand it based on the values of the options that are set for the current use of the template. An Interaction Template based task modelling tool called Model-IT is currently being developed. A preliminary screenshot of Model-IT can be seen in Fig. 9. There are plans to integrate the Enhanced Task Model Simulator into Model-IT in the near future.

Creating User Interface Prototypes. Currently, prototypes are manually built to be self adaptive to the options set for an Interaction Template. Linking events to specific tasks is also manually coded when the prototype is initially created. The manual coding is only done once, and since the adaptation logic is built in, a prototype can be reused a number of times to simulate a template. Ideally, prototypes would be automatically generated from Interaction Templates. Unfortunately, there is no obvious solution to how data can be automatically loaded into interface components, nor is there an obvious way to automatically decide on a mapping between event occurrences and tasks in the task model. It is likely that the mapping between events and tasks will always need to be manually defined once. Also, unless all interface components begin to comply to a common interface for loading data, some code will need to be written to load data into components as well as to set component attributes based on options set for an Interaction Template. In the current implementation, event-to-task mapping and adaptation logic must be manually coded once for each interface component. The amount of code needed to implement these two requirements is minimal, making the current solution a viable option.

Linking Task Models to Final Implementations. Potentially, the technique used to map interface component events to tasks in a task model could be used in the final implementation of a system. The advantages of allowing this mapping to remain in a system's final implementation include the ability to: keep track of a user's current state in the system's task model, verify the system's implementation correctly matches the task model, and to suggest help to users based on their current state.

Acknowledgements

The authors wish to thank the National Sciences and Engineering Research Council of Canada (NSERC) and Western Ag Innovations for their support.

References

1. J. Cordy, C. Halpern-Hamu, and E. Promislow. Txl: A rapid prototyping system for programming language dialects. *Computer Languages*, 16(1):97–107, 1991.
2. Anke Dittmar and Peter Forbrig. The influence of improved task models on dialogues. In *Fourth International Conference on Computer-Aided Design of User Interfaces*, pages 1–14, 2004.
3. Kris Luyten and Tim Clerckx. TaskLib: a command line processor and library for Concur-TaskTrees specifications. http://www.edm.luc.ac.be/software/TaskLib/.
4. Kris Luyten, Tim Clerckx, Karin Choninx, and Jean Vanderdockt. Derivation of a dialog model from a task model by activity chain extraciton. In *Design, Specification and Verification of Interactive Systems 2003 (DSV-IS 2003)*, pages 191–205. Springer-Verlag, 2003.
5. B. Mickael and P. Girard. Suidt: A task model based gui-builder. In C. Pribeanu and J. Vanderdonckt, editors, *Proceedings of the 1st International Workshop on Task Models and Diagrams for User Interface Design TAMODIA 2002*, pages 64–71. INFOREC Printing House, 2002.
6. David Navarre, Philippe A. Palanque, Fabio Paternó, Carmen Santoro, and Rmi Bastide. A tool suite for integrating task and system models through scenarios. In *DSV-IS '01: Proceedings of the 8th International Workshop on Interactive Systems: Design, Specification, and Verification-Revised Papers*, pages 88–113, London, UK, 2001. Springer-Verlag.

7. David Paquette and Kevin A. Schneider. Interaction templates for constructing user interfaces from task models. In *Fourth International Conference on Computer-Aided Design of User Interfaces*, pages 223–235, 2004.
8. Fabio Paternó. ConcurTaskTreesEnvironment (CTTE). http://giove.cnuce.cnr.it/ctte.html.
9. Fabio Paternó. *Model-Based Design and Evaluation of Interactive Applications*. Springer, 2000.
10. Fabio Paternó. Task models in interactive software systems. In S. K. Chang, editor, *Handbook of Software Engineering and Knowledge Engineering*, pages 817–836. World Scientific Publishing Co., 2001.
11. Kevin A. Schneider and James R. Cordy. Abstract user interfaces: A model and notation to support plasticity in interactive systems. In Chris Johnson, editor, *DSV-IS*, volume 2220 of *Lecture Notes In Computer Science*, pages 28–48. Springer, 2001.
12. R.C.M Tam, D. Maulsby, and A. Puerta. U-tel: A tool for eliciting user task models from domain experts. In *Proceedings Intelligent User Interfaces'98*, pages 77–80. ACM Press, 1998.
13. A. Wilson, P. Johnson, C. Kelly, J. Cunningham, and P. Markopoulos. Beyond hacking: A model-based approach to user interface design. In *Proceedings Human Computer Interaction'93*, pages 40–48. Cambridge University Press, 1993.

Investigating Annotation in Electronic Paper-Prototypes

Amir M. Naghsh, Andy Dearden, and Mehmet B. Özcan

Communication & Computing Research Centre (CRI),
Sheffield Hallam University,
Howard Street, Sheffield, S1 1WB, UK
{a.naghsh, a.m.dearden, m.b.ozcan}@shu.ac.uk
http://www.shu.ac.uk/schools/cms/paperchaste/index.html

Abstract. Many design activities depend on communicative activities around collaboratively produced prototypes. A common communication practice in producing text documents is to add annotation in the form of comments. Previous research indicates that electronic paper-prototyping can be used to rapidly create simple prototypes of interactive systems, such as websites. Little is known, however, about how to provide and maintain variety of communication channels around such electronic paper-prototypes to enable end-users and other stakeholders to contribute to design dialogues. This paper presents Gabbeh, an electronic paper-prototyping tool, and reports on an evaluation using the tool in a simulated design exercise.

1 Introduction

Collaboration can be facilitated by applications for sharing and annotation. Recent studies point to various ways in which the design process depends on communicative activities [1, 2, 22]. Button [3] explains that communication and transformation process involving design artefacts are key dimensions to design process.

This paper discusses annotation in electronic paper-prototypes. It reports on progress in the development of Gabbeh [15], as well as reporting on its evaluation.

2 Background

The number of potential stakeholder groups who may be involved during the design process is extensive. These groups may be external or internal to the organisation in which the design group is located. Näslund [16] discussed the different groups of stakeholders who are involved within a software development project. Members of all these stakeholder groups work together to review and discuss artefacts to improve them to reach common ground on the basis that one artefact can and should be developed. In this process, designers and other stakeholders exchange a large number of documents and models, and may spend a great deal of time meeting to resolve conflicts and specific design issues. This becomes challenging when stakeholders are distributed. On these projects much time and money may be spent on enabling different stakeholders to meet up and communicate ideas.

S.W. Gilroy and M.D. Harrison (Eds.): DSVIS 2005, LNCS 3941, pp. 90–101, 2006.

Enabling users or other stakeholders to envisage or make sense of design proposals (whether those proposals originate with 'professional designers' or from the users themselves) is an essential element of most approaches to development. Users can only make informed choices when the proposals being discussed are meaningful to them.

The use of pencil and paper is an established participatory approach for designing interactive systems [10, 24]. Whilst paper-prototyping has many advantages in promoting user participation, it also has some limitations. In particular:

- The lack of an explicit representation of the navigational structure could make it difficult for users to understand and revise the dynamic behaviour of paper prototypes [20].
- It is difficult to review a paper-prototype when users and designers are not able to arrange a face-to-face meeting.
- Paper-prototypes may be difficult to relate to other representations being used within design, such as detailed specifications of behaviour and functionality.

A feature that is particularly useful in using prototypes is the ability to simulate the dynamic behaviour of a finished system [4]. As pen-based interaction devices have become more widely available, software systems that provide support for pen-based interaction in interactive systems design have been developed. Such software systems can be described as tools which support 'electronic paper-prototyping' [9].

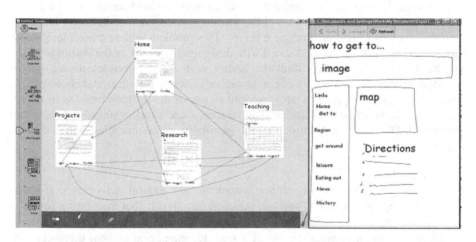

Fig. 1. The DENIM sketching environment and 'run mode' [13]

One well known example is DENIM [13, 17], which is a sketching tool used for designing websites. DENIM is usually run on a graphics tablet, such as a TabletPC or a Wacom Cintiq. In DENIM users can sketch out the overall structure of a site (a collection of pages), sketch the contents of the pages as a set of 'scribbles', define hyperlinks from scribbles in one page to another page, and then execute the resulting hypertext in a reduced functionality browser. Figure 1 depicts a screenshot from DENIM. The slider bar to the left of the screen allows the site to be viewed at different levels of detail—varying from a site overview that simply identifies the pages included, through a navigation view where the overall navigation can be examined, down to a detailed view where fine details of individual pages can be manipulated.

Other examples of electronic paper-prototyping tools include SILK [12] and Free-form [23]. Other work has also explored ways in which the benefits of paper-prototyping might be realised in software prototyping environments, without relying on pen-based interaction [18]. These approaches overcome some of the limitations of paper-prototyping by making the dynamic behaviour of the proposed system easier for users to perceive and permitting the prototype to be distributed electronically. However, the designs of these existing tools are primarily oriented towards the needs of people directly involved in creating designs, rather considering how other stake-holders can provide inputs to design.

A comparison of existing systems [8] showed that one major difference between these design environments and using a paper prototype is the lack of support provided to communicate about the prototype. Green & Petre [11] suggested that 'Secondary notation' is necessary to support communication of ideas that cannot be represented within the restricted syntax of a specific notation. In paper prototyping, post-it notes, highlighting and hand written comments in the form of scribbles can be used to indicate reasons for particular design choices, critiques of particular elements, or indications that further work is required or planned. Denim, Freeform and InDesign do not permit users or other stakeholders to give feedback directly through the medium of the prototype. Instead, any comment or feedback must be held separately (for example in an audio recording or minutes of the meeting), resulting in a difficulty in identifying the items to which any comment refers. This problem will be particularly acute if some stakeholders are not co-located with designers. The lack of the ability to annotate the design may severely limit the ability of these previous electronic paper-prototyping systems to support communication between different stakeholders [8]. Hence, these systems appear to have overlooked one of the primary benefits of paper-prototypes. Gabbeh has been designed to address these shortcomings. Gabbeh is an extension to DENIM and re-introduces the possibility of commenting within the design environment.

Uses of Annotation

Highlighting, underlining and writing comments are natural activities performed while reviewing an artefact. Previous research has shown that annotating text is a common activity when reading [14]. O'Hara and Sellen [19] found that readers use annotation to remark important parts of a text document and to help themselves to understand the text. Such remarks are also useful for future tasks. Marshall [14] found that annotations were used in many ways in college textbooks that includes highlighting or underlining the most important parts to aid the memory, book marking important sections and rephrasing the information into the readers own words to aid interpretation. These annotations are often used as a personal way of tracking references and keeping notes. Annotations are often beneficial to others as well, even when they are not purposely made to be shared.

Cadiz et al. [7] explained that annotations that are shared deliberately support communication and collaboration between members of a group. Bottoni et al. [5]

explained that the traditional notion of annotation has recently evolved from paper document to any type of digital documents such as multimedia and websites. They define the digital annotation as the production of additional information related to the document as whole or to some parts of it. *"These annotations come to constitute a new document, rather than being modifications of the original document, as occurs for manual annotations on paper documents."* The possibility of sharing digital annotations has recognized as a support to communication in cooperative works [5, 6].

Bottoni et al. [5] explains that people have developed ways of using paper documents in making design decisions, communicating comments with other members or highlighting important design issues. Such annotations have been made in the context of groups activities in order to be used later. Further Bottoni et, al. explains that annotation can support different cognitive functions such as *"remembering"* by highlighting or underlining the most important parts, *"thinking"* by adding comments containing ideas, critical remarks and questions, *"clarifying"* by changing the representation of the information in to an interpretive remark.

Current annotation research falls into two categories, either presenting prototype applications for annotating text documents or research on how and why readers annotate paper texts. So far a little attention has been given to the annotation in other areas other than text documents. Despite the fact that the importance of annotation has been realized in the design process as a support for discussion and communication around prototypes [21, 22] little has been done in understanding how and why stakeholders annotate prototypes. The development of Gabbeh offers an opportunity to investigate these key questions.

3   Gabbeh

Gabbeh [15] is an extension to DENIM. The core innovation in Gabbeh is that it allows different stakeholders to add arbitrary annotations in the form of comments either when the model is being designed or when the model is being executed. Figure 2 shows an example of comments in Gabbeh in the 'design view'.

End users may execute Gabbeh using a separate limited functionality browser to review a design. To make Gabbeh easier to be used by end-users, the design sheet is excluded from the version of 'run mode', which is installed at end-users site. It allows the end-users to work only with a simple browser with annotation features.

Furthermore, Gabbeh allows designer-users to add arbitrary scribbles (free-hand notes) to a comment using a similar free-hand writing tool used to create elements in a web page in 'design mode'. It also allows a dialogue box to be used for inserting the comments or converting the scribbles into typed text. A comment in Gabbeh can be associated with any arbitrary number of design components, such as panels, labels, texts and scribbles. Comments are given a background colour. This is intended to allow development teams to distinguish between different types of comments, or perhaps between comments from different speakers. The usage of comment is deliberately left open.

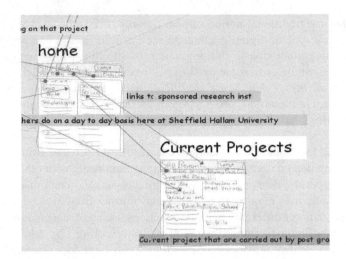

Fig. 2. Comments in the Gabbeh design view

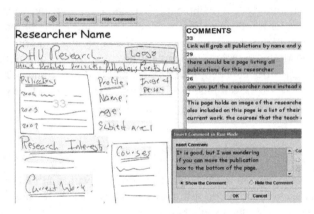

Fig. 3. Adding a comment when Gabbeh is executed

Gabbeh allows end-users to view and add comments while they are reviewing the design in 'run mode'. This functionality is intended to allow end-users to give feedback through the prototyping medium. Figure 3 shows an example of how users can view and add comment in 'run mode'. Comments are displayed in a side window adjacent to the page. Gabbeh displays the comment's location within the page using coloured numbers on the page. If the comment is only associated with the page, Gabbeh only displays the comment in the side window.

Users are able to add comments when Gabbeh is being executed, which can then be visible in the 'design view'. In the current version, comments created in 'run mode' are associated with a page, but not with a specific position on the page.

A simple filtering tool is provided in the design view to offer a way of managing the visibility of comments. The current design gives two options either to see all comments attached to the design sheet, or to see only the comments attached to one page (Fig. 4).

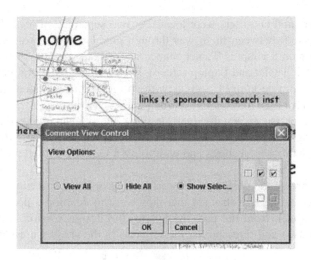

Fig. 4. Managing comments in Gabbeh

4   Evaluation

To evaluate Gabbeh, an observational study of a simulated design task was conducted. The evaluation examined the following questions:

1. Would the comments in Gabbeh be used at all?
2. Does the comment tool enable discussions?
3. How are comments used in practice?

The evaluation consisted of four simulated design exercises, each consisting of two sessions. Three participants were involved in each exercise. Participants were divided into groups of two: designers and one end-user. A design task was allocated for each of the eight sessions. Designers were asked to perform the assigned task to first session by using Denim and the task assigned to second session by using Gabbeh. The first exercise was a pilot study. The designer for the pilot study was a member of staff for the computer science department with some experience in web design, a professional developer and the end user was a member of staff from the business school. They used Denim to design a research-group website and Gabbeh to design a personal website.

The results suggested that the end-user was not engaging strongly in the design process. In particular, the end-user made very few comments about the proposed design. This may be because the user is not the real customer, and so does not really care about the design and the finished system.

Therefore, for the later exercises, one of the investigators (an author of this paper) played the role of end-user. For the remaining exercises, six participants were divided into three pairs of 'designer-users'. The first pair consisted of two members of staff of the School of Computer Science who were experienced in web design. The remaining two pairs were final year students of the Software Engineering Degree, who were experienced with designing websites. Each group was asked to design a 'visit Sheffield' site using Denim and a 'research group' website using Gabbeh.

The designers and end-users were located at two separated offices. The only communication channel between them was through email and the prototype. Designers worked together on a Graphic Tablet connected to a laptop. They had access to two displays (Graphic Tablet and Laptop screen), keyboard and an extra mouse. The end-user had access to a desktop PC to review the prototype. Two video cameras, one in each location, were used to record the participant's activities.

Prior to the exercise, each individual "designer" participant received approximately one hour training using Gabbeh and Denim. The purpose was to help designers to become familiar with tools' features and with using a Graphic Tablet, as this was a new device to some of them.

For each exercise the designers were given a task sheet describing requirements for the website and were instructed that they were to develop a preliminary design and gather feedback from the user throughout the design session. Design sessions lasted between two and three hours. Participants in the study were paid a small fee for their time.

After each session an informal debriefing session was held with the designers and to ask for their feedback and discuss any issues. This was also recorded.

5   Results

1.   Were comments used?
The results showed that all participants used the commentary feature of Gabbeh. Also, the content of emails was reduced to few lines informing the user of which comments they needed to check within the design. For example, one of the emails posted by designers contained: *"We have made the amendments....We were slightly unsure about couple of points. Please read the comment in red"*.

However, it is not the case that the commentary tool was always used when it might have been appropriate to do so. For example, analysis of the video recordings revealed the following discussion:

Designer 1: *... that would link to a research page which is then going to have all the researchers' names; I think that's what they say at the moment. Does this make sense, what do you recommend? Do you want to take a different approach?*

Designer 2: *I would go a different way to represent this, the only thing that I think of is to have all the researcher's name on the home page ... but put it like this and we will see what they (refereeing to user) going to say. We are going to get some feed back anyway. [group 1, session 1]*

In this case, the designers went ahead without adding any comments, but assumed that the user would respond if they were particularly dissatisfied. However, when working with DENIM, one of the same two designers was heard saying: *"Now we need a commenting tool to ask user what they think"*.

The result provides a clear answer to the first question that commentary tool is likely to be used when it is available.

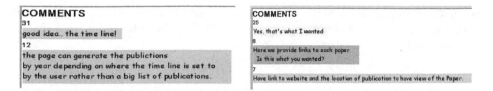

Fig. 5. Examples of discussions: "Designer initiated discussion" (Left) and "User initiated discussion" (right)

2. Were discussions supported?

To answer this second question all the comments within emails and the prototypes were reviewed. As can be seen in Fig. 5, each comment has a reference ID, automatically generated when each comment is created. A larger ID number means a comment was added later in the design process. In addition to considering the context of comments for each page, the recorded videos were also reviewed to learn about the time and situation that the comment was created. This made it possible to identify threads of comments in the form of discussion. Results showed that there were five designer-initiated discussions made in Gabbeh and one in Denim. For example, the following thread of comments was made in group 2, session 2 when participants were using Gabbeh. The thread consists of three starting with the designers

Designers: *"We provided a photograph of each researcher together with links to their profile and a quick overview of their interests at here"*
User: *"can we have a group pic instead of individual ones here?"*
Designers: *"We provided an area for some text about the group as well as a group photograph."*

3. How were comments used?

To answer this question each individual comment was identified. The recorded videos were used to retrieve the time that the comment was made, the author(s) of the comment and the key points of the discussion that was happening at the time of the creation of the comment. The comments were then clustered to identify categories of interest. The categories found are described below:

Clarifying, explaining the design. Explaining the functionality or the dynamic behavior as a part of design. This avoids the designer-users developing the design in detail, whilst indicating how the design may be developed. Examples of this category include:

> *"This page holds an image of the researcher and their interests in more detail, also included on this page is a list of their interests and current work. The courses that they teach on are also included here "*

> *"Link will grab all publications by name and year supplied as an attribute of the link"*

Verifying, designer-users report the design and request for verification. Also they might ask for the confirmation to changes that has been done based on a previously created comment by end-user.

> *"Here we provide links to each paper, Is this what you want?"*

Exploring, questions that help designers to obtain more detail about the end-users needs or desires.

> *"Can you please provide us with more details about requirement four?"*

Comments on *clarifying*, *verifying* and *exploring* categories were all made by the designer-users.

Altering, requesting an alteration in the design by end-users. *Altering* includes comments on a change or correction of the existing design or an instruction to include a new element in the design.

> *"A better and more descriptive "Title" for home page such as*
> *Sheffield Hallam University Research Group (SHURG)"*

> *"there should be a page listing all publications for this researcher"*

Confirming, feedback provided by end-users approving or disapproving of aspects of the design. (See figure 5, comment 25)

Understanding, questions which help end-users to understand the design better to relate it to his/her needs.

> *"In accommodation page, what is the search box for?"*

Altering, confirming and understanding comments were made by end-users.

6   Discussion

Analysis of the video recordings, and debriefing sessions showed a number of concerns with the current design of Gabbeh. Three important issues are considered below:

1.   Managing large numbers of comments

As a prototype evolves, the number of annotations and comments attached to it also increases and it becomes more difficult to manage them. Observations showed that of the four groups of designers-users only two groups used the filtering tool provided. One group of designer-users reported that they found it difficult to deal with the positioning of the comments in the 'design-mode'. Instead, they preferred to have all the comments shown at one place. To over come the problem these designer-users made all the comments invisible on the design sheet and instead used the 'run-mode' browser to view the comments for each page, before returning to the design mode to continue their work.

2.   Identifying and managing discussions

Analysis of the video tapes and of the comments made, showed that there were distinct discussions in which one or more comments is made in response to another.

However, it was difficult to identify these threads without referring back to the video recordings to clarify the relationships between the comments. Clearly, there is a requirement to identify comments as replies to previous comments. The colour scheme of comments was used in a variety of ways, particularly for separating designer comments from end-user comments. One group of designers used different colours for different iterations of the design. Thus, their second email to the end-user consisted of the single instruction: *"Please read the comment in red"*.

3. Supporting Progress awareness and Tracking

One problem that became apparent after a number of iterations was the need to develop some form of version control over the prototype and the comments. For example, an end-user might make a comment requesting a change, which is then implemented by the designer-users. If the comment is not removed from the design record, then it may not refer to anything in the current design. Clearly, there ought to be some way of managing the history of the comment to show that it has been addressed.

This suggests that each comment could be regarded as having a life-cycle starting with its creation. This life-cycle might be different for comments from different categories. Understanding such life-cycles will be an area for further work.

7 Conclusion

This paper has presented the design and evaluation of Gabbeh, a software tool that supports annotation in electronic paper prototyping. The ability to comment and annotate a prototype is an important property to encourage user participation in designing, but has not been possible in previous electronic paper-prototyping tools. The paper has also reported on an evaluation of Gabbeh in a simulated design exercise. The exercise has revealed that comments made in Gabbeh could be divided into seven categories. Designers-users made comments for *clarifying* design detail, *exploring* unspecified and not well understood requirements and *verify*ing the parts that were already designed. In contrast, end-users used comments for *understanding* by asking questions about the design, *altering* the design and *confirming* the changes in the design. Additionally, some comments were used to discuss the organization of the design process. The evaluation suggests that important areas for further work are the management of large collections of comments and understanding the life-cycle of comments within a larger design process. Future possible enhancements will include being able to import images of existing applications so that the tool can be used to support design evolution and redesign, as well as allowing the prototype build by Gabbeh to be associated with other representations used in design process.

Acknowledgement

This work is supported by EPSRC grant number GR/R87918.

References

1. Anderson B., Button, G. & Sharrock, W. 1993. *Supporting The Design Process Within An Organizational Context.* ECSCW "93, Milan, Italy, Kluwer Academic Publishers: 47-59.
2. Belotti, V. and Bly, S., 1996. *Walking away from desktop computer: distributed collaboration and mobility in a product design team.* In Proceedings of CSCW "96, Cambridge, Mass., November 16-20, ACM press: 209-218.
3. Button, G. and Sharrock, W. 1996. *Project work: the organisation of collaborative design and development in software engineering.* CSCW Journal, 5 (4), p.369-386.
4. Bødker, S., Greenbaum, J. & Kyng, M. 1991. Cooperative Design of Computer Systems. In, Greenbaum, J. & Kyng, M. (Eds.) *Design at Work*, pp. 139-154. Hillsdale, New Jersey: Laurence Erlbaum Associates.
5. Bottoni, P., Civica, R. & Levialdi, S. 2004. *MADCOW: a Multimedia Digital Annotation System.* Maria Francesca Costabile (Ed.): Proceedings of working conference on Advanced Visual Interfaces 2004, pp. 55–62, Gallipoli, Italy, May 25-28.
6. Brush, A.J. 2002. Annotating Digital Documents for Asynchronous Collaboration, PhD. Dissertation *Department of Computer Science and Engineering*, University of Washington, Seattle.
7. Cadiz, JJ, Gupta, A., and Grudin, J. 2000. *Using Web annotations for asynchronous collaboration around documents.* In Proceeding of CSCW'00, Philadelphia, PA, Dec 2000, pp. 309 – 318
8. Dearden. A., Naghsh. A M., Özcan. M. B. 2004. *Support for participation in electronic paper prototyping.* 18th Participatory Design Conference, University of Toronto, Canada, July 27-31, pp. 105-108
9. Dearden, A. M., Siddiqi, J. & Naghsh, A., 2003. Using Cognitive Dimensions to Compare Prototyping Notations. In *Proceedings of the Fifteenth Annual Meeting of the Psychology of Programming Interest Group.* Keele University, UK, 8th –10th April 2003. Available at: http://www.shu.ac.uk/schools/cms/paperchaste/downloads/publications/ dsn2003.pdf
10. Ehn, P. & Kyng, M., 1991. Cardboard Computers: Mocking-it-up or Hands-on the Future. In, Greenbaum, J. & Kyng, M. (Eds.) *Design at Work*, pp. 169–196, Hillsdale, New Jersey: Laurence Erlbaum Associates.
11. Green, T. R. G. and Petre, M., 1996. Usability analysis of visual programming environments: a 'cognitive dimensions' framework. *J. Visual Languages and Computing*, 7, 131-174.
12. Landay, J., 1996. *Interactive Sketching for the Early Stages of User Interface Design.* Technical Report CMU-CS-96-201, Carnegie Mellon University, Pittsburgh, PA. 1996.
13. Lin, J., Newman, M.W., Hong, J.I. & Landay J.A., 2000. DENIM: Finding a tighter fit between tools and practice for web site design. In *proceedings of CHI 2000,* pp. 510 - 517. The Hague, Netherlands: ACM Press.
14. Marshall, C., 1997. *Annotation: from paper books to the digital library.* In Proc. of Digital Libraries '97, New York, ACM Press, pp. 131-140
15. Naghsh, A. M., Ozcan M. B. *Gabbeh - a tool for computer supported collaboration in electronic paper prototyping.* Proceedings 18th British HCI Group Annual Conference, volume 2, Leeds Metropolitan University, UK 6-10 September 2004
16. Näslund, T., 1997. *Computers in Context –But in Which Context? In Kyng,* M. & Mathiassen, L. (Eds). Computers and Design in Context. MIT Press, Cambridge, MA. pp. 171 – 200.

17. Newman, M.W., Lin, J., Hong, J.I. & Landay J.A., DENIM: An Informal Web Site Design Tool Inspired by Observations of Practice. In *Human-Computer Interaction*, 2003. 18(3): pp. 259-324.
18. Nixon, B., 2001. *Design and Implementation of a Software Paper Prototyping Application*. BSc. Final year project, School of Computing & Management Sciences, Sheffield Hallam University.
19. O'Hara, K. and Sellen, A. J., 1997. *A Comparison of Reading Paper and On-Line Documents*. CHI'97, Conference on Human Factors in Computing Systems, pp. 150–170, Atlanta, GA.
20. O'Neill, E., Johnson, P. & Johnson, H., 1999. Representations and user-developer interaction in cooperative analysis and design, *Human-Computer Interaction*, 14 (1 & 2), pp. 43 - 91.
21. Obendorf, H. 2003. *Simplifying Annotation Support for Real-World-Settings: A Comparative Study of Active Reading*. In: Proceedings of the 14th ACM Conference on Hypertext and Hypermedia, Nottingham, UK, August, pp. 120-121.
22. Perry, M. & Sanderson, D. 1998. *Coordinating Joint Design Work: The Role of Communication and Artefacts*. Design Studies, 19, 273-28
23. Plimmer, B. & Apperley, M., 2003. FreeForm: A tool for sketching form designs. In Gray, P., Johnson, H. & O'Neill, E (Eds.) *Proceedings of HCI 2003, Volume 2*. Research Press International, Bristol, UK. pp. 183 – 186.
24. Preece, J., Sharp, H. & Rogers, Y., 2002. *Interaction Design*. John Wiley & Sons.

Test of the ICARE Platform Fusion Mechanism*

Sophie Dupuy-Chessa[1], Lydie du Bousquet[2], Jullien Bouchet[1], and Yves Ledru[2]

[1] CLIPS-IMAG, BP 38, 38041 Saint Martin d'Hères cedex 9, France
[2] LSR-IMAG, BP 72, 38402 Saint Martin d'Hères cedex 2, France
{sophie.dupuy, lydie.du-bousquet, jullien.bouchet,
yves.ledru}@imag.fr

Abstract. Multimodal interactive systems offer a flexibility of interaction that increases their complexity. ICARE is a component-based approach to specify and develop multimodal interfaces using a fusion mechanism in a modality independent way. As ICARE is being reused to produce several multimodal applications, we want to ensure the correctness of its fusion mechanism. Therefore, we validated it using a test architecture based on Java technologies. This paper presents our validation approach, its results, its advantages and its limits.

1 Introduction

An increasing number of applications in the field of human computer interfaces support multiple interactions such as the synergistic use of speech, gesture and eye gaze tracking. Multimodal applications are now being built in different application domain including medecine [15], military [5] or telecommunication [12]. For example, lots of mobile phones offer two input modalities, a keyboard and a voice recognizer, to interact. Although many multimodal applications have been built, their development still remains a difficult task. The major difficulty concerns the technical problem of the fusion mechanism, such as the application of R. Bolt [1], in which a speech modality "put that there" is blending with a gesture modality, specifying positions defined by the deictic "that" and "there". Here, the difficulty is to blend correctly the several data from the modalities. Thus, the fusion algorithm must be rigorously and carefully developed and validated, assuring that the multimodal action performed by the user is actually accomplished by the application. So, several frameworks are dedicated to the multimodal interactions, such as [6] and [13].

Here, we focus on a particular multimodal fusion approach: the ICARE approach described in [3]. ICARE is a component-based approach that is independent of the modalities. So it can be reused without modification in many multimodal applications. Applications described in [2] are made with ICARE components, such as one multimodal user identification system and a prototype of an augmented reality system, allowing the manipulation numeric notes in the real world.

As in any other multimodal framework, ICARE must ensure a minimum level of quality of its fusion mechanism. This need is increased by the reuse of the ICARE composition components which implements its fusion mechanism. That's why we propose

---

* Many thanks to Laurence Nigay, responsible for the INTUITION project, for providing the fusion mechanism-ICARE components.

S.W. Gilroy and M.D. Harrison (Eds.): DSVIS 2005, LNCS 3941, pp. 102–113, 2006.
© Springer-Verlag Berlin Heidelberg 2006

a validation that targets the composition components of the platform. So our objective is not to test traditional user interfaces, but to validate the way of blending modalities.

The validation is based on testing because we wanted the approach to be applicable in practice. The test architecture is composed of a tool called Tobias [10] that generates a large number of test cases from a scenario, JUnit [8] to execute these test cases and JML assertions (Java Modelling Language [9, 4, 7]) to produce automatically the verdict of test cases. The major interest of this architecture is that it fully supports the testing process: it allows testers to generate many test cases that are automatically evaluated by an oracle. The test case generation proposed by Tobias is an important point of the architecture as it can easily produce a large number of modality combinations with controlled characteristics. So we expect that ICARE can be efficiently tested.

This paper presents the ICARE platform (Sect. 2). It then details the testing infrastructure used for its validation (Sect. 3), focuses on the test methodology (Sect. 4) and reports on the test results (Sect. 5) before drawing the conclusions of the experiment (Sect. 6).

2   ICARE Platform

2.1   Presentation

ICARE is the contraction of Interaction CARE (Complementarity Assignment, Redundancy and Equivalence). It is a component-based approach that allows the easy and fast development of multimodal interfaces with assembled components. ICARE framework is based on a conceptual component model that describes the several software components. A few ICARE components are called "elementary components". Two types of elementary components are defined: "device components" (DC) and "interaction language components" (ILC). A modality is the coupling of a device and an interaction language [13]. For example, in Fig. 1, a speech modality is defined by assembly of one microphone (DC) and the "speech commands" (ILC).

Other ICARE components are called "composition components". They describe combined usages of modalities. The ICARE composition components suggest various fusion mechanisms based on the CARE properties [14]: Complementarity, Assignment, Redundancy and Equivalence. These fusion mechanisms can be applied to any subset of the available modalities. ICARE composition components do not depend on a particular modality and can merge data from two to n modalities. While Equivalence and Assignment express the availability and respective absence of choice among multiple modalities for performing a given task, Complementarity and Redundancy describe relationships between modalities for performing a given task. Thus, three composition components are defined with their own fusion mechanism: the Complementarity one, the Redundancy one and the Redundancy/Equivalence one.

These components have been used in several research applications. For each one, an assembly of components has been set to define which modalities are used and how the modalities are combined. For example, the Figure 1 shows a part of the architecture of a future French military aircraft cockpit prototype. This prototype, called FACET, is described with more details in [3]. Figure 1 shows the ICARE components assembly in FACET, allowing the pilot to mark a specific point on the ground. For performing a

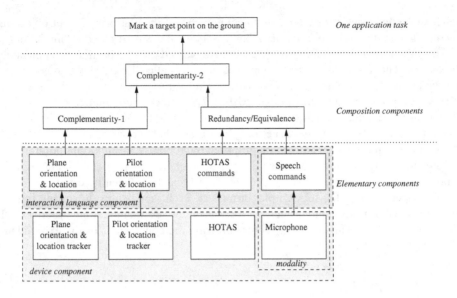

Fig. 1. Part of ICARE specification of FACET input interaction

marking command, the pilot has the choice among two modalities. The HOTAS (Hands On Throttle And Stick) modality and the speech modality are functionally equivalent and can be used separately. However, they can also be used in a redundant way, thanks to the Redundancy/Equivalence component. The HOTAS are made of two command joysticks (one for each hand) to pilot the plane and to issue commands. If the pilot presses the HOTAS button or speaks (the voice command <Mark>), one mark command is sent to the rest of the application. If the pilot uses both modalities at the same time, still one mark command is sent. In addition, to detect the target point that the pilot selected in the real world, two modalities are used in a complementary way, thanks to the *Complementarity-1* component. One modality is for the orientation and location of the pilot and the other is for the orientation and location of the plane. Finally, in order to obtain a complete marking command, the command <Mark> must be combined (*Complementarity-2* component) with the target point defined by the pilot.

2.2 Composition Components

The Complementarity component combines all complementary data close in time. For example in Figure 1, orientation and location of both, the pilot and the plane, must be merged to detect the target point on the ground. The mechanism is mostly based on a customizable temporal window, used to trigger the data fusion coming from the modalities. All data coming from the modalities have a confidence factor and a timestamp. To know if orientation and location data are in the same temporal window, the timestamp of data is used. If the timestamps are too distant, the fusion is not accomplished. The result of the fusion, in addition of the new data generated by the fusion, is a new confidence factor calculated from the merged modalities data. This factor is equal to the average of confidence factors of the merging data.

The Redundancy component is used when two or more modalities convey redundant pieces of information that are close in time. In such cases, at least one of the user actions is ignored, because the output is exactly the same. To gain more security, the Redundancy/Equivalence component in figure 1, can be replaced by a Redundancy component. In this case, if only one modality is used (HOTAS or speech), the command <Mark> is not performed, avoiding ambiguous commands and errors. The Redundancy component mechanism seems to be a Complementarity component with the substantial difference that all data coming from the several modalities must be equivalent, corresponding to the same command. As with the Complementarity component, timestamps of data arriving of the modalities are used to detect the redundancy of the command. The new confidence factor is equal to the higher confidence factor among the two modalities' data.

The Redundancy/Equivalence component is a mix of the two CARE properties Redundancy and Equivalence. It corresponds to the Redundancy component, where the redundancy can be optional. Clearly, if someone has two modalities to perform an action, he can do it in an independent way or in a redundant way. In the redundancy case, only one action is actually performed. As for other composition components, its mechanism is based on a temporal window, but it includes two different strategies: the "eager" and the "lazy" strategies. The "eager" strategy provides an efficient mechanism and the "lazy" strategy provides a safe one. Adopting an "eager" strategy, the component does not wait for further pieces of data to keep propagating data to the following connected ICARE component. Each time a piece of data is sent to another ICARE component, the component keeps its track. It starts a customizable timer in order to detect the redundant pieces of data that may be received later. The advantage of this approach is to give to the user an immediate feedback. The drawback is that the piece of data propagated is the first one received by the component and may not have the highest confidence factor. Opposed to the "eager" strategy, the "lazy" strategy waits until the end of the timer to propagate the piece of data. The advantage of this strategy is to guarantee the propagation of the data containing the highest confidence factor.

3   Test Architecture

Although ICARE is only a research prototype, a minimum level of software quality is required to reuse it in the various projects of the our team. Therefore, an effort was initiated in june 2004, in order to check the fusion mechanism of the three ICARE composition components.

As ICARE is coded in Java, we looked for a light validation architecture based on Java technologies. We chose a testing approach because it is the easiest validation technique to carry out. We wanted a test platform that would generate many cases of modality combination and automatically check whether the components react correctly.

3.1   Automated Oracle

An important topic in software testing is to decide on the success or failure of a given test. This is known as the "oracle problem". In the simplest form of test, it is the test

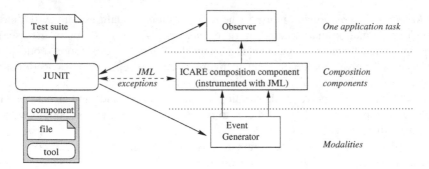

Fig. 2. The test execution infrastructure

engineer's responsibility to look at the test results and decide on their success/failure (human oracle). This approach requires a lot of effort from the test engineer and does not favour the automation of the test process. Often, the judgement of the test engineer is recorded, so that a replay of the same test can reuse this judgement, provided the output of the program under test is deterministic. In the test of the ICARE platform, it was impossible to use a human oracle:

- The behaviour of the platform is non-deterministic, due to the use of multi-threading in the implementation. It is thus impossible to reuse the results of a test when replaying it.
- The success/failure of the test cannot be decided on what is directly observed by the test engineer. Subtle timing properties must be obeyed that can only be observed by instrumenting the code.
- We intended to play a large number of tests (several thousands), which would require too much interaction for the human oracle.

In this project, the oracle is provided by an executable specification, written in JML (Java Modeling Language [9, 4, 7]). A JML specification is made up of assertions (invariants, history constraints, pre- and post-conditions) which express the properties of the classes and constrain their behaviour. JML assertions appear as comments of the java program. Their syntax is the syntax of java, augmented with several keywords. The JML compiler instruments the code of the program under test, so that assertions are evaluated before and after the execution of each method. As a result, an automated oracle is provided which raises an exception as soon as the behaviour of the code differs from the specified one.

3.2   Test Execution Infrastructure

Fig. 2 shows the various elements of our test execution infrastructure. The goal of the test is to validate composition components, like Complementarity or Redundancy/Equivalence in Fig. 1. These components take as input a series of events, generated by the elementary components, and turn them into higher level events (composed events) which are sent to the application. The test infrastructure embeds each ICARE composition component under test with two classes:

1. **An event generator** plays the role of the various modalities corresponding to the elementary components of Fig. 1. The event generator simplifies significantly the test effort, because it decouples the test activity from the concrete aspects of the modalities (e.g., voice and gesture recognition). The test of the elementary components which turn these physical phenomena into computer events, is out of the scope of the validation of the ICARE platform.

2. **An observer** collects the events produced by the ICARE composition component.

Both classes are under the control of the popular unit testing tool JUnit [8], which automates the execution of a test suite given as input.

3.3   Finding Errors with This Approach

The main purpose of the validation work was to find some errors in the code. To be more precise, we tried to find some inconsistencies between the code and the JML assertions. When an error is reported, it can correspond to an error in either the code or in the JML specification. Human analysis is necessary to give the right diagnostic.

Test execution may also lead to detect java run-time errors, e.g. when the Java Virtual Machine runs out of memory. Once again, this may correspond to an error in the java code, or can be the result of the evaluation of the JML assertions. Here again, human diagnostic is needed.

3.4   Test Suite Generation

The test execution infrastructure requires a test suite. In this project, the test suite was generated using the Tobias tool [10]. Tobias is a combinatorial testing tool which starts from an abstract test scenario and unfolds it into a large number of test cases. These test cases, named "abstract test cases", are independent of a specific target technology. Tobias then supports the translation of these abstract test cases into an input file for JUnit (concrete java test cases). Tobias was used to produce many ways to fuse modalities among which some were identified to be particularly important to validate.

4   Test Description Methodology

4.1   Approach

As said previously, we applied a combinatorial testing approach to produce a lot of tests. The idea is to (1) identify properties to be validated, (2) express interesting scenarios so as to observe behaviours with respect to these properties, and (3) use Tobias to unfold those scenarios into executable test cases. For example, one can identify that "the Complementarity component combines all complementary data close in time". The time distance has to be defined by the application designer when using the composition components. As said previously, data coming from the modalities have a confidence factor and a timestamp. Thus, the following two points have to be checked:

1. If the timestamps of the data to be merged are too distant, new data is not produced.
2. If the timestamps of the data to be merged are in the same temporal window, new data are produced having a confidence factor equal to the average of confidence factors of the merging data.

$$S_c = G.i; C1.3c; C1.d50; G.st; C1.startComplementatrity();$$
$$G.s1; G.sn; G.s2; G.sn; G.s3; G.sn; C.end;$$
$$with$$

$$\begin{cases}
i = \{G.setEvent(t)|t \in \{1\}\} \\
3c = \{CC.setNbOfComponents(v)|v \in \{3\}\} \\
d50 = \{CC.setDeltaT(v)|v \in \{50\}\} \\
st = \{setTrace(c)|c \in C1\} \\
s1 = \{sendComp(c, p, d, f, b)|c \in \{C1\}, p \in \{1\}, d \in \{0, 20\}, f \in \{66\}, b \in \{false\}\} \\
s2 = \{sendComp(c, p, d, f, b)|c \in \{C1\}, p \in \{2\}, d \in \{0\}, f \in \{66\}, b \in \{false\}\} \\
s3 = \{sendComp(c, p, d, f, b)|c \in \{C1\}, p \in \{3\}, d \in \{0, 20\}, f \in \{66\}, b \in \{false\}\} \\
sn = \{sendComp(c, p, d, f, b)|c \in \{C1\}, p \in \{1, 2, 3\}, d \in \{0, 20\}, f \in \{33\}, b \in \{false\}\} \\
startComplementatrity() \text{ is a method with parameter of Complementarity component}
\end{cases}$$

Fig. 3. One abstract scenario for Tobias

One way to do so is to produce tests which first initialise the test infrastructure (i.e., ICARE component, event generator and the observer) This is called "test preambule". Then, the event generator should send several events with different timestamps and confidence factors ("test body"). Finally, the ICARE component should be stopped ("test postambule").

This can be expressed as an abstract scenario in Tobias. In the scenario S_c (Fig. 3), the preambule is composed of the five first events ($G.i$, $C1.3c$, $C1.d50$, $G.st$, $C1.startComplementatrity()$) and the postambule is composed of the last event ($C.end$). The scenario body consists in 6 $sendComp()$ events. The $sendComp()$ event is produced by a modality. The major parameters are p the communication port and f the confidence factor. The scenario is unfolded into $2*6*1*6*2*6 = 864$ executable tests. The unfolding operation in Tobias takes only a few seconds.

4.2 Testing Strategy

To validate the 3 components, we produced 19 test schemas, which were unfolded into approximately 6000 test cases. The schemas were designed to test the components in three different ways.

First, tests were designed to check the behavior of the components in normal situations. These tests consist of sending a sequence of various events which are differentiated by their data, their delay (i.e., the difference between their initial time and the current time), their confidence factor and the port of the component where they are sent. Other parameters of these tests were the delay between two event sendings and the duration $deltaT$ that determines if an event is too old to be considered (see schema S_c).

Second, we created boundary cases that require an intensive solicitation of the component. Some of these tests initialize the components under test with a large number of input ports. Other tests sends a lot of events without delay in between.

Finally, some tests aim at considering specific aspects of the ICARE components, in particular their configuration.

We applied this strategy to the three components (Complementarity, Redundancy, Redundancy/Equivalence). In fact, the tests of the Complementarity and Redundancy components were similar as their behaviour is very close to each other: they have to choose a group of input events to determine the information to be propagated. The Redundancy/Equivalence component is different because it has to handle temporal windows. So it was tested with specific test schemas.

5   Results of the Experiment

5.1   Test Results

The results of the tests of each ICARE composition component can be summarized into three tables corresponding to the three test strategies. Each table contains four columns: the first column presents the test, the second one the number of test cases produced for this test, the third one the number of errors, the last one the error(s) found. We consider as an error anything that makes the test fail. So it can be a JML/Junit failures or a Java error. These errors are more precisely explained in the comments of the tables.

Complementarity and Redundancy components. Testing the Complementarity and the Redundancy components gives the same results. It makes it possible to find errors of different types. There are programming bugs such as an event lost (Table 1(b)) or the propagation of stale events (Tables 1(a) and 1(c)).

There is one error resulting from some differences between the specifications and the program. The Redundancy component must check if the input events contain similar data: its implementation checks that the data of input events have the same size whereas the specification requires the same data. The code of the component can be considered as correct if it is assumed that the event-sending device will always send consistent data.

Finally we found an error in the specifications. The specifications state that the number of input ports of a component is unlimited. But this runs the Java Virtual Machine out of memory (Tables 1(c)). So, the specifications and the code of the components should consider the practical constraints and limit the number of input ports.

Redundancy/Equivalence component. The Redundancy/Equivalence component is implemented differently from the other two components. But it propagates events like the Complementarity and the Redundancy components. So as with the other components, it has problems with the content of input events and the modification of parameters when it is running (Table 2(c)).

Its main difference is the use of threads in order to handle data concurrently. This is the source of several errors found in the component implementation (Tables 2(a) and 2(c)).

The processing of the component requires concurrent access to the data structure. This brings execution errors (Java errors in Table 2(a)) and an abnormal behavior of the component in lazy strategy. In some cases, calculations are made using accurate information on the state of the data structure, but the result of the calculations is wrong because the state has changed since the event arrival. In other cases, calculations are made using outdated information causing a lack of internal consistency and thus an incorrect behavior.

The eager and lazy strategies are based on the concept of temporal window. Even if boundary tests with only one temporal window (Table 2(c)) do not bring error, many

Table 1. Tests for the Complementarity and Redundancy components

Tests	nb TC	nb E	Error Description
(a) Normal situations			
sending 6 events to the component	864	1	propagated events are too old
sending 50 events in a multithreaded environment	784	10	propagated events are too old
(b) Boundary tests			
creating a large number of input ports	8	1	Java error (no more memory available)
sending 6 events to the component without delay	864	10	propagated events are too old
sending 32 events in a multithreaded environment at a high rate	1	1	one event lost
(c) Specific situations			
changing the configuration of the component while it receives events	196	10	propagated events are too old
initializing the component with various values	12	1	propagated events are too old

nb TC : number of Test Cases for each component
nb E : number of error (incorrect behaviour observed during test execution)

Table 2. Tests for Redundancy/Equivalence component

Tests	nb TC	nb E	Error Description
(a) Normal situations			
sending 4 events in the eager strategy	192	30	10 wrong behaviors 5 to 36 incorrect specification
sending 4 events in the lazy strategy	192	20	13 wrong behaviors 5 incorrect specification 2 Java errors
(b) Boundary tests			
sending 5 events during one temporal window in the eager strategy	64	0	-
sending 5 events during one temporal window in the lazy strategy	64	0	-
(c) Specific situations			
changing the configuration of the component while it receives events	196	71	66 wrong behaviors 5 incorrect specification

test failures come from temporal windows (Tables 2(a)). In some cases, an event is not processed at the end of its temporal window. In other cases, delayed events i.e. events arriving into the component some time after their creation are not processed as events arriving at their creation time: these events do not belong to the right temporal window. Moreover the component does not remove events which have a delay longer than the duration of the temporal window.

As the Redundancy/Equivalence component is complex, its specification also contains errors. They were found when the component has a correct behavior that the specifications consider incorrect. These cases are reported as "incorrect specification" in the table below.

5.2 Advantages of the Approach

The test infrastructure chosen is easy to manipulate. In approximately one week, the tester has produced his first tests without all the JML properties. The main difficulty was to write correct JML properties that can be executed. The language offers a large set of constructions. However, some construction combinations are not executable.

As expected, we fully benefit from the generation of test cases by Tobias. With test schemas, Tobias allows the tester to easily combine in many different ways several modalities. These schemas produced expected test cases, but also unthought test cases that reveal errors. So the combination approach of Tobias is appropriate for multimodality.

One of the most difficult points in testing components is the non-deterministic test execution. So adding JML assertions is a good way to obtain an automatic oracle. But assertions sometimes need access to variables or data that are not directly visible in the program. They require the introduction of new pieces of code to make the program automatically testable.

5.3 Limits of the Approach

In theory, each test case should produce a reproducible behavior. However the way components are conceived makes it difficult. In particular, the component behavior is mainly based on the timing of events. But this timing can vary from one execution to another. So the results of a given test case can change over time. That is why the numbers of failures given in the result tables must be considered as the result approximations of several executions.

The time variations can also cause problems to give a correct test result for the Redundancy/Equivalence component. Because of the use of threads in its structure, some properties are not verified at execution time even if the component behaves correctly. The shift between the results and the actual behavior occurs in three cases:

1. When the temporal window is too small compared to the processing time of an event
2. When the size of the temporal window is comparable to the time between two event arrivals
3. When an event delay is greater or equal to the size of the temporal window

In these cases, the component is likely to be processing an event while the temporal window is closing, making the JML specifications checking the existence of a removed event. To avoid these problematic situations, we chose a "long" temporal window.

Finally, failures can come from the specifications. In particular, several failures of the Complementarity and the Redundancy components are related to too old events. The JML processing time can make events become too long. So it is not possible to determine if the failures come from JML or from a too long processing in the components.

6   Conclusion

Testing the ICARE composition components has revealed several errors. As expected it permitted the discovery of errors in the fusion mechanism. But it also reveals some cases of modalities fusion that have not been anticipated. So ICARE has really been improved by the experiment which can be considered as a real progress.

The testing tools used have shown the interests of an automatic oracle and of the combinatory test generation for multimodality. Instrumenting the component code by adding JML properties is a light solution to produce an automatic oracle. But it also consumes resources and creates errors by slowing down the program. One way to avoid these problems is to lighten the instrumentation when a problem is detected. For instance, the properties that are necessary for a given test could be commented out. Then the test is played again to see if the problem comes from instrumentation. On the other hand, instrumentation can make some tests succeed by slowing down the execution. In these cases, it is difficult to know that the program is incorrect as it has bad results when it will not be possible to detect them.

In this experiment, we succeed in avoiding the traditional graphical user interface testing pitfalls [11] of automatic test case generation and test oracles. But this is partly due to the fact that we test only components and not a complete interface. So an interesting perspective is to use the same testing infrastructure to validate a whole multimodal application. Good candidates for validation are those that are built with ICARE. First it would be another way of testing the ICARE composition components. Secondly we could use JML to check some ergonomic properties. For instance, we could verify that at the end of the operation that marks a target point on the ground, the mark is really displayed. Of course we could not check that the user sees it, but we could guarantee that the application has a correct behaviour and displays the right information. It is clear that testing real applications would be much more difficult than testing components, in particular because of the multi-threading. This could require to change some parts of the testing infrastructure, particularly JUnit that executes tests.

As a conclusion, the experiment described in this paper had a very positive result: the ICARE framework is more robust than it used to be and the extensive test campaign has increased our confidence in its quality. We believe that several test techniques are now mature enough and sufficiently easy to use, to be applied to other fusion mechanisms, and that this will help master the complex development of multimodal user interfaces.

References

1. R. A. Bolt. "Put-that-there": Voice and gesture at the graphics interface. In *SIGGRAPH'80*, pages 262–270, 1980.
2. J. Bouchet and L. Nigay. ICARE: A Component-Based Approach for the Design and Development of Multimodal Interfaces. In *Extended Abstracts of CHI'04*, pages 1325–1328, Vienna, Austria, 2004.
3. J. Bouchet, L. Nigay, and T. Ganille. ICARE Software Components for Rapidly Developing Multimodal Interfaces. In *ICMI'04*, pages 251–258, State College, PA, USA, 2004.

4. L. Burdy, Y. Cheon, D. R. Cok, M. Ernst, J. Kiniry, G. T. Leavens, K. R. M. Leino, and E. Poll. An Overview of JML Tools and Applications. In *Eighth International Workshop on Formal Methods for Industrial Critical Systems (FMICS'03)*, volume 80 of *Electronic Notes in Theoretical Computer Science*, pages 73–89. Elsevier, 2003.
5. P. R. Cohen, M. Johnston, D. McGee, S. Oviatt, J. Pittman, I. Smith, L. Chen, and J. Clow. QuickSet: Multimodal interaction for distributed applications. In E. Glinert, editor, *Proceedings of the Fifth ACM International Multmedia Conference*, pages 1325–1328. ACM Press, New York, 1997.
6. F. Flippo, A. Krebs, and I. Marsic. A Framework for Rapid Development of Multimodal Interfaces. In *ICMI'03*, pages 109–116, 2003.
7. The Java Modeling Language (JML) Home Page. http://www.cs.iastate.edu/ leavens/JML.html.
8. JUnit. http://www.junit.org.
9. G.T. Leavens, A.L. Baker, and C. Ruby. JML: A notation for detailed design. In H. Kilov, B. Rumpe, and I. Simmonds, editors, *Behavioral Specifications of Businesses and Systems*, pages 175–188. Kluwer, 1999.
10. Yves Ledru, Lydie du Bousquet, Olivier Maury, and Pierre Bontron. Filtering TOBIAS combinatorial test suites. In *Fundamental Approaches to Software Engineering (FASE'04)*, volume (2984) of *LNCS*, pages 281–294, Barcelona, Spain, 2004. Springer.
11. A. Memon. GUI Testing: Pitfalls and Process. *Software technologies*, pages 87–88, 2002.
12. L. Nardelli, M. Orlandi, and D. Falavigna. A Multi-Modal Architecture for Cellular Phones. In *ICMI 2004*, pages 323–324, State College, PA, USA, 2004.
13. L. Nigay and J. Coutaz. A Generic Platform for Addressing the Multimodal Challenge. In *CHI'95*, pages 98–105, 1995.
14. L. Nigay and J. Coutaz. The CARE Properties and Their Impact on Software Design. In *Intelligence and Multimodality in Multimedia Interfaces*, AAAI Press 1997.
15. S. Oviatt and al. Designing the user interface for multimodal speech and gesture applications: State-of-the-art systems and research directions. *HCI*, 15-4:263–322, 2000.

A Method for the Verification
of Haptic Algorithms

Joan De Boeck, Chris Raymaekers, and Karin Coninx

Hasselt University, Expertise Centre for Digital Media (EDM) and transnationale
Universiteit Limburg, Wetenschapspark 2, B-3590 Diepenbeek, Belgium
{joan.deboeck, chris.raymaekers, karin.coninx}@uhasselt.be

Abstract. The number of haptic algorithms has been growing over the past few
years. However, little research has been performed in evaluating these algorithms.
This paper provides both a theoretical framework and a practical discussion of
how the correctness and performance of force-feedback algorithms can be verified. The practical discussion is necessary as the theoretical framework proves
that an infinite number of cases should be considered when evaluating a haptic algorithm. However, using statistical techniques, this evaluation can be performed
within a reasonable frame of time. The evaluation method in this paper has itself
been validated by evaluating two algorithms. From this test, we can conclude that
the evaluation method is a reliable method for verifying if haptic algorithms are
correct.

1 Introduction

Over the past few years, haptic interaction has been a growing field within the research
into virtual environments. A problem with these algorithms is the fact that they are
highly interactive: the forces that are sent back to the user must be calculated at real
time in order to achieve a realistic simulation. For instance, in most implementations,
force-feedback algorithms must be executed within a haptic loop that takes less than
0.9ms in order to achieve a 1kHz update rate and to allow other parts of the simulation
to execute. When rendering very stiff objects, an even higher update rate of 5–10kHz is
needed [7].

Contrary to this, little research into the correctness of haptic algorithms has been performed. Recently, some empirical methods were developed for the evaluation of haptic
applications [8] and virtual environments in general [18]. In this paper, we discuss an
empirical approach for the evaluation of force-feedback algorithms. For brevity, we will
refer to force-feedback algorithms as haptic algorithms, as this is currently the most
common use of haptics[1]. In the remainder of this paper, we will first discuss existing
techniques for the evaluation of haptic algorithms. Section 3 discusses our evaluation
methodology, both from a theoretical and a practical point of view. In Sect. 4 we give
an example of an empirical evaluation in order to assess the validity of our approach.
The results are discussed in Sect. 5. We will end this paper by drawing our conclusions.

---

[1] With force-feedback algorithms, we mean algorithms that relate to the mechanical production
of information sensed by the human kinesthetic system, as defined in [11].

S.W. Gilroy and M.D. Harrison (Eds.): DSVIS 2005, LNCS 3941, pp. 114–125, 2006.

2   Related Work

During the past few years, several attempts have been made to quantify the benefits of a haptic algorithm. Theoretical approaches tried to quantify the time complexity of different algorithms (e.g. [12]). Although this leads to a better understanding of the algorithms' performance, it does not allow for the comparison of two algorithms with the same time complexity. Furthermore, due to the behaviour of the end user, some optimizations are difficult to predict. Thus, these theoretical findings should be complemented with real-life measurements in order to know the exact behaviour.

In an example of an empirical approach, Acosta and Temkin compared the performance of different versions of the GHOST haptic API [1]. They looked at the implementation of polygonal meshes by loading objects with as many triangles as possible, until the system was not able to process the information within the haptic loop. In a similar manner, they measured the performance of the haptic scene graph implementation. Although, it does not take the performance at a lower load into account, this approach is suited to test the limits of an implementation, which is a valuable metric.

A third means of measuring an algorithm's performance is to use a tool which measures the haptic load (this is the processor time spent in the haptic loop to calculate the forces). The GHOST haptic API provides a graphical tool which displays the haptic load using 10% intervals, as depicted in Fig. 1. This technique was used to compare the polygon mesh implementation of GHOST and e-Touch [2]. It also has been adopted to measure the increase in haptic loop against scene and object-complexity in a dual-PHANToM setup [5]. Certainly, this gives a good insight of the algorithms' performance. In our opinion, however, this does not provide accurate numerical results which can be validated.

Of course, the above-mentioned approaches can be combined in order to draw more founded conclusions [15, 13], but in our opinion this is still not enough for a valid comparison.

One of the most important flaws in current evaluation methods, besides the lack of exact numerical results, is that they do not provide the algorithms with the same data. The haptic load is measured while interacting in real-time with the virtual environment. This means that the algorithms being compared receive different input. Hence, unintentionally, both algorithms are not compared in an equal manner. Moreover, Anderson and Brown [2] compare two object rendering algorithms which are implemented in two

Fig. 1. GHOST haptic load tool

different APIs. This adds the scene graph performance into the measurement, which may again result in an unintentional side-effect of the measurement method with implications for the results.

In this paper, we address this problem by presenting the same real-world data to different algorithms. In an interactive session, in which users explore a virtual object with a haptic device (in our case, a PHANToM device), the device's position and velocity are recorded for each loop. This data is then passed on as input for the other haptic algorithms. Different variables such as the time needed to execute one haptic loop, are recorded and compared.

3   Evaluation Methodology

Our evaluation methodology is an empirical implementation which relies on a number of definitions of algorithm performance. We will first expand upon these definitions before going into detail on their practical use.

3.1   Working Definitions

We will first define what we mean by a haptic algorithm. Please note, this is not a formal characterization; its purpose is to clarify our working definition in order to avoid confusion. Please see [16] for a good explanation of force-feedback algorithms.

Definition 1. A *geometric haptic algorithm* a is a two-fold algorithm. Its input is the current position $\overrightarrow{p}$ and velocity $\overrightarrow{v}$ of the pointer, as defined by the force-feedback device and a virtual object o, which has to be rendered. The first part, denoted *coll* $(a, o, \overrightarrow{p})$ is a collision-detection step, which calculates whether the pointer position is located inside the object. The second step, denoted by $render(a, o, \overrightarrow{p}, \overrightarrow{v})$ calculates the surface contact point (SCP) and the force that should be exerted by the force-feedback device.

The SCP is the point on the object's surface to which a user's pointer should be brought, by applying forces on the haptic device, in order to feel a realistic force. As is depicted in Fig. 2, this is in general implemented by placing a virtual spring between the pointer and the SCP.

Please note that we refer to geometric rendering, not volumetric rendering, as most volumetric rendering techniques do not make use of a SCP (see [3] for more information on volumetric rendering). Also, some haptic rendering algorithms use a SCP only in implicit calculations (e.g. the e-Touch library [10]). However, the principles stay the same in these cases. For the brevity of our definitions and explanations, we will use definition 1 as a basis for this paper. The extension of our reasoning to volumetric rendering is trivial.

We will denote the set of all possible haptic algorithms by $\mathcal{A}$.

Definition 2. The *object space* $\mathcal{O}(a)$ of an haptic algorithm a is the set of virtual objects on which the algorithm can be applied.

Not all objects belong to the object space of an haptic algorithm, as these cannot be applied to every possible object (for instance a rigid-body algorithm cannot perform

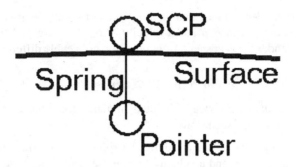

Fig. 2. Surface Contact Point

soft-body computations). It is worth remarking, however, that an algorithm's object space contains an infinite number of virtual objects.

Definition 3. A *path* is a collection of points in space which are followed by a user's pointer and the velocities of the pointer in those points.

Definition 4. The *length* of a path p, denoted by $length(p)$, is the duration in time, that the users need to explore the path. The position on the path on a certain point in time t ($t \in [0, length(p)]$) is denoted by $\overrightarrow{p}_t$; its velocity by $\overrightarrow{v}_{pt}$.

When users explore a certain object, there are many possible paths they can follow. For instance a solid rigid body cannot be penetrated (although practical implementations of course allow a slight penetration). On the other hand, a deformable object cannot be deformed in all possible manners: a virtual football can be slightly squeezed, but it is impossible to reach its centre.

All possible paths that a user can follow when working in an empty virtual environment is called the path set $\mathcal{P}$.

Definition 5. The *path space* $\mathcal{P}(o) \subset \mathcal{P}$ of a virtual object o is the set of paths that can be followed by a user when exploring that object and thus touches the object.

An object's path space contains an infinite number of paths. Furthermore, a path can belong to the path spaces of an infinite number of objects.

3.2   Equivalence of Algorithms

Before defining the equivalence of algorithms, we first introduce the equivalence of the different parts of the algorithms.

Definition 6. The *collision-detection* steps of two haptic algorithms a and b are *equal* for a certain object o and a point in space $\overrightarrow{p}$ if either both collision-detection steps return true or they both return false. We denote this by

$$coll(a, o, \overrightarrow{p}) \simeq coll(b, o, \overrightarrow{p}).$$

Definition 7. The *render* steps of two haptic algorithms a and b are *equivalent* for a certain object o, a point in space $\overrightarrow{p}$ and a velocity $\overrightarrow{v}$ if the difference between the *SCPs* returned by both render steps is smaller than the just noticeable difference[2] (JND). We denote this by

$$render(a, o, \overrightarrow{p}, \overrightarrow{v}) \cong render(b, o, \overrightarrow{p}, \overrightarrow{v}).$$

We use the term "equivalent" instead of "equal" in definition 7 because two equivalent render steps can return a different force.

Definition 8. The *render* steps of two haptic algorithms a and b are *equal* for a certain object o, a point in space $\overrightarrow{p}$ and a velocity $\overrightarrow{v}$ if these render steps are *equivalent* and if the difference between the *forces* returned by both steps is smaller than the JND. We denote this by

$$render(a, o, \overrightarrow{p}, \overrightarrow{v}) \doteq render(b, o, \overrightarrow{p}, \overrightarrow{v}).$$

Using definitions 6 through 8, we can now define the equivalence of haptic algorithms.

Definition 9. We call two haptic algorithms *collision equivalent* if their collision-detection steps are equal in all cases:

$$\forall a, b \in \mathcal{A} : (\mathcal{O}(a) = \mathcal{O}(b)) \wedge (\forall o \in \mathcal{O}(a), \forall p \in \mathcal{P}(o), \forall t \in [0, length(p)] :$$
$$coll(a, o, \overrightarrow{p}_t) \simeq coll(b, o, \overrightarrow{p}_t)) \Rightarrow a \simeq b.$$

Definition 10. Two haptic algorithms are *render-equivalent* if their render steps are equivalent in all cases:

$$\forall a, b \in \mathcal{A} : (\mathcal{O}(a) = \mathcal{O}(b)) \wedge (\forall o \in \mathcal{O}(a), \forall p \in \mathcal{P}(o), \forall t \in [0, length(p)] :$$
$$render(a, o, \overrightarrow{p}_t, \overrightarrow{v}_{pt}) \cong render(b, o, \overrightarrow{p}_t, \overrightarrow{v}_{pt})) \Rightarrow a \cong b.$$

Definition 11. Finally, two haptic algorithms are *equal* if their render steps are equal in all cases:

$$\forall a, b \in \mathcal{A} : (\mathcal{O}(a) = \mathcal{O}(b)) \wedge (\forall o \in \mathcal{O}(a), \forall p \in \mathcal{P}(o), \forall t \in [0, length(p)] :$$
$$render(a, o, \overrightarrow{p}_t, \overrightarrow{v}_{pt}) \doteq render(b, o, \overrightarrow{p}_t, \overrightarrow{v}_{pt})) \Rightarrow a \doteq b.$$

We define the three levels in definitions 9 through 11 because different algorithms can have different purposes. For instance, a new algorithm can be created in order to be faster. In that case, the new algorithm should be equal to existing implementations.

It is also possible that a new algorithm modifies the force vector in order to implement a haptic texture [9]. This algorithm can be render-equivalent to existing algorithms.

Finally, a new algorithm could be created which rounds certain edges by modifying the SCP. This algorithm can be collision equivalent to existing algorithms.

3.3 Correctness of Algorithms

Comparing a new algorithm to all existing algorithms that share the same object space is very time consuming. We therefore propose that for each possible rendering problem a

---

[2] The just noticeable difference is the smallest change in pressure, position, ... that can be detected by a human and depends on the body area where the stimulus is applied [4]. As an example, one cannot tell the difference between two orientations of one's wrist if they are less than $2.5°$ apart.

reference algorithm is defined. Such a reference algorithm is generally accepted to solve the rendering problem in a correct manner. At this moment, no reference algorithms are defined, but one can use the widely accepted implementations that are used in SDKs, such as GHOST [17].

Definition 12. The set of all possible *reference algorithms* is denoted by $\mathcal{R}$, where $\mathcal{R} \subset \mathcal{A}$.

We can now define if an algorithm is correct with respect to a certain reference algorithm and a certain operator.

Definition 13. $\forall a \in \mathcal{A} \backslash \mathcal{R}, \forall r \in \mathcal{R}, \forall op \in \{\simeq, \cong, \doteq\} : correct_{r,op}(a) \Leftrightarrow a \ op \ r$.

The operator used in the definition depends on the problem that has to be solved. Collision equivalence is the minimal requirement in order to guarantee that the comparison of algorithm performance, as defined in the next subsection, is fair.

3.4 Algorithm Performance

Based on the definitions of Sect. 3.2, we can now define the mutual performance of two algorithms. We will first define how the performance of one algorithm can be measured in order to define the comparison of two algorithms.

Definition 14. The *rendering time* of an algorithm a for a virtual object o, a point in space $\overrightarrow{p}$ and a velocity $\overrightarrow{v}$, denoted by $time(a, o, \overrightarrow{p}, \overrightarrow{v})$ is the time needed to calculate $coll(a, o, \overrightarrow{p})$ and $render(a, o, \overrightarrow{p}, \overrightarrow{v})$.

One can now state that an algorithm is better than another algorithm if they are both correct (we do not take incorrect algorithms into account) and the former's rendering time is smaller than the latter's.

Definition 15. $\forall a, b \in \mathcal{A}, \forall op \in \{\simeq, \cong, \doteq\} : a \ op \ b \wedge \forall o \in \mathcal{O}(a) : \forall p \in \mathcal{P}(o), \forall t \in [0, length(p)] : time(a, o, \overrightarrow{p}_t, \overrightarrow{v}_{pt}) \leq time(b, o, \overrightarrow{p}_t, \overrightarrow{v}_{pt}) \Rightarrow a \geq_{op} b$

Definition 16. $\forall a, b \in \mathcal{A}, \forall op \in \{\simeq, \cong, \doteq\} : a \geq_{op} b \wedge \exists o \in \mathcal{O}(a), \exists p \in \mathcal{P}(o), \exists t \in [0, length(p)] : time(a, o, \overrightarrow{p}_t, \overrightarrow{v}_{pt}) < time(b, o, \overrightarrow{p}_t, \overrightarrow{v}_{pt}) \Rightarrow a >_{op} b$

Of course, an algorithm that is in some rare case slower than another algorithm and has an overall better performance is still better than the latter algorithm. This is not reflected in definitions 15 and 16. We therefore take this fact into account in our last definition.

Definition 17. An algorithm a has *a better overall performance* than algorithm b for an operator $op \in \{\simeq, \cong, \doteq\}$ if $a \ op \ b$ holds true and if the rendering time of a is significantly less than the rendering time of b (when comparing both rendering times using a relevant statistical technique). We denote this by $a \succ_{op} b$.

Please note that the following always holds true:

$$a >_{op} b \Rightarrow a \succ_{op} b$$

3.5   Practical Implications

When bringing the definitions of Sect. 3.1 through 3.4 into practice, a number of issues arise. Although we define a set of reference algorithms that are assumed to be correct, it is very hard to prove the correctness of an algorithm without having a basis to compare to. A reference implementation may not even exist yet. Indeed, in order to verify if an algorithm is correct, one must evaluate an infinite number of situations (each object space contains an infinite number of objects and each path space contains an infinite number of paths).

Secondly, if we assume to have a reference algorithm, we have to compare an infinite number of objects and paths to prove the correctness of another algorithm.

In order to evaluate a new algorithm, as mentioned before, we propose to use an empirical method and use statistical techniques to draw conclusions. As a reference algorithm, we therefore propose to use an algorithm that already has proven its "correctness" in practice.

Next, a number of reference objects (n_o), with different shapes and different numbers of polygons have to be chosen. We recommend to choose both concave and convex objects with a varying number of triangles. For each object, a number of paths can be generated by letting a number of users (n_u) explore the object for a certain amount of time (t_e), expressed in seconds. In order to measure differences in the user's behaviour, we suggest to chose several differently skilled subjects (such as novice, experienced and expert users).

We now sample the paths of all users using the reference algorithm and store the pointer positions and velocities. If we assume f_{sr} as the update rate of the haptic loop (in Hz), this makes a total of

$$n_o \times n_u \times t_e \times f_{sr}$$

samples per algorithm that need to be tested. Next, the recorded samples are played back using another algorithm and the results are logged. For each algorithm, one can now statistically compare the execution time (e.g. using the student t-test), the result of the collision step, the surface contact point and the force vector. This allows us to make judgements about the performance and the correctness as described in 3.2 and 3.4.

For instance if we define a test with 5 objects ($n_o = 5$), explored by 6 users ($n_u = 6$) for a time of 40 seconds ($t_e = 40$) and if we assume a sample rate of 1000Hz ($f_{sr} = 1000$), we will end up with 1.200.000 samples per experiment. Although the researcher is free to choose the size of the experiment, this number of observations allows to draw statistically sound conclusions.

To sum up, we propose a four-fold solution in order to test an haptic algorithm:

1. Choose a reference algorithm and n_o objects.
2. Let n_u users explore the objects and record the paths by their positions and velocities during a given time t_e.
3. Apply the algorithms that are to be tested on the acquired data set.
4. Use statistical techniques to sample the differences.

4   Example Evaluation

In order to evaluate the proposed technique, a comparison between two algorithms has been conducted in practice. As GHOST is currently integrated in our research framework [6], we have chosen to record the playback data using the GHOST API. In order to allow the recording of our samples, GHOST has been extended by deriving a new class from the polymesh implementation class. The derived class invokes a first callback function before starting the collision step and a second callback after the SCP calculation. The callback functions write the position and velocity of the virtual pointer to one file and the results of the haptic calculation to another file.

As GHOST does not permit insertion custom code for measuring purposes at any particular place, and as it is nearly impossible to know what calculations exactly are performed in the executed interval (scene graph calculations, object rendering calculations, or even other calculations), the logged results from GHOST were not formally evaluated. Instead, they were used as a basis for the evaluation of two test algorithms.

Two test algorithms were developed within HAL, a haptic library we developed for research purposes [14]: an algorithm, based on the God-object algorithm [19], and a second algorithm, which optimizes the previous algorithm by implementing spatial partitioning using an octree [2].

Two specialized classes were written for HAL. A pseudo haptic device reads the positions and velocities from file and acts as if it was an haptic device using the recorded data. A scene graph with logging features measures the time that an algorithm needs for haptic calculations and saves the result of the algorithm and the time that was needed. The measurements were made using the Windows high-performance timer. Although Microsoft Windows is not a real-time operating system, we made the calculations more precise by executing the test algorithms within a high-priority thread, as a regular haptic device would do. Just before the execution of a new loop, the measurement scene graph lets the other processes execute by releasing its time slice. This decreases the chance that a context switch occurs in the middle of the haptic calculations. Finally, the pseudo-haptic thread is bound to one processor in order to avoid problems with the high-performance timer[3].

As this is a proof of concept validation of our measurement method, we did not perform a full evaluation of the test algorithms. This means we didn't explicitly choose a reference algorithm from which we can be 100% sure it is correct. We also chose the values of our parameters to be relatively small to end up with a manageable amount of data. We have tested three objects ($n_o = 3$), a cube, consisting of 12 triangles, a sphere, consisting of 182 triangles and a sphere consisting of 562 triangles. Only one expert user ($n_u = 1$), one of the authors, tested the objects during 40 seconds ($t_e = 40s$). The haptic update rate was 1000Hz ($f_{sr} = 1000$), resulting in a set of 120.000 samples per algorithm. All the values were stored in a SQL database, which allows us to easily select and combine results and export parts to statistical applications.

---

[3] The high-performance timer can give results that deviate slightly when a thread migrates from one processor to another.

5   Discussion

This section discusses the results from the example evaluation. First, we will compare the results from both algorithms. Next, we will generalize our results and explain some other benefits of our evaluation method.

5.1   Comparison

Lets assume the correctness of algorithm 1, which is based on the God-object algorithm described in [19]. First the collision equivalence of both algorithms has to be verified. If two algorithms are not collision equivalent, one cannot unambiguously draw conclusions from this test. Collision equivalency can be very easily checked by performing a query that only selects those samples in which the collision result of both algorithms was different. From our values we can even conclude the equality of both algorithm, which could be expected since algorithm 2 is an optimized version of the same algorithm 1. Note that to conclude the correctness of an algorithm, we don't require render equivalence or equality.

If we compare the calculation times for the samples in which both algorithms have collision, and the times of the samples in which no collision occurs, and we compare both algorithms using one-way ANOVA, we can conclude a significant improvement for the optimized algorithm ($p < 0.001$). Since we could predict this result in advance, the proposed approach shows a statistically founded conclusion.

Table 1. Average calculation times for the spheres

Triangles	Algorithm 1	Algorithm 2
182	0.01029ms	0.00746ms
562	0.03175ms	0.00783ms

Moreover, if the test has been conducted by a variety of objects or a variety of skilled users, the database allows us to select a subset of samples and draw conclusions about special conditions. In our example we have sampled two spheres, one with 182 and one with 562 polygons. If we compare the improvement of calculation time of the low-resolution object, with the improvement of the high-resolution object, we can conclude that algorithm 2 has a higher improvement for complex objects. This result can also be checked against the theoretical time complexity of the algorithm. The average calculation times for calculating the collision detection and the SCP is summed up in table 1. As one would expect, the calculation time increases with the number of triangles in algorithm 1, while the octree of algorithm 2 causes the calculation time to stay near-constant.

5.2   Generalization

Although our proposed measurement method has been tested with an early version of our haptic library, we are convinced that the results are far more general. We want to stress that this test can be implemented in any haptic API that is open enough to implement the necessary recording or play-back features.

To record values of a path, it is sufficient to read the device's position, velocity and collision result at the given sample rate. All current available APIs support this feature. To measure the calculation time, it is necessary to capture the high-performance timer before and after the calculation. In the GHOST API we can do this by deriving a new object. It is impossible to measure different scene graph algorithms as those timings don't take any scene graph calculation into account. Other APIs such as e-Touch, which are open source don't suffer from this problem since their code can be extended at any point.

To play back values, a new device has to be created in order to read the recorded paths from file. For this feature we need an API that not only allows multiple devices, but also allows the developer to implement a pseudo device. This requirement makes it impossible for new algorithms to be tested in an implementation within the GHOST API. New algorithms that have to be tested therefore must be implemented in an API that is open enough to support these features.

5.3 Other Benefits

Since our method allows us to record a path and replay exactly the same data with other algorithms, and since we are recording the results to a database, we are able to quickly find those samples where erroneous differences between the algorithms occur. Using the same recorded paths and identical values, results in a deterministic system which makes it easier for the programmer to reproduce the same errors instead of searching for the same coincidental situation. By debugging the algorithm with just a subset of the recorded path, the error can be traced line by line. In preparation of this paper we have used this method to eliminate some implementation errors in the collision detection algorithm and in the octree algorithm.

6   Conclusions

In this paper we presented a theoretical framework and a practical discussion for an empirical method for comparing haptic algorithms. The proposed method addresses some flaws in currently known methods as there are the difficulties to obtain exact numerical results, and the problem to offer identical input to the algorithms to be compared.

We tested our approach with two algorithms of the HAL haptic library, in which the latter is an optimization of the former. We showed that statistical analysis on the results proved the result as could be expected. We also found that our methodology can proof its benefits when debugging new algorithms as specific situations can be "replayed" as often as necessary in order to find implementation problems.

We can conclude this paper with our believe that the evaluation method, proposed in this paper, can now and in the future contribute to a better and more efficient evaluation of current and new haptic algorithms.

Acknowledgements

Part of the research at EDM is funded by ERDF (European Regional Development Fund), the Flemish Government and the Flemish Interdisciplinary institute for Broadband technology (IBBT).

The measurement methodology was developed as part of our contribution in the European Network of Excellence "Enactive Interfaces" (FP6-IST 002114).

The authors would like to thank Lode Vanacken, Tom De Weyer and Erwin Cuppens for their help with our implementation.

We would especially like to thank Prof. Dr. Roel Braekers of the LUC Center for Statistics (Censtat) for discussing the statistical design with us.

References

1. Eric Acosta and Bharti Temkin. Scene complexity: A measure for real-time stable haptic applications. In *Proceedings of the sixth PHANToM Users Group Workshop*, Aspen, CO, USA, October 27–30 2001.
2. Tom Anderson and Nick Brown. The activepolygon polygonal algorithm for haptic force generation. In *Proceedings of the sixth PHANToM Users Group Workshop*, Aspen, CO, USA, October 27–30 2001.
3. Ricardo S. Avila. *Haptics: From Basic Principles to Advanced Applications*, chapter Volume Haptics. Number 38 in Course Notes for SIGGRAPH '99. ACM, August 8–13 1999.
4. Grigore C. Burdea. *Force And Touch Feedback For Virtual Reality*. Winley Inter-Science, 1996.
5. Joan De Boeck, Chris Raymaekers, and Karin Coninx. Assessing the increase in haptic load when using a dual phantom setup. In *Proceedings of the seventh PHANToM Users Group Workshop*, Santa Fe, NM, USA, October 26–39 2002.
6. Joan De Boeck, Chris Raymaekers, and Karin Coninx. Aspects of haptic feedback in a multi-modal interface for object modelling. *Virtual Reality*, 6(4):257–270, July 2003.
7. Zdeněk Kabeláč. Rendering stiff walls with PHANToM. In *Proceedings of the 2nd PHANToM Users Reserach Symposium 2000*, volume 8 of *Selected Readings in Vision and Graphics*, Zurich, CH, July 6–7 2000.
8. Arthur E. Kirkpatrick and Sarah A. Douglas. Application-based evaluation of haptic interfaces. In *Proceedings of the 10th Symposium on Haptic Interfaces for Virtual Environment and Teleoperator Systems*, pages 32–39, Orlando, FL, USA, March 24–25 2002.
9. Marylin Rose McGee, Phil Gray, and Stephen Brewster. The effective combination of haptic and auditory textural information. *Lecture Notes in Computer Science*, 2058:118–126, 2001.
10. Novint. *e-Touch Programmers Guide*, 2000–2001.
11. Ian Oakley, Marilyn Rose McGee, Stephen Brewster, and Phill Gray. Putting the feel in 'look and feel'. In *Proceedings of CHI 2000*, pages 415–422, The Hague, NL, April 1–6 2000.
12. Chris Raymaekers, Koen Beets, and Frank Van Reeth. Fast haptic rendering of complex objects using subdivision surfaces. In *Proceedings of the sixth PHANToM Users Group Workshop*, Aspen, CO, USA, October 27–30 2001.
13. Chris Raymaekers and Karin Coninx. Improving haptic rendering of complex scenes using spatial partitioning. In *Proceedings of Eurohaptics 2003*, pages 193–205, Dublin, IE, July 6–9 2003.
14. Chris Raymaekers, Joan De Boeck, and Karin Coninx. An empirical approach for the evaluation of haptic algorithms. Accepted for First Joint EuroHaptics Conference and Symposium on Haptic Interfaces for Virtual Environment and Teleoperator Systems (WorldHaptics 2005), Pisa, IT, March 18–20 2005.
15. Chris Raymaekers and Frank Van Reeth. Algorithms for haptic rendering of CSG trees. In *Proceedings of Eurohaptics 2002*, pages 86–91, Edinburgh, UK, July 8–10 2002.

16. Diego Ruspini. *Haptics: From Basic Principles to Advanced Applications*, chapter Haptic Rendering. Number 38 in Course Notes for SIGGRAPH '99. ACM, August 8–13 1999.
17. SensAble. *GHOST Programmers Guide*, 1996–2001.
18. Alistair Sutcliffe and Brian Gault. Heuristic evaluation of virtual reality applications. *Interacting with Computers*, 16(4):631–849, August 2004.
19. C. B. Zilles and J. K. Salisbury. A constraint-based god-object method for haptic display. In *Proceedings of the International Conference on Intelligent Robots and Systems, Volume 3*, pages 146–151, August 1995.

A Specification Language and System for the Three-Dimensional Visualisation of Knowledge Bases

El Mustapha El Atifi and Gilles Falquet

CUI University of Geneva, 24 Rue Général-Dufour, 1211. Geneva - Switzerland
{elmustapha.elatifi, gilles.falquet}@cui.unige.ch

Abstract. In this paper we present models and languages to specify 3D interfaces for accessing knowledge bases. In this approach, a specification has an abstract and a concrete level. The abstract specification language describes the contents of nodes, obtained by selecting knowledge base objects, and different categories of links on these nodes. It serves to generate an abstract interface which is a 3D spatial hypertext. The concrete specification language associates styles and layout managers to the abstract interface components, so as to produce a concrete interface in which the nodes have a presentation and a position. This concrete interface is then easily translated in a 3D scene representation language such as VRML or X3D to be displayed.

1 Introduction

The use of knowledge organisation systems is spreading rapidly to support or enhance new computerized applications. For instance, the implementation of the semantic web idea will require the development of ontologies, multi-agent systems must refer to common ontologies to communicate and many e-learning environments include knowledge representation components for modelling the domain, the user profiles and so on. In addition, traditional databases or document repositories are often complemented with a knowledge representation layer to form machine treatable knowledge bases.

Several authors have shown that 3D visualisation techniques can enhance the usability of user interfaces, at least for certain tasks. In addition, 3D spaces offer a wide spectrum of opportunities to develop visual metaphors and interaction objects. However, the 3rd dimension has rarely been used to represent knowledge bases. This comes probably from the lack of tools to specify and implement such interfaces.

The aim of our work is to develop a specification language and system to produce three-dimensional interfaces to view and search the content of knowledge bases. Moreover, we require that the generated interfaces have all the navigation and representation features of 3D spatial hypertexts. That is, it must be possible to navigate the scene by activating hypertext links, and the geometric positions of the objects must represent some semantic relationship that hold between the knowledge base elements they represent.

In the rest of this section we give some background on knowledge representation and visualisation and on interface specification. In Sect. 2, we introduce the abstract interface model and the abstract specification language. In Sect. 3 we present the concrete model and language. In Sect. 4 we briefly show the current implementation strategy. Section 5 gives our conclusion.

S.W. Gilroy and M.D. Harrison (Eds.): DSVIS 2005, LNCS 3941, pp. 126–136, 2006.

1.1   Knowledge Representation and Knowledge Bases

"Knowledge base" is a general term for a place that contains organized information about a chosen topic. There are many different kinds of knowledge bases. In artificial intelligence, they typically contain formal information on objects, facts or rules; it is thus possible to apply automatic processing to them. Knowledge bases that are used in companies for knowledge management purposes tend to be less formal. They are often made of an indexed document base describing "lessons learned", "best practices", FAQs and so on. [8], [20].

The knowledge elements present in knowledge bases may have different level of formalisation and abstraction. For instance, domain ontologies contain abstract formalized knowledge while text documents may contain factual (concrete) non-formalized knowledge, and databases contain factual formalized knowledge. To deal with this diversity, we selected the RDF-RDFS family of data/knowledge representation models [17].

RDF is a very simple semi-structured data model based on (subject, predicate, object) triples that form a semantic graph. The subject and object are resources (identified by their URI (Universal Resource Identifier)). The predicate is a name that indicates the relation holding between the subject and the object. RDF is mainly intended to create a semantic layer to describe web resources (e.g. HTML pages). It can be considered as the data layer of the semantic web.

RDFS adds a schema layer on top of RDF. RDFS mainly adds the notions of class (of resource), class instance, subclass, and property. RDFS schemas are similar to class specifications in object-oriented systems and languages. The RDFS layer is expressed in terms of RDF triples. For instance, a triple (R, rdf:type, C) indicates that the resource R is an instance of the class C.

Several query languages have been proposed for RDF, the most recent one being SPARQL [22]. They are mostly based on triple patterns. A triple pattern is a triple in which zero or more components are replaced by variables. Such a pattern matches all the RDF triples that have the same constant values as the pattern. For instance, the pattern (?X author Bob) matches all the triples with predicate author and object Bob. And thus a query of the form SELECT ?X FROM (?X author Bob) returns all the resources X such that the author of X is Bob. In the rest of this paper we will consider that a knowledge base consists of document fragments (resources) described by an RDF/RDFS layer. The documents are intended to store the non-formalized knowledge, while the RDF/RDFS layer stores the formalized facts (data) and general knowledge (concept definitions).

1.2   Data and Knowledge Visualization

During the last decade, human-computer interaction researchers have invented various visualization techniques to efficiently present and interact with different data types (linear structures, two-dimensional maps, three-dimensional worlds, temporal structures, multi-dimensional data, trees, and networks). Here we are particularly interested in techniques for visualizing the network structure of a formal ontology. The techniques used until now remain simple and traditional (hypertext interfaces, tabular views, graphs, etc.). As mentioned by Shneiderman [26], there is still much to do in this area. Apart from basic graph drawing, one can mention general techniques like fisheye views [25], or lenses to visualize large networks on a single screen. When a tree structure exists (or can be extracted from the network), techniques like hyperbolic trees [18] or 3-dimensional embedded objects can be used. These techniques have been evaluated with users to assess their effectiveness—see, for instance, [14] and [7].

The SemNet system [11] is one of the rare attempts at proposing a 3-dimensional view of a knowledge base. It represents concepts and their semantic links as a 3D graph. Another system called MUT [30] proposes a virtual museum metaphor with nested boxes for representing nodes and links from network-structured knowledge bases. Some systems let the user rearrange the visual elements according to their own cognitive model, for instance Workscape [1] or Web Forager [6].

Another knowledge visualization technique is the spatial hypertext. Spatial hypertexts are hypertext systems in which the usual hypertext navigation links are complemented with implicit spatial links [27]. The idea is that the spatial proximity of two nodes implicitly indicates a semantic relationship between these nodes. In spatial hypertexts the nodes are generally (rectangular) objects that lie on a 2D surface. However, some 3D spatial hypertext have been recently developed [13].

1.3   Interface Specification Techniques and Languages

Although formal specification techniques have been extensively studied in the software engineering field, there are only few works on formal specification languages for user interfaces. Among these works we can cite [15] in which Jacob defines a language for specifying direct manipulation interfaces. Other authors have incorporated formal specification techniques (transition diagrams, Petri nets, grammars, etc.) in the interface specification or in dialogue specification, see for instance [5], [2], [21], [3] or [16]. In fact most of the interface specification languages can be found in an interface development environment. In particular, model based environments such as MECANO [23], MOBI-D [24], MASTERMIND [29], TRIDENT [4] or Teallch [12] have a declarative specification language. They generally include a domain model, a task model, a dialogue model, a presentation model, and a user model. These models have often an abstract level and a concrete level that associates abstract elements to concrete interface objects (widgets, Java components, etc.). More recently, interface specification language have been defined with XML, see for instance [19]. Nevertheless, these languages generally have no formal semantics and describe interfaces in terms of "standard" widgets (menus, input fields, buttons, etc.).

In the database interface field, several tools have been proposed for the declarative specification of Web interfaces, for instance Strudel [10] or Lazy [9].

1.4   A Two-Level Approach to the Specification of 3D Interfaces

Our aim is to specify and generate a 3D spatial hypertext that represents the content of the knowledge base.

The distance between the knowledge representation in the knowledge base model and its representation in the 3D interface model can be large. In particular if we consider 3D representations that are not just graphical views of the objects and relations of the knowledge base (KB). The 3D representation can, for instance, utilize metaphors or geometric relations to convey the meaning of the knowledge base. Thus it is difficult to directly specify the concrete representation of each KB element in the interface. In addition, we want to isolate the general structure of the interface (the semantic content of the interface objects and their links) from the presentation itself (object properties like color, shape, position, etc.). For this purpose, an interface specification consists of two levels: the specification of an abstract interface and the specification of a concrete interface.

The abstract interface specification defines a mapping from a knowledge base content (state) to abstract interface objects, which are abstract spatial hypertext nodes and links. It is expressed in terms of the knowledge base model and the abstract interface model. The concrete specification maps abstract interface components (nodes and links) to concrete components (3D objects and navigation actions).

2   Specification of the Abstract Interface

At the abstract level, the specification of a 3D interface for a knowledge base consists in specifying how to build a spatial hypertext that represents the content of the knowledge base.

2.1   Abstract Interface Model

The abstract interface model is based on a three-dimensional version of the spatial hypertext paradigm. In a 3D hypertext each hypertext node is presented as a three-dimensional object in a 3D scene. Each node can have active elements to trigger link following actions.

An abstract hypertext node can be simple or compound, in this last case the node includes other nodes. The inclusion link between a compound node and a component can have attributes that will play a role in the positioning of the node.

Formally, an abstract spatial hypertext is a quadruple (N, I, V, S) where N is a set of nodes, and $I, V,$ and S are sets of inclusion, navigation, and semantic links respectively.

A node is a pair (i, c) where i is a node identifier c is a node content, which is a hierarchy of typed elements. The element contents will be interpreted in the concrete interface where they can give rise to geometric or appearance properties, texts, references to other resources and so on.

The different kinds are defined as follows:

1. A navigation link is a pair (s, d) where s is the identifier of the source node, and d is the identifier of the destination node.
2. An inclusion link is a quadruple (s, a, u, v) where s is the compound node, a is the element in which the node u is to be included, and v is a set of attribute-value pairs. The attribute values are indications that can be used at the concrete level to position the included node or to determine some presentation attribute.
3. A semantic link is a 4-tuple(s, d, t, v) where s is the source node, d is the destination node, t is the type of the link, and v is set of attribute-value pairs. Here again, the attribute values will be interpreted at the concrete level for positioning or presenting the linked nodes.

2.2 Abstract Interface Specification

An abstract specification is a set of node type specification. A node type specification is a 4-tuple (*name, parameters, selection, content*). An abstract specification can be viewed as a parameterized query to the knowledge base, the results of which are then used to build the node content and links to other nodes. The selection expression is a selection expression of the knowledge base query language. Its free variables represent objects (resources) of the knowledge base.

The content specification is an ordered tree of element specifications. An element specification is a triple (t, l, c) where t is the element's type, l is a, possibly empty, link specification, and c is a content specification. The content specification can be

1. A literal specification
2. A formal parameter name
3. A knowledge base variable
4. A list of element specifications

In addition, the content specification c may contain a subtree c_{iter} called the iterated content. All the elements under the root of the iterated content belong to the iterated content. The purpose of the iterated content is to define a part of the content that will be instantiated for each result yielded by the selection expression. Knowledge base variables may appear only in this subtree.

A link specification is made of a link category (*inclusion, navigation,* or *semantic*), a target node designation, a link type name, and a set of link attribute specifications.

Semantics. The semantic function I maps a knowledge base state K, a node specification $N = (n, p, s, c)$, and a list of parameter values $A = (p_1 = a_1, \ldots, p_k = a_k)$ to an abstract node and a set of abstract links of the abstract interface model.

This function is formally defined as follows. Let $S = \langle s_1, \ldots, s_l \rangle$ be the result of the selection expression (with the parameter names replaced by their actual values) evaluated on the current state of the database. If the selection has n free variables $x_1, \ldots, x_n$, its evaluation's result is a list of n-tuples of the form $(x_1 : v_1, \ldots, x_n : v_n)$.

The following table defines the interpretation $I^r(e)$ of a content element for a given result tuple $r = (x_1 : v_1, \ldots, x_n : v_n)$ (and for the given parameter assignment A)

element	$I^r(e)$
constant c	c
parameter p_i	a_i
KB variable x_i	v_i
function $f(e_1, \ldots, e_m)$	$I(f)(I^r(e_1), \ldots, I^r(e_m))$
$<type>(e_1, \ldots, e_p)$	$<type>(I^r(e_1), \ldots, I^r(e_p))$

If the element contains a link specification $(cat, target, type, attr)$, its interpretation will yield a link of the appropriate category to the target node, with the specified type and attribute values. The target node designation is composed of a node type name n and a list of parameter specifications $(e_1, \ldots, e_k)$, where each e_i is an atomic element specification (constant, node parameter name, KB variable name, or function call). The target node is thus $(n, (I^r(e_1), \ldots, I^r(e_k))$. The attribute list is interpreted similarly (each attribute value is an atomic element).

2.3   An Example

In this example we start with a simple knowledge base that contains concepts, relations between these concepts, and typed links from these concepts to URI of documents (a document can be an *example* or a *description* of a concept). The goal is to create a scene that is like an exhibition hall. In the exhibition, each concept is a stand with a large sign on top and posters with examples and descriptions on the walls. The examples must be on the left wall and the descriptions on the right one.

The abstract specification is as follows:

```
abstract-node: Exhibition
selection: (?c rdf:type rdf:Class)
content: { inclusion-link: to: ConceptPresentation[c] }
```

The iterated content of the node is placed between { and }.

```
abstract-node: LabelAndSuperClassesOf [c]
selection: (c rdfs:label ?l).(c rdfs:subClasseOf ?c2)
content:
    <label>(l),
    {navigation link: to: ConceptPresentation[c2]
        type: "subsumption"
        attributes: (position: "top")
    }
```

```
abstract-node: ConceptPresentation [c]
selection: (c ?r ?c2)(?c2 rdf:type rdf:Class)
content:
    inclusion-link: to: LabelAndSuperClassesOf[c]
        attributes: (position: "center")
    inclusion-link: to: ExamplesOf[c]
        attributes: (position: "left")
    inclusion-link: to: DescriptionsOf[c]
        attributes: (position: "right")
```

```
abstract-node: ExamplesOf [c]
selection: (c ex:example ?d)
content: { inclusion-link: to: TextPanel[d] }
```

```
abstract-node: TextPanel [d]
content: <theText>(d)
```

3   Specification of the Concrete Interface

The concrete interface is a 3D spatial hypertext this means that the information is conveyed by node (3D) objects that have a shape, a color, a position, etc. and by their linking structure. In spatial hypertext there are implicit links, which are represented by the geometric proximity of nodes, and explicit navigation links, which are represented by anchor objects (buttons) that can lead the user to other nodes when activated. Explicit links can also have a graphical representation (for instance solid lines, or tubes, or roads).

The aim of the concrete specification is to define the interface objects that will represent the knowledge base. A concrete specification determines a mapping from an abstract interface to the concrete 3D objects and actions that form a spatial hypertext. A concrete specification is similar to a style sheet for document presentation. But it must be more sophisticated about the positioning of sub-objects. For this reason, we have chosen to separate this aspect of the concrete interface from the rest, we take a layout manager approach, i.e. we consider that there exist layout managers that will take care of all the necessary computation to determine the position of each element of the scene. More precisely, each concrete node has its own layout manager that places all its sub-nodes.

A layout manager is essentially an algorithm that takes as input a set of (sub-)nodes and computes their location according to their content and to constraints represented by semantic links.

A layout manager can have two kinds of parameter:

1. Global parameters, for instance, to set the minimum distance between two objects, or to set the number of lines and columns in a grid style layout
2. Constaints that will be associated to implicit links.

3.1   Concrete Interface Model

What distinguishes the concrete model from the abstract one is the addition of a geometry, an appearance, and a position for each node. The main difficulty in going from the abstract to the concrete interface is to compute the position of each node so as to represent the inclusion (of subnodes into nodes) and the semantic relationships of the abstract model. The positioning of nodes is represented by associating a layout manager to each node. The association between a node and its layout manager is in fact a binding of the layout manager parameters with values which can be constants (numeric or texte) or semantic relations.

Formally, thus a concrete spatial hypertext is a 6-tuple (N, I, V, S, M, B) which denotes (nodes, inclusion links, navigation links, semantic links, layout managers, a node to layout managers bindings).

N, I, V, and S are as in the abstract model, except that nodes are triples (i, c, p) where i is the node identity, c is its content tree, and p is a set of attribute-value pairs used for presentation, such as shape, color, visibility.

A binding b from a node to a layout manager is a set of pairs (p, v) where p is a parameter of the layout manager and v is a value. The value of a parameter is either a simple value (number, string, etc.) or the name of a semantic link type.

Although we call it "concrete", this model is still more abstract than models like VRML, X3D, or Java3D because the positioning of the objects is not given by 3D coordinates but left to layout managers.

There are two strategies to translate a concrete interface into a 3D scene in one of these implemented models. In the static approach, the concrete interface is given as input to the different layout managers that compute the node positions and create a static scene. In the dynamic approach, the 3D scene is created with "active" components that dynamically recompute the object positions each time an event occurs. For instance, a hyperbolic tree layout manager must recompute the positions each time the user selects a new object to become the center of the view.

3.2   Concrete Interface Specification

A concrete specification is a triple (n, a, l) where n is the abstract node type to which this specification applies; a is a list of *attribute*: *value* pairs; and l is a layout specification.

The attribute values are either constants (as in `shape: Box, position: (5, 3, 2.5)`) or expressions computed from some values found in the abstract node (element contents or element attribute values), as in `size: ./size`.

The layout specification is comprised of a layout name and a list of bindings that determine either parameter values or which semantic relation to use for which type of geometric constraint. The binding may include some value translation. For instance, if the `color` attribute takes its value from a content element that has a text value, each possible text value must be associated to a color.

The semantics of a concrete specification is quite straightforward. The value of expressions is obtained by evaluating literal values, path expressions in the abstract node contents, and functions on these values.

3.3   Example (cont. from Sect. 2)

```
concrete-node: Exhibition
shape: Box;
layout-manager: 2DSpringDistances(spring => "semanticRel")

concrete-node: ConceptPresentation[c]
shape:Box
layout-manager:BoxBorder(location => position("left"-> north,
    "rigth"-> south, "center"-> center))

concrete-node: LabelAndSuperClassesOf
shape: Panel
layout-manager:layout-clrtb-LinksRes(linkObject: "cone")

concrete-node: ExamplesOf
shape: Wall
layout-manager: Sequence

concrete-node: TextPanel
shape: Panel
layout-manager:HTMLViewer(content: ./theText)
```

Figure 1 shows a 3D interface generated from a knowledge base and the specifications shown here.

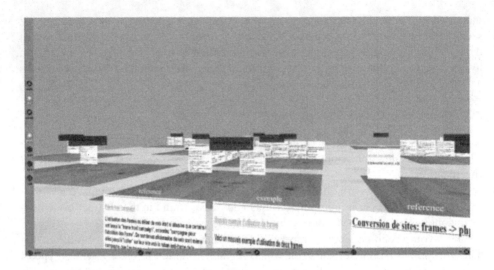

Fig. 1. A 3D view of a hyperbook knowledge base as an exhibition hall

4 Implementation

We have developed specification interpreters for abstract and concrete specifications. The abstract specification interpreter takes as input an abstract specification and a knowledge base and produces an abstract interface. The interpretation starts with a parameterless root node and then recursively interprets the nodes that are referred to (through any kind of link).

In order to re-use existing generation tools, the knowledge base is stored in a relational database and the abstract node specifications are translated to Lazy[1] node specifications. Then the Lazy system is invoked to generate the abstract interface as an XML file.

The interpretation of the concrete specification consists of invoking the selected layout managers to compute the concrete node positions. This is a static approach (as mentioned in the concrete model description), the positions are defined once and for all. The concrete specification interpreter is a Java program that loads the abstract interface through an XML parser, transforms the abstract nodes to (partial) X3D nodes and then invokes the layout manager. The layout manager are Java classes that implement the `Layout` interface.

5 Conclusion

We have shown that a relatively simple specification language is sufficient to generate arbitrarily complex 3D scenes to represent the content of knowledge bases. The specification process has two phases: the abstract specification produces an abstract hypertextual interface and then the concrete specification generates the factual 3D objects

---

[1] Lazy is a declarative hypertext view specification language. It produces XML or HTML contents by querying the database and assembling the query results.

and actions. These languages are declarative, and therefore more abstract than other procedural (even object-oriented) frameworks.

References

1. Ballay J.M. Designing Workscape: An Interdisciplinary Experience, In ACM Conference on Human Computer Interaction (CHI'94), pp. 10–15, 1994
2. Bastide, R., Palanque, P., A Petri Net Based Environment for the Design of Event-Driven Interfaces, 16th International Conference on Application and Theory of Petri Nets (ATPN'95), Torino-Italy, 20–22 June 1995.
3. Berstel Jean, Crespi Reghizzi Stefano, Roussel Gilles, San Pietro Pierluigi, A scalable formal method for design and automatic checking of user interfaces, Proceedings of the 23rd international conference on Software engineering, p.453-462, Toronto, Ontario, Canada, May 12–19, 2001.
4. Bodart F., Hennebert A.-M., Leheureux, J.-M., Vanderdonckt, J. Computer-Aided Window Identification in TRIDENT, in Proc. of 5th IFIP TC 13 Int. Conf. on Human-Computer Interaction INTERACT'95 (Lillehammer, 27–29 juin 1995), K. Nordbyn, P.H. Helmersen, D.J. Gilmore and S.A. Arnesen (ds.), Chapman & Hall, Londres, 1995, pp. 331–336.
5. Bumbulis, P., Alencar, P.S.C., Cowan, D.D., Lucena, C.J.P. Combining Formal Techniques and Prototyping in User Interface Construction and Verification, in 2nd Eurographics Workshop on Design, Specification, Verification of Interactive Systems (DSV-IS'95). 1995, Springer-Verlag Lecture Notes in Computer Science.
6. Card, S., Robertson, G., York, W, The WebBook and the Web Forager: An Information Workspace for the World-Wide Web, In Proceedings of CHI'96, ACM Conference on Human Factors in Software, 1996.
7. Cockburn, A., McKenzie, B.3D or not 3D?: evaluating the effect of the third dimension in a document management system. In Proc. of the ACM CHI conference on Computer-Human Interaction, pp. 434–441, 2001.
8. Conklin, J. Designing Organizational Memory: Preserving Assets in a Knowledge Economy, Group Decision Support Systems, 1996.
9. Falquet G., J. Guyot J., Nerima L., In *The World Wide Web and Databases*, International Workshop webDB'98, Valencia, Spain, March 1998, selected papers, LNCS 1590, 1998.
10. Fernandez, M., Florescu, D., Kang, J., Levy A., Suciu, D. Catching the boat with Strudel: experience with a web-site management system, In Proceedings of SIGMOD'98 Conference, 1998.
11. Fairchild, K. M., Poltrock, S. E., Furnas, G. W. SemNet: Three-Dimensional Graphic Representation of Large Knowledge Bases, in Guidon, R. (Ed.), Cognitive Science and its Application for Human-Computer Interaction, Lawrence Erlbaum, Hillsdale, NJ, USA, 1988.
12. Griffiths, T. et al. Teallch: a model-based user interface development environment for object databases, In User Interfaces to Data Intensive Systems, pp. 86–96, 1999.
13. Grønbæk, K. Mogensen, P. Hypermedia in the virtual project room - toward open 3D spatial hypermedia. Proceedings of the eleventh ACM on Hypertext and hypermedia, San Antonio, Texas, United States, 2000.
14. Hornbk, K., Frkjr, E. Reading of electronic documents: the usability of linear, fisheye, and overview+detail interfaces. In Proc. of the ACM CHI conference on Computer-Human Interaction, pp. 293–300, 2001.
15. Jacob Robert J.K, A specification language for direct-manipulation user interfaces, in ACM Transactions on Graphics (TOG), Volume 5, Issue 4, pp. 283–317, 1986.

16. Jan Van Den Bos, Abstract interaction tools: a language for user interface management systems, in ACM Transactions on Programming Languages and Systems(TOPLAS), Volume 10, Issue 2, P.215-247, 1988.
17. Klyne, G., Caroll, J. (Eds.) *Resource Description Framework (RDF): Concepts and Abstract Syntax.* W3C Recommendation. Retrieved from http://www.w3c.org/TR/rdf-concepts/ on February 5, 2005.
18. Lamping, J., Rao, R. , Pirolli, P. The Hyperbolic Browser: A Focus+Context Technique for Visualizing Large Hierarchies, in Proc. ACM CHI'95 Conf., New York, 1995.
19. XML Markup Languages for User Interface Definition, In The OASIS Cover Pages, Retrieved from http://xml.coverpages.org/userInterfaceXML.html on January 02, 2004
20. O'Leary, D. E. Enterprise Knowledge Management, in IEEE Computer, volume 31, 1998.
21. Palanque, P. Towards an integrated proposal for Interactive Systems design based on TLIM and ICO. In F. Bodart and J. Vanderdonckt, editors, Eurographics Workshop on Design, Specification and Verification of Interactive Systems: Informal Proceedings, pp. 69–85, Belgium, 1996.
22. Prud'hommeaux, E., Seaborne, A. SPARQL Query Language for RDF. W3C Working Draft , Retrieved from http://www.w3c.org/TR/rdf-sparql-query/, on February 22, 2005.
23. Puerta, A. R. The MECANO Project: Comprehensive and Integrated Support for Model-Based Interface Development, In Proc. of the 2 Int. W. on Computer-Aided Design of User Interfaces CADUI'96 Namur, 5–7 June 1996.
24. Puerta, A.R., and Maulsby, D. Management of Interface Design Knowledge with MOBI-D, in proc of International Conference on Intelligent User Interfaces (IUI97), pp. 249–252, Orlando, January 1997.
25. Schaffer, D., Zuo, Z., Greenberg, S., artram, L., Dill, J., Dubs, S., Roseman, M. Navigating hierarchically, clusetered networks through fisheye and full-zoom methods, ACM Transactions on Computer-Human Interaction, 3 (2), pp. 162–188, 1996.
26. Shneiderman, B. Designing the User Interface: Strategies for Effective Human-Computer Interaction. 3rd ed. Addison-Wesley, Reading, Mass., USA. 1998.
27. Shipman, F., Marshall, C. Spatial hypertext: an alternative to navigational and semantic links. ACM Computing Surveys, Vol. 31, No. 4, December 1999.
28. Sowa, J. F. Principles of Semantic Networks: Explorations in the Representation of Knowledge, 1991.
29. Szekely, P. et al. Declarative Interface Models for User Interface Construction Tools: the MASTERMIND Approach. In Engineering for Human-Computer Interaction, L.J. Bass and C. Unger (eds), Chapman & Hall, London, 1995, pp. 120–150.
30. Travers,M., A visual representation for knowledge structures, Proceedings of the second annual ACM conference on Hypertext, pp. 147–158, November 1989.

A Calculus for the Refinement and Evolution of Multi-user Mobile Applications

W. Greg Phillips[1], T.C. Nicholas Graham[2], and Christopher Wolfe[2]

[1] Electrical and Computer Engineering, Royal Military College of Canada,
Kingston, Ontario, Canada K7K 7H6
greg.phillips@rmc.ca
Voice: +1-613-541-6000 ext. 6491; Fax: +1-613-544-8107
[2] School of Computing, Queen's University,
Kingston, Ontario, Canada
{graham, wolfe}@cs.queensu.ca

Abstract. The calculus outlined in this paper provides a formal architectural framework for describing and reasoning about the properties of multi-user and mobile distributed interactive systems. It is based on the Workspace Model, which incorporates both distribution-independent and implementation-specific representations of multi-user and mobile applications. The calculus includes an evolution component, allowing the representation of system change at either level over time. It also includes a refinement component supporting the translation of changes at either level into corresponding changes at the other. The combined calculus has several important properties, including locality and termination of the refinement process and commutativity of evolution and refinement. The calculus may be used to reason about fault tolerance and to define the semantics of programming language constructs.

1 Introduction

Recent years have seen the introduction of numerous architectural models and associated tools for the high level design of interactive systems. Interest in architectural models has continued with the advent of new styles of user interface such as groupware systems that allow users to collaborate asynchronously or in real time, mobile systems allowing users access to a wide variety of devices such as tablet PCs, PIMs and smart phones, and ubiquitous systems which are sensitive to the user's context.

While many architectural models have been proposed (e.g., [2, 3, 4, 7, 8]; see [9] for detailed discussion), there is as yet little underlying theory to explain their semantics, to allow comparison of different models or to serve as a guide for implementing tools or applications based on these models. In this paper we provide such a theory, called the Workspace Model, formalized via an evolution calculus and a refinement relation.

The full formal specification of the model is available as [10]. In this paper we outline the formal underpinnings of the Workspace Model and illustrate its utility via two applications. The novel aspects of the model include

S.W. Gilroy and M.D. Harrison (Eds.): DSVIS 2005, LNCS 3941, pp. 137–148, 2006.

- Its recognition that the structure of interactive systems change over their run times as the users of the system change, as their intentions change and as the physical run time platform changes
- Its linkage of a conceptual architectural view to an implementation architecture, allowing high-level design to be mapped in a principled manner to a run time implementation, while avoiding premature commitment to a distributed implementation
- Its treatment of partial failure as a first-class consideration in architectural models
- Its ability to represent the use of multiple devices and device types in a single interactive session

The paper is structured as follows. In Sect. 2 we provide an overview of the Workspace Model, including the key elements of the conceptual level, the implementation level, the refinement rules and the evolution calculus. Section 3 presents key properties of the model. Finally, in Sect. 4 we present two applications of the model, the first characterizing mechanisms for dealing with partial failure, and the second showing how the model can be used to give the semantics of a language supporting the development of groupware applications.

2   Elements of the Model

In this section, we provide an overview of the Workspace Model including its two architectural levels, the evolution operations, and the refinement relation.

Figure 1 shows the key elements of the workspace model and how they relate to one another. Architectures may be expressed at a conceptual level and at an implementation level. A conceptual architecture expresses the structure of the elements making up an interactive system, but does not specify how they are to be implemented as a distributed application. Conceptual architectures are illustrated in Sect. 2.1 using a small example.

A refinement relation R composed of individual refinement rules r maps conceptual architectures to implementation architectures. In general, a given conceptual architecture can be mapped to many implementation architectures. R therefore captures a space of possible implementations. $R(c, i)$ indicates that i is a valid refinement of c. Refinement is discussed in Sect. 2.2 and implementation architectures are presented in Sect. 2.3.

Finally, an evolution operator e expresses runtime evolution of conceptual and implementation level architectures. In Fig. 1, $e_c(c)$ produces c', a modified conceptual architecture, and $e_i(i)$ produces i', a modified implementation level architecture. Evolution is discussed in Sect. 2.4.

The two architectural levels have previously been described at greater length in [11][1] and the full definitions of evolution and refinement may be found in [10]. Here we present the architectural levels in the form of a small example and provide sample evolution operations and refinement rules, in order to give a flavour of the complete system.

---

[1] The visual notation used in the workspace model has been modified from that used in [11] based on the results of an informal usability study.

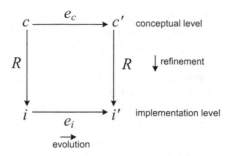

Fig. 1. Key elements of the Workspace Model

2.1 Conceptual Architecture

We present the conceptual level using an example in which a presentation is attended by multiple audience members, some local and some remote. The presenter has a private view of the presentation including the current slide and associated notes, as well as controls affecting the presentation flow. Local audience members sit in an auditorium, view the presentation on a large screen, and hear the presenter's voice directly. Remote audience members view the presentation on their personal computers and listen to the presenter by means of a networked voice system. The remote audience members' slide view shows the same slide as the local audience members'.

A conceptual architecture supporting this example is depicted in Fig. 2, using the Workspace notation. There are two *workspaces*, indicated by the dotted lines, which represent distinct contexts of use. Within the workspaces we may find *people*, software and hardware *components* (rectangles; only software components are illustrated), and *connectors* between them. Components are attached to connectors at *ports* (circles, which we occasionally omit from the diagrams where this has no effect on semantics). Workspaces may also contain *nodes*, which are identifiable computational elements

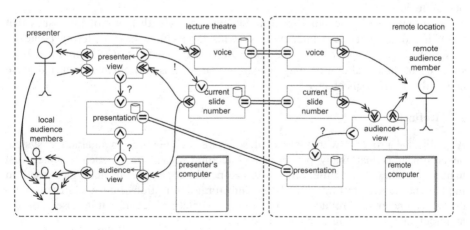

Fig. 2. Conceptual level view of the presentation example

such as the presenter's computer. A node's presence in a workspace indicates that components in the workspace may be implemented on the node; nodes thus provide a bridge between the conceptual and implementation levels.

The conceptual level includes three kinds of components. *Actors* (not shown) have independent threads of control and may therefore initiate activity in a workspace. *Reactors*, such as the presenter view and audience view components, react to input calls or messages arriving on connectors but are otherwise inert. Finally, *stores* such as the presentation and voice components are purely passive and are analogous to the model of the model-view-controller architecture [6], with the added feature that they may be used to represent shared state.

The conceptual level also includes three kinds of connectors. *Calls* (single arrow head) are point to point, blocking, and analogous to procedure calls. Calls which modify the state of the called component are *updates* and are indicated by an ! annotation; calls which return values are *requests* and are indicated by a ?. Complementing calls are *subscriptions* (double arrow head), which are asynchronous and provide multi-source to multi-target *message* delivery. The third connector type is the *synchronization* (double line), which provides an abstract representation of data sharing. Stores that are *synchronized* (such as the presentation components in Fig. 2) respond the same way to requests and emit consistent message streams; that is, they may be thought of as representing "the same thing."

The architecture depicted in Fig. 2 supports our example as follows. The presenter acts as the source of three subscriptions, two delivering voice to the local and remote audience members and one providing mouse and keyboard inputs to the presenter view component. Inputs to the presenter view may result in modifications to the state the current slide number via the call connector. Since the two current slide number components are synchronized, a change to the current slide number in the lecture theatre workspace will result in a message being delivered to the presenter view and to both audience views via the outgoing subscription connectors. The presenter view and audience view components will react to this message by querying their respective presentation components for the current slide and displaying it on their associated output devices.

In summary the conceptual level architecture deals with many of the issues that arise in modeling modern interactive systems. Users may have differing contexts; may use different devices; may be collocated, distributed, or even mobile; and the structure of the collaboration may change in real time as participants enter and leave and as the users' goals change.

2.2 Refinement

A traditional problem with the use of software architectures in interactive system development is that many proposed architectural styles are of such a conceptual nature that they bear little obvious correspondence to the technologies used to implement the system (e.g., [3, 7]). Architectural descriptions rarely address how to refine a conceptual architecture to an implementation, leaving it to users of the architectural style to determine how best to do so.

The Workspace Model provides a refinement relation R that precisely defines the legal implementations of any conceptual architecture. This helps developers by providing rules that they can follow in the implementation of their conceptual architectures, helping in the transition from conceptual to implementation view. The refinement relation also helps toolkit builders by providing precise semantics for implementation decisions embodied in the toolkit.

The refinement relation defines the space of possible implementations for any given conceptual architecture. The relation is specified via a graph grammar showing how conceptual elements may be rewritten to implementation elements. The graph-grammatical rules each specify one step of a refinement. The refinement relation R is therefore the reflexive transitive closure of this set of refinement rules.

Figure 3 shows example refinement rules for the implementation of components on nodes. Analogous rules specify the possible refinements for ports and connectors. All 29 refinement rules are specified in [10].

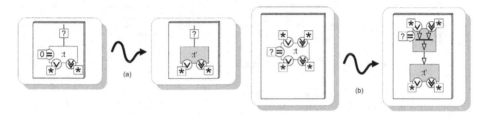

Fig. 3. Example refinement rules for implementation of components

A refinement rule consists of a left-hand side *pattern* that may be matched in the current architecture. When a pattern is matched, it is replaced by the result found in the right-hand side of the rule. The wavy arrow between the two sides is pronounced "may be refined to".

Rules (a) and (b) specify the implementation of an anchored component of type t onto a node. Rule (a) says that an anchored component with no synchronization port and at most one incoming connector (call or subscription) may be refined to an implementation-level component (shaded) with corresponding type t'. The rule specifies that the matched component may have zero or more outbound ports of the call and subscription types, which are preserved in the implementation component.

Rule (b), whose pattern will also match any architecture satisfying rule (a)'s pattern, specifies that any anchored conceptual component may be implemented by a combination of an implementation level component matching type t' and a *concurrency control and consistency maintenance* component (CCCM) which mediates conflicting calls and messages. The conceptual component's incoming and synchronization ports are allocated to the CCCM while its outgoing ports are allocated to the t' component. In the case of infrastructure components inserted into an architecture by a refinement, the rule does not specify precisely how these components are implemented. For example, a CCCM may be based on locking or on one of may optimistic concurrency control protocols [5].

These examples give a flavour of the rules making up the refinement relation. Other rules match a partially refined architecture and refine it to more completely refined architecture, ultimately resulting in an implementation architecture.

2.3 Implementation Architecture

As shown in Sect. 2.2, a conceptual architecture is refined to an implementation architecture by the application of a series of rules. These specify the allocation of components to computational nodes, the refinement of conceptual connectors into the types of physical connectors available in real distributed systems, and the introduction of special components to deal with concurrency control, consistency maintenance, message broadcasting, the marshalling of network calls and return values, and caching.

Figure 4 shows one valid implementation of the conceptual-level architecture of Fig. 2. In Fig. 4 we have instantiated components on the two computational nodes that were shown as available in Fig. 2.

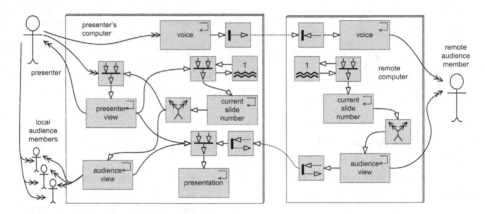

Fig. 4. One possible implementation of Fig. 2

In this example we have made the decision to implement the **presentation** store solely on the presenter's node. The remote node's **audience view** component accesses it over the network, using *transceiver* components to marshal and unmarshal calls and return values. The network link is indicated by the dashed arrow.

Conversely, we have fully replicated the **current slide number** store, maintaining one copy on each node. The two copies' CCCMs maintain consistency by the execution of some replica consistency maintenance algorithm (e.g., locking or a distributed operation transform [12]). The two CCCMs communicate by means of a *shared channel*, implemented using *channel endpoints* (the components with the wavy lines). Channel endpoints are provided by many group communication frameworks, including for example Spread [1] and Horus [13], and provide a useful multipoint message distribution service with ordering and performance guarantees.

Finally, to implement subscription connectors, which have an asynchronous semantics and many-to-many topology, we introduce *message broadcaster* components in the connectors' implementation.

It is important to note that Fig. 4 represents just one valid refinement of the conceptual architecture of Fig. 2. For example, different decisions could have been made on the allocation of components to nodes or on the replication strategy for shared data; similarly a cache might be introduced on the remote node to retain local copies of the slides as they are taken from the presentation, improving responsiveness when previously viewed slides are revisited.

2.4 Evolution Calculus

An important characteristic of modern interactive systems is their support for runtime evolution. Evolution can come as a result of participants entering or leaving a collaborative session, as a result of participants moving from one location to another, perhaps using different devices, as a result of participants' goals changing, affecting their tools and how they are used, and as a result of changes to the underlying distributed system such as network failure or the introduction of a new node.

The Workspace Model's evolution calculus allows us to model change resulting from any of these stimuli. Changing users, locations, tasks or goals typically result in change at the conceptual level while distributed system changes typically result in change at the implementation level. When a change occurs at one level, the refinement rules are used to find a sequence of evolutions at either or both levels such that the refinement relation R between the levels is restored.

The evolution calculus consists of a set of operations at each of the two levels. Operations are defined using a graph grammar notation similar to that used for refinement rules. Each definition consists of an operation signature, a pattern and a result. When the operation is invoked on an architecture that matches the pattern the architecture is transformed such that the elements of the pattern now match the result. Where an operation fails to match a pattern the architecture is not modified.

Two sample operations are shown in Fig. 5, one at the conceptual level and one at the implementation level. There are a total of 49 operations in the calculus [10].

Figure 5(i) partially defines the **attach** operation for synchronization groups. The operation's signature is **attach(A, k, p)** where A is the architecture to which the operation is applied and p and k are the identifiers of a synchronization port and a synchronization connector respectively. The pattern for this operation will match if A contains a synchronization port p (identifiers are shown in diamonds) that is not attached to any synchronization connectors (the zero in the box) and a synchronization connector k that is attached to no ports. The result of the operation is identical to A except that k is attached to p. There is another rule with the same signature allowing a store to attach to a synchronization connector that is already attached to other stores.

Figure 5 (ii) shows a **disconnect** operation at the implementation level. This evolution might be invoked in response to a conceptual level change or as a result of a network failure. Note that whereas conceptual level connectors exist independent of any connections, implementation level connectors are destroyed by a **disconnect**.

In response to evolutions at the conceptual and evolution level, further evolutions may be carried out at one or both levels that return the system to a state where the current conceptual architecture refines to the current implementation architecture. In this way, traceability between the two levels is retained. Additionally, it is possible to apply evolutions at either the conceptual or implementation level, depending on which is more appropriate for the evolution being specified. For example, adding a new participant to a collaboration would initially be reflected as a change at the

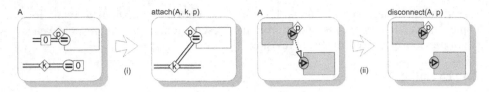

Fig. 5. Sample evolution specifications

conceptual level (with corresponding changes to the implementation), whereas the addition of a cache to a link in order to improve performance would be an evolution at the implementation level only.

3 Properties

As stated in the introduction, the Workspace Model has been designed to possess three properties that are critical to its practical application. These properties are straightforward to prove for our formalism via structural induction over the refinement rules and evolution calculus operations.

Refinements are Local. This property states that the composition of refinement steps is commutative. That is, if A is an architecture and r_1 and r_2 are refinement rules such that r_1 and r_2 match non-overlapping portions of A, then $r_1(r_2(A)) = r_2(r_1(A))$.

The primary consequence of this property is that refinement rules can be applied locally (without reference to the context of their matches), whether the refinement is being carried out statically by a developer or automatically by some runtime agent.

Refinements Terminate. This property states that any non-trivial refinement sequence will eventually lead to a ground architecture. An architecture is *ground* if it consists only of implementation level elements and no further refinement rules match. A refinement r over a is *non-trivial* if r's pattern matches in a.

More precisely, the termination property states that for all architectures a, there exists some number n such that for every set of non-trivial refinements r_1 through r_n, $r_n(r_{n-1}(...(r_1(a)...)$ is ground.

This property is critical to automated implementations of refinement as it implies that any refinement sequence will eventually lead to an implementation architecture. Of course, the termination of refinements does not guarantee that all refinements will be appropriate choices!

Evolution and Refinement is Commutative. This property states that following an evolution in the conceptual or implementation architectures, there exists some sequence of evolutions at the conceptual or implementation level or both, such that the new conceptual architecture refines to the new implementation architecture.

More precisely, for any e_{i0} or e_{c0} resulting in a new combination of c_0 and i_0, there exists some finite set of e_i and e_c such that $R(e_{cm}(e_{cm-1}(...(c_0)...)), e_{in}(e_{in-1}(...(e_i(i_0)...)))$ where R is the reflexive transitive closure of r.

This property is trivially true as the sequence of evolutions could simply be to delete all workspace elements at both levels. However, as shown in section 4, achieving this traceability property with minimal changes to the architecture is the root of a good fault tolerance strategy.

4 Applications

In previous work, we reported on the use of the Workspace Model to support scenario modeling and automatic runtime distribution of real-time groupware systems [11]. In this section we present two further applications of the Workspace Model: reasoning about fault tolerance and the use of the model to define an extension to the C++ programming language.

4.1 Fault Tolerance

In the Workspace Model, a partial failure manifests itself as one or more un-requested evolutions at the implementation level. For example, the loss of contact with a node will initially be recognized as the disconnection of any remote connectors targeting components on that node.

The response of a running system to partial failure may be either *restoral* or *recovery*. The best case is a restoral, in which all user-visible system functions are restored, for example by re-establishing the failed network connection. Where this is impossible, the aim of a recovery is to put the system into a semantically coherent state with the minimum impact on the users. The Workspace Model representations of these two possible responses are illustrated in Fig. 6.

Both parts of Fig. 6 begin with an implementation level architecture i that is a refinement of the current conceptual architecture c; that is, $R(c, i)$. The initial failure is represented as a series of evolutions e_{if} at the implementation level that result in a new implementation architecture i_f where i_f is not a valid refinement of c.

Part (a) represents a *restoral*. Here, a further series of evolutions e_{i1} through e_{in} are applied to i_f such that $R(c, e_{in}(...(e_{i1}(i_f)...)))$ —that is, such that the resulting implementation level architecture i_r is a valid refinement of c.

Where restoral is not possible, it is generally necessary to modify the conceptual architecture in some way in order to effect a recovery.

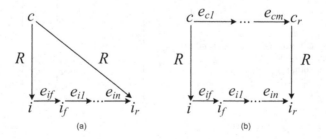

(a)   (b)

Fig. 6. Workspace model representations of (a) restoral and (b) recovery

This is represented in Fig. 6(b). Here, a series of evolutions e_{c1} through e_{cm} are applied to c while a series of evolutions e_{i1} through e_{in} are applied to i_f, such that $R(e_{cm}(...(e_{c1}(c)...),\ e_{in}(...(e_{i1}(i_f)...)))$.

As noted in Sect. 4 it is always possible to find such a series of evolutions, with the trivial solution being one in which all elements of c and i_f are deleted to arrive at empty architectures at both levels. However, Fig. 6(b) is far from vacuous. Rather, it suggests initial criteria on which the appropriateness of a restoral may be judged: the number (and nature) of conceptual level evolutions required to reestablish coherence between the conceptual and implementation levels.

4.2 Extension to C⁺⁺

A second application of the Workspace Model is its use to provide a rigorously defined alternative semantics for an existing programming language. Currently we are working with C⁺⁺. The aim is to enable conventionally written programs to be used in a mobile multi-user distributed setting with little or no modification, while maintaining a predictable, precise, "natural" semantics.

As an example, consider the C⁺⁺ code C *x = new C(); executed in the context of some object q. The normal C⁺⁺ semantics of this statement creates a new instance of class C and declares a pointer x within the scope of q such that x refers that instance.

However, this is inadequate if we wish to be able to migrate the new instance across process boundaries or to refer to it from multiple processes. In effect, what we want is a pointer equivalent that allows the target to be remote and mobile, but with a well-defined semantics and fault tolerance strategy. This is precisely what the Workspace Model's call connector provides, so we can define the semantics of this code as shown in Fig. 7.

The text in the box shows the series of Workspace-level evolution operations defining the semantics of the given code. In the definition the architecture is an implicit parameter to each evolution and the semi-colons represent composition.

The diagram on the right side of the figure illustrates the complete effect of this series of evolutions on an initial architecture. A new conceptual level component of the appropriate type is created, source and target ports for a call connector are created on the appropriate components, and a call connector is created and attached to those ports.

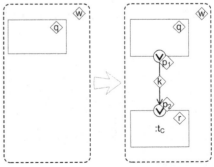

```
Let
    q be the component in which the code is executed
    w  be the workspace containing q
    tc be the conceptual component type for class C
    r, k, p1 and p2 be identifiers unused in the initial
        architecture

Then C *x = new C(); executed in q is defined as:
    createComponent(tc, w, r) ;
    createCallSource(q, p1) ;
    createCallTarget(x, p2) ;
    createCall(w, k) ;
    attach(k, p1) ;
    attach(k, p2) ;
where the port p1 is associated with the variable x.
```

Fig. 7. Definition of the C⁺⁺ new operator in terms of workspace conceptual evolutions

As discussed in Sect. 2.4, this change at the conceptual level will cause the current implementation architecture to no longer be a valid refinement of the conceptual level. The run-time system will respond by computing and executing a series of evolutions at the implementation level to reestablish the refinement relation. In the end result the syntactic variable x will be a pointer either directly to the implementation of the new component (if it was in fact instantiated on the same node as q) or to a run-time provided component that acts as a remote proxy.

The implementation of these semantics for C^{++} is provided by means of a pre-processor and a runtime support system.

5 Conclusion

In this paper, we have presented the Workspace Model and its associated refinement relation and evolution operations. The Workspace Model provides precise semantics for reification of conceptual architectures as distributed systems, and for the sorts of runtime evolution that occur over the lifetime of groupware or mobile applications. We have shown two applications of the model, one characterizing fault tolerance in distributed interactive systems, and the other providing semantics of a C^{++}-like programming language.

Two implementations of toolkits based on the workspace model are underway, one in Python and one in C^{++}. With these toolkits, we hope to gain further experience with the expressiveness of the workspace model, and to determine whether the refinement relation and evolution calculus provide an effective basis for formally-specified implementation of distributed interactive systems.

References

1. Y. Amir, C. Danilov and J. Stanton. A low latency, loss tolerant architecture and protocol for wide area group communication. In *Proceedings of the International Conference on Dependable Systems and Networks* (DSN 2000), p.327, IEEE Computer Society, June 2000. Also available from www.spread.org.
2. L. Braubach, A. Pokahr, D. Moldt, A. Bartelt, and W. Lamersdorf. Toolsupported interpreter-based user interface architecture for ubiquitous computing. In *Proceedings of the Ninth International Workshop on Design, Specification and Verification of Interactive Systems* (DSV-IS '02), pages 89–103. Springer-Verlag, 2002.
3. P. Dewan. Architectures for collaborative applications. In M. Beaudouin-Lafon, editor, *Computer Supported Co-operative Work*. John Wiley & Sons Ltd., January 1999. ISBN 0-471-96736-X.
4. W.K. Edwards. *Core Jini*. Prentice Hall PTR, 2nd edition, 2000. ISBN 0-13089-408-7.
5. T.C.N. Graham, T. Urnes, and R. Nejabi. Efficient distributed implementation of semi-replicated synchronous groupware. In *Proceedings of the ACM Symposium on User Interface Software and Technology* (UIST '96, Seattle, WA, USA, Nov. 6–8), pages 1–10. ACM Press, 1996.
6. G.E. Krasner and S.T. Pope. A cookbook for using the Model-View-Controller user interface paradigm in Smalltalk-80. *Journal of Object- Oriented Programming*, 1(3):26–49, August/September 1988.

7. Y. Laurillau and L. Nigay. Clover architecture for groupware. In *Proceedings of the ACM Conference on Computer-Supported Cooperative Work* (CSCW '02, New Orleans, LA, USA), pages 236–245. ACM Press, 2002.
8. R. Litiu and A. Prakash. Developing adaptive groupware applications using a mobile component framework. In *Proceedings of the ACM Conference on Computer-Supported Cooperative Work* (CSCW '00, Philadelphia, PA, USA), pages 107–116. ACM Press, 2000.
9. W.G. Phillips. Architectures for synchronous groupware. Technical Report 1999-425, Queen's University, Kingston, Ontario, Canada, May 1999. Available from www.cs.queensu.ca.
10. W.G. Phillips and T.C.N. Graham. Workspace Model Specification, version 1.0. Technical report 2005-493. Queen's University, Kingston, Ontario, Canada. March, 2005. Available from www.cs.queensu.ca.
11. W.G. Phillips and T.C.N. Graham. Workspaces: A multi-level architectural style for synchronous groupware. In *Proceedings of the Tenth International Workshop on Design, Specification and Verification of Interactive Systems* (DSV-IS '03), number 2844 in LNCS, pages 92–106. Springer-Verlag, 2003.
12. C. Sun and C. Ellis. Operational transformation in real-time group editors: Issues, algorithms, and achievments. In *Proceedings of the ACM Conference on Computer-Supported Cooperative Work* (CSCW '98, Seattle, WA, USA), pages 59–68. ACM Press, 1998.
13. R. van Renesse, K.P. Birman and S. Maffeis. Horus, a flexible group communication system, *Communications of the ACM*, volume 39, issue 4, pp.76–83,April 1996.

A Taxonomy for Migratory User Interfaces

Silvia Berti, Fabio Paternò, and Carmen Santoro

ISTI-CNR,
Via G. Moruzzi, 1 56100 Pisa, Italy
{Silvia.Berti, Fabio.Paterno, Carmen.Santoro}@isti.cnr.it
http://giove.isti.cnr.it

Abstract. Migratory user interfaces are particularly promising for forthcoming ubiquitous environments enabled by the evolution of wireless technology and the proliferation of a wide variety of interactive devices. In this paper we present a logical framework and some fundamental concepts and dimensions that can be useful to help user interface designers and developers understand migratory interfaces, analyse the state of the art, and identify areas which need further research. A number of works in this area are compared and referred to such framework and dimensions, so as to identify the advantages and drawbacks of the various approaches.

1 Introduction

Migratory interfaces are a fundamental aspect in forthcoming ubiquitous environments. Indeed, in the near future many users will access several types of devices in smart environments that allow them to actively and effortlessly switch among them (e.g., from a PC to a mobile phone), so as to furnish the best combination of application functionality and device mobility, and continue their work from where they left off. Therefore, migratory interfaces require session persistence and user interfaces able to adapt to the changing context (device, user, and environment).

On the one hand, the effect of migratory interfaces is to make user interactions more natural and effective since they allow users to move about freely and still complete their tasks with the dynamic set of available devices. On the other hand, their design and implementation raises a number of non trivial issues that need to be carefully addressed. Thus, in order to aid understanding of the relevant problems to consider we have identified a reference framework composed of the logical phases characterising the migration process and a set of logical dimensions capturing the relevant aspects.

In recent years, research addressing migratory user interfaces has started in several centres. One early paper by Bharat and Cardelli [7] considered similar issues. They presented a programming model and an implementation of a tool for developing migratory applications, placing no restriction on the kind of application that can be built. In this approach agents carry pieces of code and the state of the migratory application from one host to another, where a server allows the agent to rebuild the migrating application. Such an approach is unsuitable for supporting migratory interfaces, in particular in multi-device environments. In this context the goal is to

S.W. Gilroy and M.D. Harrison (Eds.): DSVIS 2005, LNCS 3941, pp. 149–160, 2006.

support several types of platforms, from powerful stationary PCs to PDAs and cell phones. Most of them are mobile platforms, having to cope with power consumption issues, low storage and processing capabilities. The processing load involved with using agents that migrate to a platform hosting an agent server, where the application is rebuilt at runtime, would be too heavy for most of these platforms. Instead, in this paper we analyse, compare and contrast architectures and tools that tackle the challenges of user interface migration that can occur across heterogeneous devices. To this end, a taxonomy for migratory interfaces is proposed and discussed. It is worth pointing out that not all the approaches mentioned cover the whole migration process; often they just focus on a portion of it. In closing, we discuss the approaches considered and indicate areas that require further research in the near future.

2 Basic Concepts

Migratory interfaces are interfaces that can transfer among different devices, and thus allow the users to continue their tasks. This definition highlights important concepts: task performance continuity, device adaptation and interface usability.

The diversity in features of the devices involved in migration, such as different screen size, interaction capabilities, processing and power supply, can make a user interface developed for a desktop unsuitable for a PDA and vice versa. For example, an interface layout designed for a desktop platform does not fit in the smaller screen of a PDA, or a graphic interface running on a desktop system must be transformed to a voice interface when the application migrates to a car. Thus, an interface cannot migrate as is from one device to another (except in case of homogenous devices), and needs an intelligent engine in order to adapt it to the different features of the target platform taking into account usability principles.

By task performance continuity we mean that when migration occurs users do not have to restart the application on the new device, but they can continue their task from the same point where they left off, without having to re-enter the same data and go through the same long series of interactions to get to the presentation they were accessing on the previous device.

Moreover, the devices involved in the migration can belong to different platforms. The concept of platform groups sets of devices that share similar interaction resources (such as the graphical desktop, the graphical PDA, vocal platform). Interaction resources are atomic input and/or output channels (such as the screen, the microphone, the mouse). A device is a system able to run an application and support user interaction through a set of interaction resources. In the migration process there are one or multiple source devices and one or multiple target devices. In total migration the interface migrates wholly from one device to another. In partial migration, only a part of the interface migrates to the target device. In distributing migration the interface migrates to multiple target devices, which is different from a distributed user interface, where the interface runs in one device and is allocated to multiple interaction resources connected to that device (for example, two screens). In dynamic distributed user interfaces the allocation of the user interface parts to the interaction resources is dynamic (for example, moving one window from one screen to another or changing from graphical to vocal modality), but they are not migratory interfaces because the interface is always executed on the same device. In aggregating migration the user interface of multiple devices migrate into one device.

3   The Reference Framework

In the migration process two types of models are relevant (see Fig. 1):

– **Context model.** This refers to the description of aspects related to environment, user and device; for example, ambient noise, level of brightness; description of user profile and of the device features in terms of screen size, type of operating system.

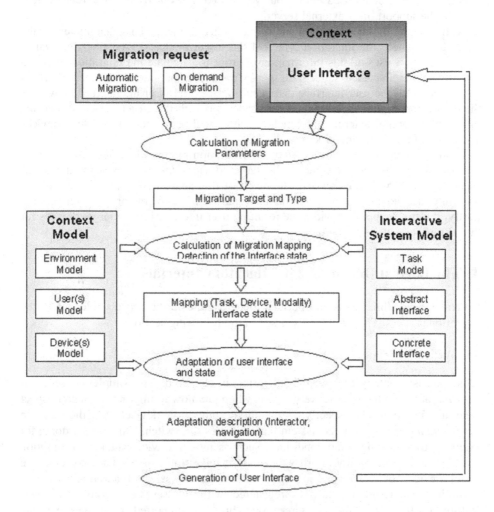

Fig. 1. The main steps and components of the migration process

- **Interactive system model.** This refers to the description of user interfaces at different levels of abstraction, from the task model to the concrete interface description.

Figure 1 shows the steps in the migration process, where the ovals represent the activities and the rectangles the data manipulated and produced during the various phases. One key aspect in the migration process is the ability to capture the state of the migrating interface, which is the result of the history of user interactions with the application, including pages visited, data submitted and results of previous data processing. We suppose that there is a migration engine that collects the necessary information regarding the context, user interface, and requests for migration. In some settings (for instance, with peer-to-peer migration architectures), such activity is not allocated to one, centralised entity, but will be carried out by the different devices without the support of an external server.

At the beginning, the migration engine has to determine the basic parameters of the migration, namely the migration type and the target device(s) (see first top oval in Fig. 1). Then, it uses all this information in order to calculate the migration mapping and detect the interface state. This phase produces the interface state, which is composed of all the user interface data resulting from the user interactions as well as the interaction resources and modalities associated with the target device(s); and the migration mapping, determining which activities will be supported by which devices as a result of the migration process.

In the adaptation performance step, the migration engine identifies how to adapt the user interface and its state to the target devices taking into account various aspects, such as user preferences. The result of this phase is the specification of the user interface adaptation to perform, in terms of both interactors and navigation. Lastly, run-time support provides the resulting user interfaces in the target devices for the current state at migration time.

4   The Logical Dimensions in Migratory Interfaces

Several logical dimensions can be identified to indicate the aspects relevant to the migration process. They will be discussed in the following sections.

4.1   Activation Type

This dimension analyses how the migration is triggered. The simplest case is *on demand*, in which the user actively selects when and how to migrate (the latter aspect generally involves also specifying the target migration device(s)). Otherwise, in *automatic migration*, it is the system that activates the switch. This can be done, for example, by checking some conditions, such as mobile device battery consumption level and device proximity in order to decide if migration is needed and to select the target device. In *automatic migration*, the target is selected automatically; for example, considering the devices registered with the service according to their features (stationary or mobile, screen size, browser supported, etc.), device usage (whether personal or suitable for shared use) and location (exploiting various tracking technologies). CamNote, an application complying with Cameleon-RT infrastructure described in [1], supports migration on demand when the user resizes the window and provides users with visual mechanisms aimed at making them aware of (the state of) the occurring migration (e.g., users can see the application progressively disappear from one device and appear on another). Other approaches such as ISTI migration [5] support both on demand and automatic triggering. However, the vast majority of existing approaches supports only on demand migration. For instance, in the approach of ICrafter [15] the type of migration request considered is only on demand because the user is supposed to request a user interface for a specific service and for a specific device. The same type of activation is also supported in [16], where the user is allowed to save and restore multiple independent snapshots of web sessions on a browser and to retrieve them at a later time to continue any one of the sessions saved in any order.

4.2 Type of Migration

This dimension analyses the 'extent' of migration, as there are cases in which only a portion of the interactive application should be migrated. It is worth pointing out that a fine-grained migration (e.g., partial) does not necessarily imply that a coarse-grained migration (e.g., total) is possible as well, since this dimension generally defines the scope of the possible migrations allowed by a certain approach. We identified five types of migration: *total, partial, distributing, aggregating* and *multiple*. Total migration basically allows the user to change the device used to interact with the application. In this case, the system is in charge of keeping interaction continuity and supporting interface adaptation to the different platforms.

Partial migration is the ability to migrate a portion of the user interface, while the remaining portion remains in the source device. In *partial control migration*, there is a clear distinction of the portions (one for user interaction and one for information presentation) in which the migration occurs. An example of partial control migration obtained by analysing the logical description of the user interface is presented in [4]. Another example, in which the control part of one (or even more than one) service can migrate to a single device, can be found in the ICrafter approach [15], where the control part of different devices existing in an interactive workspace can migrate to a single device. If the client application is partially split into several parts (both concerning control and presentation), and such parts are distributed over target and source devices, we refer to *mixed partial* migration.

In distributing migration the user interface is totally distributed over two or more devices after migration. This is different from distributed user interfaces (such as those considered in [17]) for which the user interfaces are originally generated as distributed among various interaction resources connected to the same device. Aggregating migration performs the inverse process: the interface of multiple source devices are grouped in the user interface of a single target device. Multiple migration occurs when both the source and the target of the migration process are multiple devices.

4.3 Number/Combinations of Migration Modalities

This dimension analyses the modalities involved in the migration process. *Mono-modality* means that the devices involved in the migration adopt the same modality interaction. *Trans-modality* means that the user can migrate by changing the interface modality. An example of migration from graphical interface to vocal interface is the case of users navigating the Web through a PDA or Desktop PC and afterwards migrate the application to a mobile phone supporting only vocal interaction. Lastly, with *multi-modality* the migratory interface contemporaneously supports two or more interaction modalities at least in one device involved in the migration. Work in this area often has mainly focused on graphical interfaces, investigating how to change the graphical representations depending on the size of the screens available. For instance, both papers [8, 13] focus on how to adapt a user interface originally designed for a large screen to a small screen. In [5] there is an example of transmodal migration where conversion from graphical to vocal modality or vice-versa while migrating is obtained by exploiting task descriptions of the user interfaces and mapping the task support in a way appropriate to the interaction resources available.

Another work that started to consider the vocal modality and the possibility of generating voice interfaces is ICrafter [15], although still at a preliminary stage, since a lot of work must be done manually by the designer in order to provide suitable constructs for speech interactions.

4.4 Type of Interface Activated

This dimension specifies how the user interface is generated in order to be rendered on the target device(s). With *precomputed user interfaces* the user interface has been produced in advance for each type of device. Thus, at runtime there is no need for further adaptation to the device but only for adaptation of the state of the user interface. On the contrary, if a *runtime generation of user interfaces* is considered, the migration engine generates the user interface according to the features of the target device at the time migration occurs. Between the two approaches, an *intermediate* one is still possible, in which the migration engine adapts dynamically to the different devices using some 'templates' or logical descriptions that have been previously created. The first version of the ISTI approach [3] used pre-computed user interfaces obtained through logical descriptions of the user interfaces generated for each platform through the TERESA tool. However, a more general solution has been designed and implemented in [2]: it starts with the desktop version of a Web application and when accesses from different platforms or requests of migration to different platforms are identified by a proxy server, then the underlying logical abstractions are rebuilt through a reverse engineering tool and they are used to dynamically generate the version of the user interface adapted for the target platform. In the approaches analysed, the most common style used is the intermediate one (see [1], [9], [10], [15]) which seeks a trade-off between the availability of pre-computed solutions and the ad-hoc support of the runtime generation.

4.5   Granularity of Adaptation

The adaptation process can be affected at various levels: the entire application can be changed depending on the new context or the user interface components (presentation, navigation, content). An example of adaptation at the *application* level occurs in the Aura approach [11]. In this case, suppliers provide the abstract services, which are implemented by just wrapping existing applications and services to conform to Aura APIs. For instance, Emacs, Word and NotePad can each be wrapped to become a supplier of text editing services. So, the different context is supported through a different application for the same goal (for example, text editing can be supported through MS Word or Emacs depending on the resources of the device at hand). By adaptation at the *presentation* level we mean, for example, when the presentation layout changes. *Navigation* refers to the connections among the different presentations: for example, when the number of presentations increases or decreases, then the connections between them have to change. *Content* adaptation refers to when some information is removed, or added, or modified (e.g.: summarised) in order to produce a user interface more usable depending on the resources of the device. In *component* adaptation different representations of the same interaction object are supported. For example, the selection of elements can be obtained through list box, radio button, check box, etc. As for the layout and navigation adaptation, approaches such as [1], [8] and [9] support them. Furthermore, in the approach described in [6], the (Web) page is adapted and converted into a two level hierarchical organisation with a thumbnail page at the top level to provide a global view, and an index page to a set of sub-pages at the bottom level, so as to allow the user to select a particular region to zoom into for detailed information. Roam [9], CamNote [1], Dygimes [10] and ISTI [5] also operate at an interactor-based level by suppressing/replacing/transforming interactors. An example of interactor replacement is when a graphical link is replaced with a textual link. It is worth pointing out that in [13] there is no change either in the content or in the layout of the original page.

4.6   How the UI Is Adapted

There are several strategies regarding how to adapt user interfaces after a migration process occurs:

- **Conservation.** This strategy maintains the arrangement and the presentation of each object of the user interface: one possible example is the simple scaling of the user interface to different screen sizes.
- **Rearrangement.** In this case all the user interface objects are kept during the migration but they are rearranged according to some techniques (e.g., using different layout strategies).
- **Increase.** This is when the user interface migrates from one device with limited resources to one offering more capabilities, the user interface might be improved accordingly, by providing users with more features.
- **Reduction.** This technique is the opposite of increase and it can be applied when the user interfaces migrates from desktop to mobile device because some activities that can be performed on the desktop might result unsuitable for mobile device support.

- **Simplification.** In this case all the user interface objects are kept during the migration but their representation is simplified, for example, different resolutions are used for figures or figures are substituted with textual descriptions.
- **Magnification.** This technique represents the opposite of simplification (e.g., a textual description might be substituted with multimedia information).

Examples of rearrangement can be found in [8], where the original Web page might be split into different sub-pages. It is worth pointing out that in techniques such as those supported in [6], it is the user who is in charge of interactively performing further adaptation, by collapsing irrelevant information so as to get more space for interesting data which are consequently magnified. Such an adaptation can also be saved for future uses.

4.7 The Impact of Migration on Tasks

The impact of migration on tasks depends on how the user interface is adapted because reduction and increase can produce some change on the range of tasks supported by each device. Differently, conservation and rearrangement do not produce any effect on the set of tasks supported. Then the possible cases are (1) after a partial or distributing migration some tasks can be performed on two or more devices in the same manner (*task redundancy*), which means, for instance, that the decomposition of the different tasks into subtasks is unchanged, as well as the temporal relationships (sequencing, concurrency, etc.) occurring among them; (2) after a partial or distributing migration a part of a task can be supported on one device and the other part/s is/are available on different devices (*task complementarity*). Additional cases are when the number of tasks supported (3) increases (*task increase*) or (4) decreases (*task decrease*) after migration. Obviously, a final case might be identified when the migration has no impact on tasks, as they remain substantially unchanged. The possibility that tasks increase/decrease has been taken into account in several approaches such as [9], [1], [5]. For instance, in Roam [9] there is a dedicated module (the *task manager*) whose job is to choose the appropriate tasks for the target device platform, and to remove widgets belonging to tasks inappropriate for the target device platform. For example, considering an e-shopping application, if UI designers specify that the *Add Shopping Item* task is not suitable for cell phones the corresponding widgets are removed by the task manager and not displayed on the cell phone presentation. A particular example of task increase has been identified in ICrafter, whose main novelty claimed by authors is to produce UI not only for services, but also for on-the-fly aggregation of services. Other approaches do not seem to pay particular attention to this dimension. For example, in the approach described in [13], the authors focus on five types of general, Web-oriented tasks such as finding information and re-finding information, which are reasonably expected to be supported on most devices.

4.8 Context Model

During adaptation of the user interface the migration process can consider the context in terms of description of device, user and environment. Not surprisingly, the variable that is taken into account by all the approaches is the device and its properties. Sometimes the knowledge of the surrounding environment together with its characteristics has also been taken into account (see [15] and [1]) with the aim of producing more usable user interfaces. Information about the user is considered only in BSR. Indeed, one of the main contributions of BSR service is that it decouples association between browser state and a device, in favour of an association between browser state and the user. It introduces the concept of a *personal* repository where a user can store multiple snapshots and retrieve them anytime on any device. The benefits of this new association are that (1) it allows a user to switch devices in the middle of an active web session without losing state and having to restart on a new device, and (2) it allows a user to keep track of multiple active web sessions and freely save and continue any active Web sessions at any time from any device

4.9 Implementation Environment

The migration process can involve different types of applications: Web-based (static/dynamic pages), Java, Microsoft etc. Probably due to their diffusion, the most recurrently considered applications are web-based applications ([5], [6], [8], [16], [12], [13]). The approaches that broaden their focus not only to web-based applications are CamNote [1], which is a slides viewer, ICrafter [15], which considers services in a workspace (projectors, scanners, etc.), Roam [9], which considers seamless applications in general (defined as applications that can run on heterogeneous devices and migrate at runtime between heterogeneous devices) and [10], which focuses on .NET and Java applications. In addition, some requirements often need to be satisfied by the underlying software implementation, for example custom web plug-in, Java VM, etc. As this aspect is strongly dependent on the type of the approach used and the supposed goals, it might encompass a wide range of possibilities. For instance, the goals of Multibrowsing [12] are minimal configuration and robustness (dynamic discovery of displays in the vicinity enables the system to work transparently without workspace configuration even when target displays freely enter and leave the workspace). In addition, since it uses Web standards, multibrowsing accommodates any device or platform supported by the Web and leverages the vast existing body of Web content and services. The consequence is that in Multibrowsing a quite minimal pre-environment configuration is supposed to be carried out (a custom plug-in should be installed on clients so as to capture meaningful data). In other approaches the requirements might require little more effort. For instance, in ICrafter the applications, in order to be able to migrate have to extend the ICrafter APIs, while in Roam they have to support Java networking -based mechanisms like RMI and serialisation, since the system is based on the exchange of messages between the different components. Finally, approaches like BSR [16] put quite strong limitations to the kind of migration allowed as they only support migration between devices/browsers with similar capabilities (no multiplatform migration is allowed so far).

4.10 Architecture

With regard to the architecture of the migration service we can consider two different strategies: *client/server*, in which there is an intelligent unit managing all migration requests and sending all data to target devices; *peer to peer*, where the devices directly communicate and negotiate the migration parameters. Examples of client/server approaches are [5] and [15], in which the architecture is centred on a component called *Interface Manager* functioning as the intelligent engine of the system. On the other hand, an example of peer-to-peer approach can be found in Roam, where it is up to the Roam agents installed on both the source and the target devices to negotiate and decide in which terms the migration will be carried out. The architecture has an impact on how capturing and saving the application execution state. First of all, we have a *client*-side approach where some mechanisms such as plug-in or applets collect the state on the client side and afterwards they send the entire data to the migration engine. Then, there is a *server-side* approach where a server detects each event on the client side and stores suitable information consequently. Lastly, we have a *mixed* approach, in which some mechanism on the client side periodically captures the runtime data and sends them to the server. The most common approach is the client-based, used in [12] and [16]. For instance, in Browser State Repository Service [16] a client-based approach is used for capturing session state through a browser state snapshot.

4.11   Usability Issues

The adaptation and generation of user interfaces are performed following the main principles of usability such as web page layout consistency and support of appropriate tasks depending on different device. With respect to this dimension, we can say that all the approaches in which task adaptation to the device is carried out, might be considered attentive to the usability issue of selecting for the user only the tasks that are appropriate for each device. A more original aspect has been taken into account by [13], in which *transformation volatility* is considered. In this approach, the need for not changing too much the web pages in order not to change consequently the cognitive user's model is identified, so as not to disorientate/confuse the users that are already familiar with a certain web site.

5   Discussion and Conclusions

If we compare the different approaches with respect to the various dimensions that have been identified, it is possible to note that many approaches are unable to support automatic detection of context's changes and only address on-demand migration. In addition, the information from the context is often limited to that regarding the device(s). Moreover, Web-based applications are the most commonly considered applications in such approaches and only a few of them address a modality other than the graphical one (more than one approach simply focuses on moving from a large to a small-screen device). Furthermore, the problem of saving the application execution state, when addressed, is generally carried out on the client side. As for the adaptation, a number of techniques have been highlighted, and a great deal of attention has been paid especially to those techniques focussing on how to adapt pages originally targeted at desktop systems, so as to guarantee adaptation coverage for desktop-based applications. Lastly, the importance of considering how tasks might vary depending on the different contexts has been analysed, and various techniques to manage such variation highlighted (the most common situation considered is the decrease in tasks due to a from-large-to-small device migration/adaptation).

In conclusion, we have presented a taxonomy for migratory interfaces, which allows designers to understand the relevant concepts and logical dimensions. In the discussion, we have also considered various approaches that have been proposed in this area. Our goal is also to highlight how the different issues raised by such interfaces have been addressed, in order to analyse advantages and disadvantages of the various methods. An analysis of how the considered approaches address the various dimensions can be useful to identify areas that are still problematic and require further research in the near future. For example, no approach has been able to address distributing migration involving multi-modal user interfaces or migrations where both the source and the target are composed of multiple devices, and there is still a lack of solutions able to support migration through peer-to-peer architectures.

Acknowledgments

This work has been partially supported by Vodafone and by the ISTI Curiosity-driven project MIGRANTES. We also thank colleagues from the previous EU IST CAMELEON project for useful discussions on the topics of this paper.

References

1. Balme, L., Demeure, A., Barralon, N., Coutaz, J., Calvary, G., CAMELEON-RT: a Software Architecture Reference Model for Distributed, Migratable, and Plastic User Interfaces, EUSAI 2004, pp. 291-302.
2. Bandelloni, R. Mori, G. Paternò, F., Dynamic Generation of Migratory Interfaces, Proceedings Mobile HCI 2005, pp.83–90, ACM Press, Salzburg, September 2005.
3. Bandelloni, R., Paternò, F., Migratory User Interfaces able to Adapt to Various Interaction Platforms, International Journal of Human – Computer Studies, 60, pp. 621-639. Elsevier, 2004.
4. Bandelloni, R., Paternò, F., Flexible Interface Migration, Proceedings ACM IUI 2004, pp.148-157, ACM Press, Funchal, January 2004
5. Bandelloni, R., Berti, S., Paternò, F., "Mixed-Initiative, Trans-Modal Interface Migration", Proceedings Mobile HCI 2004, Glasgow, September 2004, Lecture Notes Computer Science 3160, pp.216-227, Sprinter Verlag.
6. Baudisch, P., Xie, X., Wang, C., and Ma, W.-Y.Collapse-to-Zoom: Viewing Web Pages on Small Screen Devices by Interactively Removing Irrelevant Content. Proceedings of UIST 2004 (technote), Santa Fee, MN, Nov 2004, pp. 91-94.
7. Bharat K. A. and Cardelli L.., Migratory Applications. In proceedings of User Inteface Soft-ware and Technology (UIST '95). Pittsburgh PA USA. November 15-17, 1995. pp. 133-142.
8. Chen, Y., Ma, W.-Y., Zhang, H.-J. Detecting Web Page Structure for Adaptive Viewing on Small Form Factor Devices. WWW2003, May 20-24, 2003, Budapest, Hungary. ACM 1-58113-680-3/03/0005

9. Chu, H.-H., Song, H., Wong, C., Kurakake, S., Katagiri, M. Roam: a seamless application framework. The Journal of System and Software 69 (2004), pp 209-226.
10. Coninx, D., Luyten, K., Vandervelpen, C., Van den Bergh, J., and Creemers, B. Dygimes: Dynamically Generating Interfaces for Mobile Computing Devices and Embedded Systems. MobileHCI 2003, LNCS 2795, pp.256–270, Springer Verlag.
11. de Sousa, J., Garlan, D. Aura : an Architectural Framework for User Mobility in Ubiquitous Computing Environments. Proc. of the IFIP 17th World Computer Congress/3rd IEEE/IFIP Conference on Software Architecture: Systenm Design, Development and Maintenance, IFIP Conference Proceedings vol. 224, pp.29–43, Montreal, 2002.
12. Johanson, B., Ponnekanti, S., Sengupta, C., Fox, A Multibrowsing: Moving Web Content across Multiple Displays. Ubicomp2001, pp 346-353.
13. MacKay, B., Watters, C., Duffy, J. Web Page Transformation When Switching Devices. MobileHCI 2004, LNCS 3160, pp 228-239, Springer Verlag.
14. Nichols, J. Myers B. A., Higgins M., Hughes J., Harris T. K., Rosenfeld R., Pignol M.. "Generating remote control interfaces for complex appliances". Proceedings ACM UIST'02, pp.161-170.
15. Ponnekanti, S., Lee, B., Fox, A., Hanrahan, P., Winograd, T. ICrafter: A Service Framework for Ubiquitous Computing Environments. Ubicomp2001, pp 56-75.
16. Song, H., Chu, H.-H., Islam, N., Kurakake, S., Katagiri, M.. Browser State Repository Service. Pervasive Computing 2002, LNCS 2414, pp 253-266.
17. Vandervelpen, C., Coninx, K., Towards Model-based Design Support for Distributed User Interfaces, Proceedings NordiCHI 2004, October 2004, Tampere.

Solving the Mapping Problem in User Interface Design by Seamless Integration in IDEALXML

Francisco Montero[1,2], Víctor López-Jaquero[1,2], Jean Vanderdonckt[2],
Pascual González[1], María Lozano[1], and Quentin Limbourg[2]

[1] Laboratory on User Interaction & Software Engineering (LoUISE),
University of Castilla-La Mancha, 02071 Albacete, Spain
{fmontero, victor, pgonzalez, mlozano}@info-ab.uclm.es
[2] Belgian Laboratory of Computer-Human Interaction (BCHI),
Université Catholique de Louvain, 1348 Louvain-la-Neuve, Belgium
{Montero, lopez, vanderdonckt, limbourg}@isys.ucl.ac.be

Abstract. The mapping problem has been defined as the way to map models involved throughout the development life cycle of user interfaces. Model-based design of user interfaces has followed a long tradition of establishing models and maintaining mappings between them. This paper introduces a formal definition of potential mappings between models with its corresponding syntax so as to create a uniform and integrated framework for adding, removing, and modifying mappings throughout the development life cycle. For the first time, the mappings can be established from any source model to any target model, one or many, in the same formalism. Those models include task, domain, presentation, dialog, and context of use, which is itself decomposed into user, platform, and environment. IDEALXML consists of a Java application allowing the designer to edit any model at any time, and any element of any model, but also to establish a set of mappings, either manually or automatically based on a mapping model.

1 Introduction

One of the existing approaches in development of software consists in establishing a model of the future software to be developed and to produce code from this model. This approach is the cornerstone of the Model-Driven Architecture (MDA) [3] and largely contrasts with traditional approaches where the software is directly coded without any model or specifications. The development of the User Interface (UI), one component of the software, does not escape from this observation [16]. Typically, A *UI model* is referred to as a set of concepts, a representation structure and a series of primitives and terms that can be used to explicitly capture knowledge about the UI and its related interactive application using appropriate abstractions [33].

Models provide abstractions of a physical system that allow engineers to reason about that system by ignoring extraneous details while focusing on relevant ones [22]. The models can be developed as a precursor to implementing the physical system, or they may be derived from an existing system or a system in development as an aid to understanding its behaviour. The most recent innovations have focused on notations and tools that allow users to express systems perspectives of value to software archi-

S.W. Gilroy and M.D. Harrison (Eds.): DSVIS 2005, LNCS 3941, pp. 161–172, 2006.

tects and developers in ways that are readily mapped into the programming language code that can be compiled for a particular operating system platform. The current state of this practice employs the Unified Modelling Language (UML) [15, 26] as the primary modelling notation. However, despite UML Use Cases, Activity Diagrams and other notations can effectively capture functional requirements or specify detailed behaviours, UML does not specifically support the modelling of user interface aspects [19]. So, the last generation of model-based approaches to user interface design agree on the importance of task models [18, 20].

In this paper, we present an initial pattern-based general solution to the mapping problem in model-based interface development. The main function of a model-based interface development system (MB-UIDE) is to provide the software tools that allow developers to construct user interfaces by means of creating and refining an interface model [23]. The success of MB-UIDE systems has been limited. On one hand, there are systems that can generate specific-type interfaces with a high degree of automation. On the other hand, none of the knowledge based approaches for interface generation used by model-based systems is applicable beyond its intended narrow target domain nor can they be generalized to other targets [1, 2, 4, 14, 24]. In our proposal knowledge in form of patterns is used in the development process to help the developer in the model process. We are working in three directions methodologies [8, 22, 29], languages [25, 27, 31] and tools to support both.

The structure of the paper is as follows: the first section deals with related works and then User Interface extensible Markup Language (UsiXML) [13] and IDEALXML environment are presented using an example. Models of a MB-UIDE are introduced using this example, and screenshots of IDEALXML are shown in terms of the same example. We finish the paper by outlining the conclusions.

2 Related Works

To uniformly present work related to the mapping problem [9, 11, 23], we will select some significant and representative efforts made in already existing environments supporting a model-based approach and present them according to a similar framework that represents the various levels and models where a UI development process may appear.

Puerta [23, 24] presented a general framework to solve the mapping problem in model-based interface development systems. They identified the nature of the mapping problem as one of bridging levels of abstraction in an interface model, by explicitly representing mappings in an interface model, by providing tools that allow developers to set and inspect the mapping, and by affording developers knowledge-based approaches to prune the design space of potential mappings. MOBI-D [23], the interface development environment, deals with only a few of the interesting mapping situations in any user interface design. MOBI-D provides a decision-support tool called TIMM for the abstract-to-concrete mappings.

The Mastermind Dialog Language (MDL) [28] is a deterministic notation for expressing task hierarchies and the binding of task and presentation models. MDL has a syntax for specifying task models and additional features for binding tasks with presentations. The high-level syntax of MDL is a collection of module declarations.

MDL defines three categories of module, each of which represents a different technique for defining a process. In a *task*, a process is defined as a hierarchy of user tasks, the leaves of which denote actions. In an *extern*, a process is defined implicitly as a continuously available collection of anonymous actions. Finally, in a *binding*, a process is defined as the coordination of one task and one or more externs.

Teallach [12] uses mapping rules in several places in its architecture to allow mappings between the various models. For example, a set of mapping rules exist between the task model and its abstract presentation model counterpart. In addition to these mappings, an additional set of rules exist between the abstract and concrete presentation models. These mapping rules take into consideration the information captured in the user model, to provide the intended users of the system with a generated interface suitable to their requirements.

Vampire [7] enables designers to manually establish relationships between parts or whole of UIs drawn in a UI builder and a task model presented in a lateral window. In this way it is more easy to understand how each task is presented by which UI components, such as windows, dialog boxes and how leaf nodes of such tasks are mapped onto widgets. However, the relationships remain manual without any further exploitation in the rest of the development life cycle.

The next section introduces a language and a tool—UsiXML [13] and IDEALXML—using an example. Patterns [21] are used when we want to write models using IDEALXML. A *pattern* is an abstraction of a doublet, triplet, or other small grouping of entities that is likely to be helpful again and again in MB-UIDE. An entity is any element that we use in building a model, for instance if we want to model a domain, we will use a class diagram. In this context, patterns consist of classes, attributes and methods, but if we want to model a use case, we will have tasks and relationships between them. Patterns can be gathered using UsiXML. Patterns are found by trial-and-error and by observation [5]. By building many user interfaces models and by observing many applications of the lowest-level building blocks and the mappings established between them, one can find patterns. With such patterns, as Alexander observed, *the things which seem like elements dissolve*, and we are able to use a higher-level building block for modelling (task, domain, abstract UI or mapping).

As we can see in this section we have not an integrated method or tool to address the mapping problem or to use experience gathered using patterns in general in a way that is uniform and rigorous. This work tries to give a step forward in this sense.

3 UsiXML and IDEALXML Environment

MB-UIDEs [8, 22, 29] seek to describe the functionality of a user interface using a collection of declarative models. In such a context, constructing a user interface involves building and linking a collection of models. So, a model-based approach to UI design and implementation provides multiple, separate models of different facets of the UI. This approach is complicated by the multi-model binding problem, which concerns how a designer is able to bind behavior that is described in another model. Many user interface description languages have been introduced so far that address different aspects of a User Interface. This proliferation results in many XML-compliant dialects that are not widely used and that do not allow interoperatibility between tools that have been developed around the UIDL.

IDEALXML is a tool to support UsiXML[13], like GrafiXML or VisiXML. UsiXML consists of a User Interface Description Language allowing designers to apply a multi-directional development of user interfaces at multiple levels on independence, and not only device independence. IDEALXML consists of a Java application allowing the designer to edit any model and element of any model at any time where experience, using patterns, can be used. But also to establish a set of mappings, either manually or automatically based on a mapping model.

In order to develop a UI using UsiXML and IDEALXML environment we follow these steps: (1) requirements analysis, (2) edit the task model, (3) edit the domain model, (4) identify patterns in the domain model according to the task model, (5) derive an AUI by application of patterns and generalization of relevant mappings, (6) from the AUI, retrieve a pattern CUI thanks to transformation by patterns, (7) repeat this until all parts of the task model are gone and, finally, (8) assemble the code generated by GrafiXML. Our example will be a typical page in many website. A page where a user can request one or several catalogs filling a form where that user provides his/her name, address, email and reference of his/her preferences of information. Baring these steps in mind, in UsiXML are considered different models.

A *task model* describes the various tasks to be carried out by a user in interaction with an interactive system. A version of ConcurTaskTrees (CTT) [20] has been selected to represent user's tasks along with their logical and temporal ordering. IDEALXML provides tools to specify UsiXML in a graphical way. In Fig. 1 we can see tasks and relationships between those tasks.

Fig. 1. Toolbox associated with task model tab

Using a CTT notation and IDEALXML we can specify our use case (Fig. 2). We have abstract tasks ( ) (AskCatalog, SendRequest). These tasks consist of several actions related with interactive tasks ( ) that involve an active interaction of the user with the system (selecting, editing, etc.) and system tasks ( ) are actions that are performed by the system (validation, send, etc.). Relationships are established between tasks for instance parallelism ( ) where T1 is interleaved with T2 (T1 and T2 are tasks) or enabling ( ) where T1 has to be finished in order to initiate T2 and T2 is synchronized with T1 on some piece of data. By building many task models and by observing many applications of the lowest-level building block and the relationships established between them, we can find patterns. Many patterns [30, 32, 34] can be modeled using the UsiXML language and edited using IDEALXML. So, patterns that can be found in [34] (Web design patterns section) such as login, registering, simple search, advanced search, breadcrumbs and main navigation can have an associated UsiXML description. In general, any pattern related with a task can be modeled using CTT notation and UsiXML. Many of these patterns have an associated user interface as well—this aspect will be dealt with in the abstract UI model. Tasks are mapped to domain elements (attributes and methods) following *manipulate* relationships.

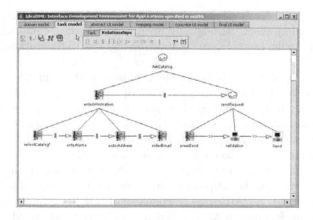

Fig. 2. Task model editor using a variant of CTT notation

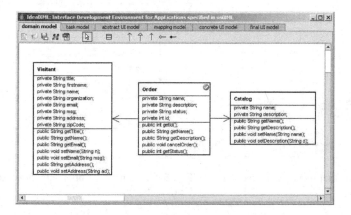

Fig. 3. Domain model editor in IdealXML

A *domain model* describes the real-world concepts, and their interactions as understood by users and the operation that are possible on these concepts. Domain model concepts are classes, attributes, methods and domain relationships (Fig. 3). The IDEALXML environment allows the user to construct class diagrams. In our example, we have three entities: Visitant, Order and Catalog (Fig. 3). In each of these classes we have attributes and methods. Attributes enable a description of a particular feature of a class and methods are presences which are called either by objects of the domain or by interface components.

The development of a domain model can be supported by using patterns. Patterns for business object modelling [7, 17] are not the same as design patterns which aim to increase reuse and framework *pluggability*. Business patterns, also known as analysis patterns [10], focus on creating an object model that clearly communicates the business requirements. The key to modelling business processes is not to focus on the steps of the process, but instead to focus on the people, places, things and events involved in the process. So, Nicola [17], for instance, gathered twelve collaboration patterns that are used for developing domain models. Examples of these patterns are: actor-role, outerPlace-place, item-specificItem, assembly-part, container-content, and role-transaction. In the example, role-transaction and specificItem-transaction patterns were used.

An *Abstract User Interface* (AUI) model is a user interface model that represents a canonical expression of the renderings and manipulation of the domain concepts and functions in a way that is as independent as possible from modalities and computing platform specificities. An AUI is populated by *Abstract Interaction Objects* and Abstract user interface relationships. *Abstract Interaction Objects* (AIO) may be of two types: Abstract Individual Components (AIC) and Abstract Containers (AC). An *Abstract Individual Component* is an abstraction that allows the description of interaction objects in a way that is independent of the modality in which it will be rendered in the physical world. An AIC may be composed of multiple facets. Each facet describes a particular function an AIC may endorse in the physical world.

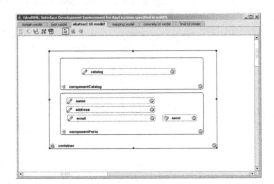

Fig. 4. Contextual menu in abstract UI model editor

Fig. 5. Containers, components, facets and abstract UI models

Four main facets are identified (Fig. 4): an *input* facet describes the input action supported by an AIC, an *output* facet describes what data may be presented to the user by an AIC, a *navigation* facet describes the possible container transition a particular AIC may enable, and a *control* facet describes the links between an AIC and system functions (i.e., methods from the domain model when existing). An AC is an entity allowing a logical grouping of other abstract containers or abstract individual components. AC are said to support the execution of a set of logically/semantically connected tasks. They are called presentation units in [33]. AIC and AC may be reified at the concrete level, into one or more graphical containers like windows dialog boxes, layout boxes or time slots in the case of auditory user interfaces. In this model it is possible to establish relationships. An important relationship is the Dialog control relationship. This relationship allows a specification of a flow of control between the abstract interaction objects and can be derived from task model relationships.

In a similar way, like other models, patterns can be used here to build abstract UI. Many patterns that can be found in the literature and in websites can be described using UsiXML and edited in IDEALXML, and these drafts using abstract components are mapped with task following *isExecutedIn* mappings.

In Fig. 5, we can see a container with two components, one of them is associated with *catalogs* and the other with the *user information*. The second component has several facets because these facets are related with an entity, in other case each component normally has one facet.

A *mapping* model is a well-known issue in transformation driven development of UI [23]. Rather than proposing a collection of unrelated models and model elements, our proposal provides a designer with a set of pre-defined relationships allowing a mapping of elements from heterogeneous models and viewpoints. This may be useful, for instance, for enabling the derivation of the system architecture, for traceability in the development cycle, for addressing context sensitive issues, for dialog control issues, for improving the preciseness of model derivation heuristics. Several relationships may be defined (Table 1) to explicit the relationships between the domain model and the UI models:

Table 1. Mappings in UsiXML

Relationship	Description
observes	It is a mapping defined between an interaction object and a domain model concept (ex. A mapped attribute is modified or a mapped method is executed)
updates	It is a mapping defined between an interaction object and a domain model concept (specially, an attribute)
triggers	It is a mapping defined between an interaction object and a domain model concept (specifically, an operation)
isReifiedBy	Indicates that a concrete object is the reification of an abstract one through a reification transformation
isAbstracteInto	Indicates that an abstract object is the reification of a concrete one through an abstraction transformation
manipulates	Maps a task to a domain concept. It may be an attribute, a set of attributes, a class, or a set of classes
isExecutedIn	Maps a task to an interaction object allowing its execution
hasContext	Maps any model element to one or several context of use

Puerta, [23] identified different kinds of mappings. Some of them are considered in the selected notations used for specifying models. For instance, CTT notation is used in our proposal because it includes relationships between tasks where task-dialog mappings are gathered. Analogously, presentation-dialog mappings are included in the Abstract UI notation where dialog control relationships allow a specification of a flow of control between the abstract interaction objects.

IDEALXML, considering these mappings (Table 1), can handle the mapping problem between models thanks to the UsiXML language that serves as a uniform language between heterogeneous models (Fig. 6). Users can select elements (attribute, method, task or AIO) and define mappings between them. In IDEALXML we can define *observes*, *updates*, *manipulates* and *isExecutedIn*. Other mappings (*isAbstract-edInto*, *isReifiedBy* and *hasContext*) will be considered when integration between IDEALXML and GrafiXML is done.

A *Concrete User Interface* (CUI) model is a UI model allowing a specification of an appearance and behavior of a UI with elements that can be perceived by users. A CUI model is composed of Concrete Interaction Objects (CIO) and concrete relationships. Concrete interaction objects and relationships are further refined into graphical objects and relationships and auditory objects and relationships. A CIO is defined as an entity that users can perceive and/or manipulate. Dialog control defined in an Abstract UI model allows a specification of a flow of control between the concrete interaction objects. The philosophy of our proposal is shown in the Fig. 8. We have experience (patterns) [7, 17, 30, 32, 34], it is gathered and documented using UsiXML and it is used in IDEALXML in user interface development process following a MB-UIDE.

Furthermore, in IDEALXML, two tools make it possible to obtain a graphical rendering from a CUI specification. GrafiXML is equipped with an export module that allows a generation XHTML code and Java Swing objects. TransformiXML allows an interpretation of a CUI specification directly in flash. In this case a CUI may be assimilated to the final user interface. (Fig. 7).

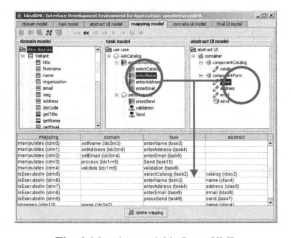

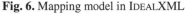

Fig. 6. Mapping model in IDEALXML   **Fig. 7.** Final UI with Java Swing objects

Editing a concrete UI in UsiXML directly can be considered as a tedious task, for this reason a specific editor called GrafiXML [13] has been developed to face the development of CUI models. Associated with each element in domain, task, abstract UI or concrete UI we have information that finally is gathered in a declarative way using UsiXML. Different specifications may be useful to adapt it to different categories of users or different environments. At the moment, different transformations are possible: from task and domain to task and domain, from abstract UI to abstract UI, and from concrete UI to concrete UI. It may be done using TransformiXML [13] (tool

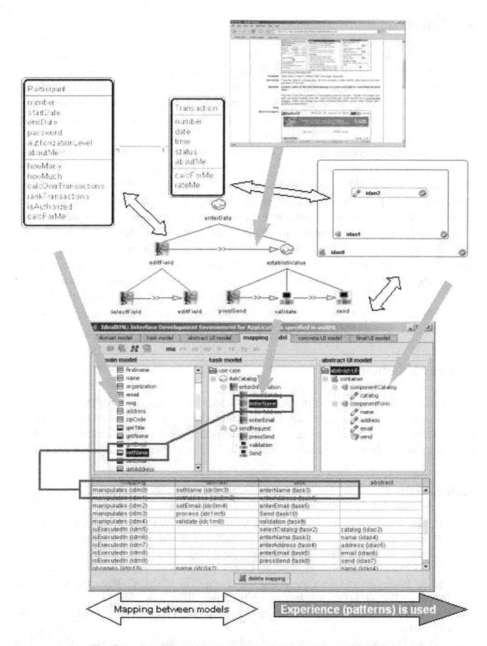

Fig. 8. IDEALXML environment: experience and mapping problem

under development). With this tool a user chooses an input file containing models to transform, generated using IDEALXML or GrafiXML. Patterns are a good source of inspiration for atomic transformation techniques because most patterns are based on a combination of several simpler techniques. That's why patterns aren't always easy to understand in depth.

4 Conclusion

The related work section emphasizes that so far no integrated method or tool exists to address the mapping problem in general in a way that is both uniform and rigorous. In this paper, we present an integrated environment tool, IDEALXML, that can handle the mapping problem (Fig. 8) using UsiXML language. IDEALXML makes it possible to specify in a WYSIWYG manner the task model, the domain model, the abstract user interface model and the mapping model.

The task model is based on the CTT notation introduced by [20]. The domain model is represented with a class diagram. The abstract UI model has the form of a hierarchical structure of embedded boxes whose leaves are abstract individual components and their facets. Mapping model establishes relationships between models, it is useful for enabling the derivation of the system architecture and for traceability in the development cycle. This paper integrates all of the traditional models: task, domain, abstract UI, mapping, concrete and final into one single environment with their respective editing environment. This integration makes is possible to establish mappings in a logical way (rather than being implicitly coded in the tools). These mappings can then be exploited manually thanks to a pattern-based approach or automatically thanks to a transformation engine (TransformiXML). In this way, we can achieve some continuity, some seamlessness through the development life cycle.

Acknowledgments

This work is partly supported the Spanish PBC-03-003 and CICYT TIN2004-08000-C03-01 grants. Also, we gratefully acknowledge the support of the SIMILAR network of excellence (http://www.similar.cc), the European research task force creating HCI similar to human-human communication of the European Sixth Framework Program.

References

1. Ali, M.F., Pérez-Quiñones M.A., Abrams M. Building Multi-Platform User Interfaces with UIML. In: Seffah, A., Javahery, H. (eds.): *Multiple User Interfaces: Engineering and Application Framework*. John Wiley and Sons, New York, 2003
2. Berti, S., Mori, G., Paternò, F., Santoro, C. A Transformation-Based Environment for Designing Multi-Device Interactive Applications. *Proc. of 9th Int. Conf. on Intelligent User Interfaces IUI'2004* (Funchal, January 13-16, 2004). 2004, 352–353.
3. Brown, A. An introduction to model driven architecture. Part I: MDA and today's systems. IBM. 2004
4. Calvary, G., Coutaz, J., Thevenin, D., Limbourg, Q., Bouillon, L. and Vanderdonckt, J. A Unifying Reference Framework for Multi-Target User Interfaces. *Interacting with Computers 15*, 3 2003, 289–308.
5. Coad, P. Object-oriented patterns. Communications of the ACM, Sep. 1992, vol. 35, no. 9, pp. 152–159.
6. Coad, P., North, D., Mayfield, M. Object Models: Strategies, Patterns and Applications. Prentice Hall, 1997.

7. Eisentein, J., Rich, C. Agents and GUIs from task models. In proceedings of 7th ACM Conference on Intelligent User Interfaces IUI 2002, pp. 47–54. ACM Press. New York, 2002
8. Eisenstein, J., Vanderdonckt, J., Puerta, A. Applying model-based techniques to the development of UIs for Mobile Computers. Proceedings IUI'01: International Conference on Intelligent User Interfaces, pp. 69–76. ACM Press. 2001
9. Elnaffar, S., Graham, N. Semi-automated linking of user interface design artifacts. In *Proceedings of Computer Aided Design of User Interfaces (CADUI '99)*, pp. 127–138, Kluwer Academic Publishing, 1999.
10. Fowler, M., Analysis Patterns: Reusable Object Models. Addison-Wesley. 1996
11. Fowler, R. Direct Mapping and User Interface. Technology of Object-Oriented Languages and Systems. *In: Proceedings of the Technology of Object-Oriented Languages*, p. 574, IEEE Computer, 1999
12. Griffiths, T., Barclay, P., Paton, N.W., McKirdy, J., Kennedy, J., Gray, P.D., Cooper, R., Goble, C., and Pinheiro da Silva, P. Teallach: a Model-based User Interface Development Environment for Object Databases. *Interacting with Computers 14*, pp. 31–68, 2001.
13. Limbourg, Q., Vanderdonckt, J., Michotte, B., Bouillon, L. and López-Jaquero, V., USIXML: a Language Supporting Multi-Path Development of User Interfaces. *Proc. of 9th IFIP Engineering Human Interaction and Interactive Systems*, 2004
14. López-Jaquero, V., Montero, F., Molina, J.P., Fernández -Caballero, A. and González, P. Model-Based Design of Adaptive User Interfaces through Connectors. *Proc. of 10th Int. DSV-IS'2003*. 2003, 245–257.
15. Markopoulos, P., Marijnissen, P. UML as a representation for Interaction Design. Proceedings OZCHI 2000, 240-249.
16. Myers, B., Hudson, S., Pausch, R. Past, Present and Future of user interface software tools. ACM Transactions on Computer-Human Interaction (TOCHI), vol. 7, no. 1, pp. 3–28, 2000.
17. Nicola, J, Mayfield, M., Abney M. Streamlined Object Modeling. Prentice Hall. 2002
18. Paris, C., Lu, S., Vander Linden, K. Environments for the Construction and Use of task models. In *The Handbook of Task Analysis*, D. Diaper and N. Stanton (eds), 2003, chapter 23, pages 467-482.
19. Paternò, F. ConcurTaskTrees and UML: how to marry them?. http://giove.cnuce.cnr.it/Guitare/ Document/ConcurTaskTrees_and_UML-new.htm
20. Paternò, F. Model-based design and evaluation of interactive application. Springer-Verlag. 1999
21. Pescio, C. Principles Versus Patterns. IEEE Computer. September, 1997.
22. Puerta, A.R. A Model-based Interface Development Environment. *IEEE Software 14*, 4. 1997, 40–47.
23. Puerta, A.R. and Eisenstein, J. Towards a General Computational Framework for Model-Based Interface Development Systems. *Knowledge-based Systems* 1999
24. Puerta, A.R. and Eisenstein, J. XIML: A Multiple User Interface Representation Framework for Industry. John Wiley & Sons, New York 2003.
25. Rumbaugh, J., Jacobson, I., Booch, G. The Unified Modeling Language Reference Manual. Addison-Wesley, 1999
26. Souchon, N. and Vanderdonckt, J. A Review of XML-Compliant User Interface Description Languages. *Proc. of 10th Int. DSV-IS'2003*. 2003, 377–391.
27. Stirewalt, R.E.K. and Rugaber, S. The Model-Composition Problem in User-Interface Generation. *Automated Software Eng. 7,* April 2000, 101–124.

28. Szekely, P., Sukaviriya, P., Castells, J., Muthukumarasamy and Salcher, E. Declarative Interface Models for User Interface Construction Tools: The MASTERMIND Appproach. *Proc. of 6ᵗʰ IFIP EHCI'95*, pp. 120–150, Chapman Hall, 1996
29. Tidwell, J. UI Patterns and Techniques. http://www.mit.edu/~jtidwell/
30. Trætteberg, H., Molina, P.J., Nunes, N.J. Making Model-Based UI Design Practical: Usable and Open Methods and Tools, *Proc. of IUI'2004* (Funchal, January 13-16, 2004), pp. 376–377, ACM Press, New York. 2004
31. Van Duyne, D., Landay, J., Hong, J. The design of sites: patterns, principles and proceses for crafting a customer-centered web experience. Addison-Wesley, 2002
32. Vanderdonckt, J. and Bodart, F. Encapsulating Knowledge for Intelligent Automatic Interaction Objects Selection. *Proc. of the ACM INTERCHI'93*. ACM Press, New York 1993, 424–42
33. Welie, M., Patterns in interaction design. http://www.welie.com

Concept Analysis as a Formal Method
for Menu Design

Guo-Qiang Zhang[1], Gongqin Shen[1], Ye Tian[1], and Jiayang Sun[2]

[1] Department of Electrical Engineering and Computer Science
[2] Department of Statistics,
Case Western Reserve University, Cleveland, Ohio, USA
gqz@eecs.case.edu,
http://newton.case.edu

Abstract. The design and construction of navigation menus for websites have traditionally been performed manually according to the intuition of a web developer. This paper introduces a new approach, FcAWN (pronounced "fawn") – Formal concept Analysis for Web Navigation – to assist in the design and generation of a coherent and logical navigation hierarchy for a set of web documents. We provide an algorithmic process for generating multi-layered menu models using FcAWN and demonstrate its feasibility with an experimental case study. Our study reveals a fundamental difference between the traditional tree-based menu structure and the lattice-based menu structure by FcAWN: a FcAWN-generated lattice structure is more general than a tree structure and yet is mathematically sound and uniquely suited for menu design and construction. FcAWN is the first mathematical principle for menu *design and generation*, providing a practical basis for human-computer interaction.

1 Introduction

In presenting any sufficiently large amounts of content, such as that contained on a web site, it is essential to structure and categorize the content in some useful way. The structure of hypermedia can lend itself to a hierarchical navigation structure where the content of a website can be divided into general categories, which can in turn be divided into more specific subcategories, each encompassing a set of one or more documents residing on the site.

Taking the navigation bar on the New York Times website www.nytimes.com, for example: the most general categories include labels such as *News*, *Opinion*, and *Features*. Under the category of *Opinion* fall the links *Editorials* and *Reader's Opinions*. Clicking on the *Editorials* link will reveal the sub labels of *Columnists*, *Contributors*, and *Letters*. Clicking on the *Columnists* link will take one to the main Columnists web page, which in turn has a list of hyper-linked New York Times columnists' names. In the same manner, when clicked on, these names will list articles that the specified columnist has written.

The layout of hierarchical menu-driven navigation interfaces such as this for large web sites is often a task that is left exclusively to the intuition of the site designer [9, 12]. For a multi-tiered menu design, a designer must make qualitative decisions as to what

S.W. Gilroy and M.D. Harrison (Eds.): DSVIS 2005, LNCS 3941, pp. 173–187, 2006.

consists of a suitable set of labels and the hierarchy that such labels compose in order to give the broadest and most accurate presentation of a site's overall content.

A problem with this manual approach is that it may require expert knowledge and can be subjective and labor-intensive, and therefore is unsuited for automation and quality control. More often than not, a web designer may subconsciously impose a tree structure for menu hierarchies, making sub-menu categories mutually exclusive and non-overlapping. The common perception and preference on tree structures is more out of familiarity with the structure than anything else. As our case study in Section 4 shows, a main difference between a manual site and a FcAWN site is that the former has a hierarchical *tree structure*, created manually by a webmaster over a period of time, while the latter has a *lattice structure* generated automatically by our Java tool which is guaranteed to provide complete coverage.

In our case study, the lattice structure provided better "logical" coverage of contents than the standard tree structures in a number of areas. For example, items related to *research facilities* are accessible from either the *Research* upper menu, or the *Facilities* upper menu in the new FcAWN design – see left of Fig. 1. This entails a diamond-shaped structure which is part of a lattice and not part of any tree because sub-branches in a tree do not overlap. Using a tree structure (see right of Fig. 1 – original site), items related to research facilities are forced to reside in either *Research* or *Facilities*, but not both. Thus a tree structure can lead to increased incidents of miss-hits.

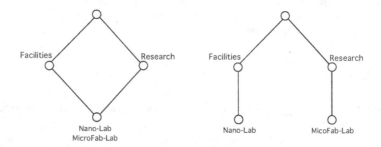

Fig. 1. Left: a lattice structure which allows research facilities such as Nano-Lab to be accessed by navigating down from both Research and Facilities. Right: a tree structure which forces research facility items to reside either in Research or in Facilities, but not both.

The situation pictured in Fig. 1 is not an isolated incident. *Documents in general have multiple attributes, and should be accessible from the root through multiple paths.* Yet multiple paths to a node are precisely what is not allowed in a tree. Manual remedies are possible, once the problem has been identified (*e.g.*, the symbolic-link mechanism in UNIX has been around for a while). It is important to take a *principled, systematic approach* so that multiple uplinks are not added as an after-thought (if there is any such thought) based on an ad hoc manual process, but become an integrated part of the design.

FcAWN is developed precisely to fill this methodological void. Based on Formal Concept Analysis [6, 10, 24], FcAWN overcomes the inherent difficulty associated with misclassification using trees by organizing documents according to their attributes or properties in a systematic and automatic way (what kind of attributes needs to be included is a matter left to the judgment of a designer). Menus correspond to certain sets of attributes – mathematical entities characterized as formal concepts. These concepts form a complete lattice and not a tree – the lattice structure does not require sub-menus to be disjoint (for example, in our case study mentioned in Fig. 1, research facilities such as MicroFabrication and NanoDevices are accessible both under the *Research* menu and the *Facilities* menu). More important, such a structure is automatically generated and systematically derived from algorithms based on FCA. Note that multiple occurrences of a submenu does not entail a physical duplication; each submenu simply contains a hyper-link to the URL associated with the document.

Here is a summary of the key features of FcAWN:

- It offers a method based on a sound mathematical principle for menu design.
- Menu structures can be automatically generated from FCA-based algorithms.
- FcAWN -generated menu structures are lattices, more general than trees. This is because trees become lattices when a superficial bottom element is added and connected to all the leaves. However, the converse is not true: removing the bottom element from a lattice may not give a tree.
- Multiple document attributes imply the need for a document to be accessible from multiple paths from the root, which is naturally and systematically captured in the lattice structure generated using FcAWN.
- Because FcAWN is a general method, it can be used for the design/redesign of device menu-interfaces such as those coming with consumer electronics and other equipments. FcAWN may also leverage the unique dynamic nature of the web to achieve dynamic web-menu configuration based on user preferences and interests. Personalized web-menus, rather than "one size fits all", should be the future of the web for which FcAWN becomes as an enabling technology.

There are two key modalities in human-computer interaction: searching and browsing. FcAWN advocates a concept-guided interactive navigation. Its basic thesis is that navigation menu-hierarchy, for the browsing modality, is an important mechanism for *higher-level information organization*. Menu-structures, in their abstract sense as ordered-structures, can be constructed using order-theoretic methods as well as knowledge-rich ontological techniques (the correspondence between ordered structures and ontological structures is also advocated in [15]). FcAWN models

- documents as objects,
- document categories as attributes, and
- menu-structures as lattices.

Each node in the lattice corresponds to a (sub)menu; and the navigation goes from upper layers to lower layers. The coverage relation of the lattice determines the structural locations of submenus. Although FCA is completely general in that there is no limitation on the depth of a lattice, its use for web-menus suggests that only the structure of the top layers of the lattice is needed. *The bottom element has no significance here.*

Related work. Research on document organization and web navigation [4, 9, 12, 21, 23, 26, 27, 28] sets a broad background for our work. Specially relevant to our results are creative FCA based works on *document classification and* *information retrieval*; however, most of them are innovative in either using lattice diagrams as an explicit *augmented* part of a user-interface modality [1, 2, 3, 5], or as an aid in clustering and in formulating queries for document retrieval [22]. Our approach is unique in that *it uses FCA as a formal method for the design of (web) menus*, instead of augmenting the user-interface with lattice diagrams. The insight behind our approach is the recognition that common navigation menu-hierarchies can be abstracted as mathematical structures by taking the submenus as nodes, and menu-submenu relation as the coverage relation in a lattice. Thus the principles of FCA become applicable for the design of structurally sound navigation menus without any changes made in the familiar human-machine interaction modality. The precursor of the work reported here first appeared as a position paper [34]. Our related application in automatic file organization appears in [35].

The rest of the paper is organized as follows. Section 2 provides a brief account of Formal Concept Analysis, to provide basic ideas of the subject area and to fix terminologies used in the rest of the paper. Section 3 presents the main steps of FcAWN. Section 4 describes a case study on our departmental website `www.eecs.case.edu` and discusses observations based on a pilot user evaluation study. Concluding remarks are given in the end.

2   Formal Concept Analysis

FCA is a lattice-based method for the mathematical analysis of symbolic/categorical data, pioneered by German scientists Wille and others [29] in mid 80's. The idea of FCA is the clustering of attributes or objects based on the algebraic principle of Galois connection, forming a partially ordered set called *concept lattice*. The clustering determines which collection of attributes or objects forms a coherent entity called *a concept*, by the philosophical criteria of unity between *extension and intension*. The *extension* of a concept consists of all and exactly those objects belonging to the concept, while the *intension* of a concept consists of all and exactly attributes shared by all the objects belonging to the concept. This section gives an introduction to FCA from the point of view of menu-layout with examples; readers interested in learning more about it should consult [6].

FCA starts with a *formal context* (or context), (O, A, R), where O is a collection of objects (e.g. documents), A a collection of attributes (e.g. categories, keys), and R is a binary relation from O to A, often specified by a table (see Fig. 2, incorporated from [30]). FCA systematically transforms this low level classfication to a higher level lattice diagram, capturing a concept hierarchy in a visualizable format – see the lattice diagram in Fig. 3.

In this example,

$$O = \{lion, finch, eagle, hare, ostrich\},$$
$$A = \{predator, flying, bird, mammal\}.$$

A "×" in the table entry indicates that the "satisfaction" relation holds between the object at the beginning of the row and the attribute on top of the column. For example, the first entry in the table indicates that a lion is a predator and a mammal. Reading off from the table, one obtains another presentation of a binary relation as a set of pairs:

R	A (attributes)			
	predator	flying	bird	mammal
lion	×			×
finch		×	×	
eagle	×	×	×	
hare				×
ostrich			×	

O (objects) labels the object rows.

Fig. 2. A formal context

$$R = \{ \ (lion, predator), (lion, mammal),$$
$$(finch, flying), (finch, bird),$$
$$(eagle, predator), (eagle, flying), (eagle, bird),$$
$$(hare, mammal),$$
$$(ostrich, bird) \ \}$$

Nodes in the lattice diagram are *concepts*, characterized by sets X of attributes which agree with the attributes shared by all objects with properties in X, i.e., Intension(Extension(X)) = X. Here, Extension is a function that maps a set of attributes to a set consisting of all objects that share all the attributes in the given attribute set. The dual function, Extension, maps a set of objects to a set consisting of all attributes that are shared by all the objects in the given object set. Following FCA's tradition, the two functions Intension and Extension are both denoted by the unary function ( )':

$$(X)' := \{a \mid \forall x \in X, \ (x, a) \in R\}, \qquad (intension)$$
$$(Y)' := \{o \mid \forall y \in Y, \ (o, y) \in R\}, \qquad (extension)$$

for all $X \subseteq O$ and $Y \subseteq A$ with respect to a context (O, A, R).

For example, the set $\{predator\}$ is a concept because objects which are predators form the set $\{lion, eagle\}$, according to the table in Fig. 2. Inspecting all the attributes shared precisely by all objects in $\{lion, eagle\}$ gives us $\{predator\}$, the attribute set we started with.

This defining property of concept guarantees *complete* coverage of attributes for a given node in the corresponding lattice diagram. Hence, when we use these lattice diagrams as menu structures in FcAWN, they help ensure that FcAWN-based web menus are complete automatically, and they do cover the contents suggested by their labels.

Another important aspect of FCA, which provides *flexibility* for menu-labeling by FcAWN, is that concepts may also be determined by a set of objects using the intension-extension transformation in a similar way. The resulting structure is reverse-isomorphic to attribute-based concepts, a dual notion which mutually determines each other. To make the object-attribute duality explicit, a concept is often equivalently defined as a pair (X, Y), such that the extension of X is Y, and the intension of Y is X, i.e., a pair (X, Y) is a concept if $(X)' = Y$ and $(Y)' = X$.

FCA has additional qualities [2, 3, 6, 22, 16, 17, 32, 33] that make them well-suited for menu design and automation. An important aspect that motivated FcAWN's development is that in many scientific applications of FCA for data analysis (e.g. [11, 25, 19]), FCA's notion of concept aligns consistently with *human's ontological notion of con-*

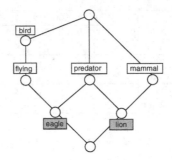

Fig. 3. The corresponding, partially labeled, lattice diagram for the context given in Fig. 2

cepts. Furthermore, the structural property of concept lattices is characterized by Wille's fundamental theorem [6]. This theorem states that with respect to a context (O, A, R), the pair $((\ )', (\ )')$ forms a *Galois connection, i.e.,* for each set of objects $X \subseteq O$ and each set of attributes $Y \subseteq A$,

$$(X)' \supseteq Y \text{ if and only if } X \subseteq (Y)'.$$

As a consequence, the concepts of (O, A, R) form a *complete lattice* under the order given by $(U, V) \leq (X, Y)$ if and only if $U \subseteq X$ and $V \supseteq V$.

3   FcAWN Menu Design

FcAWN consists of these steps:

1. select an attribute set A of categories and classify (manually or automatically) web documents O into a *document context* (O, A, R);
2. generate a concept lattice L from (O, A, R) according to algorithms based on FCA;
3. extract the top layers of L, according to the depth of nodes starting from the root (e.g. 4 to 5 layers);
4. label (automatically) the selected nodes in step 3 and extract a menu structure from the selected nodes with labels corresponding to menu items and edges corresponding to containment of menus and submenus.

These steps can be translated into three relatively independent modules (see Fig. 4):

– A. an online document classification module,
– B. a concept analysis module, and
– C. a menu-structure generation module.

The three modules are cascaded one after another with four kinds of data produced and consumed at each stage:

– a. a document collection and a set of categories/keywords,
– b. document classification table,
– c. document subgroups ordered around FCA's notion of concepts, and
– d. output menu- or folder-hierarchies representing a higher-level organization of the input collection.

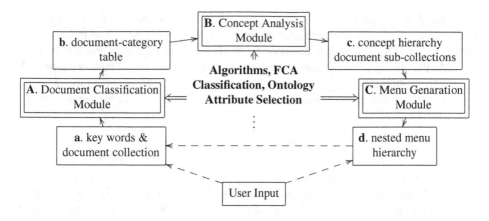

Fig. 4. Main steps of FcAWN. Dotted arrows are optional data paths; the center contains key enabling areas that impact the three modules.

Because of the modularized data-flow, FcAWN can take advantage of the state-of-the-art, and knowledge in several areas can be applied to improve the performance of each module. For example, techniques in document-classification can be modified and adapted for the online document classification module (**A**); advanced data structures and algorithms can be used to speed up special-purpose concept lattice construction algorithms (**B**); and ontological engineering techniques can be used for both intelligent document classification (**A**) and user-system interaction (**C**).

The main steps of FcAWN are presented in more detail in the following subsections.

3.1   Developing the Document Context

To develop the document context, we will need a set of *objects* and a set of *attributes* assigned to those objects. For our purpose, we will take the objects to be web documents we wish to organize but other kinds of objects in other applications are also possible. The attribute set will be a set of properties we wish to associate with this set of documents. There may be several possibilities to formulate the attribute set, such as keywords appearing in documents and other metadata. Attributes can also be selected automatically using IR (information retrieval) and Statistical techniques. Once a set of documents and a set of attributes are selected, the incidence table (R) can be built manually or automatically. Automated document classification techniques can be used here to build the document context. The design decision made may result in multiple possible document contexts, reflecting user preferences possible personalized site menu configuration, a topic of future investigation.

3.2   Generating Concept Lattices

There are a number of FCA algorithms; we apply Ganter's *Next-Concept* algorithm [7, 8] for our purpose here because this has been used successfully in several applications.

Ganter's algorithm finds all the upper neighbors (with respect to the coverage relation) of a given finite concept. Starting from the bottom element, one can compute and enumerate all the concepts upwards, resulting in a set of coverage pairs indicating the ordering among different concepts. More specifically, let (X, Y) be a concept with respect to a context (O, A, R), where $X \subseteq O$ and $Y \subseteq A$. If (X, Y) is not the top element, a set containing all possible upper neighbors can be obtained by adjoining one object at a time for all possible single additions:

$$S = \{((X \cup \{x\})'', (X \cup \{x\})') \mid x \in (A \setminus X)\}.$$

However, although every element of S is a concept and is obtained by adding only one object to X, it is not necessary an upper neighbor. A member $((X \cup \{x\})'', (X \cup \{x\}))'$ of S is an upper neighbor of (X, Y) if and only if for each a in $((X \cup \{x\})'' \setminus X)$, we have $(X \cup \{x\})'' = (X \cup \{a\})''$. This guarantees that there are no other concepts strictly in between $((X \cup \{x\})'', (X \cup \{x\})')$ and (X, Y): adding any other element in $(X \cup \{x\})'' \setminus X$ gives the same set. The time complexity for calculating a concept's upper neighbors is $(|O|^2 \times |A|)$.

Ganter's algorithm only gets the upper neighbors of a concept; to build a web-menu we need an additional "global" algorithm to compute not only all the concepts, but also the *explicit links* among the concepts. In our Java-implementation, each concept is associated with a list containing its upper neighbors. This list is initially set to be empty. Our algorithm works by starting from the bottom element, computing all the upper neighbors of the current concept using Ganter's *NextConcept* algorithm as a subprocedure, and updating the list of upper neighbors accordingly for each concept. This process is repeated until we reach the top concept - one that does not have any upper neighbors. The time complexity for our algorithm is $(|O|^2 \times |A| \times |L(O, A, R)|)$ where, $L(O, A, R)$ is the generated concept lattice. Note that even though the size of $L(O, A, R)$ is exponential in the worst case, our algorithm can be made efficient since we are only interested in nodes in the top layers.

3.3   Extracting the Top Layers

From the lattice generated in the previous step, we "peel off" the structure 3 to 5 edges deep from the top, yielding a directed graph of the upper level concepts. Concepts contained in this upper graph will be the basis for our menu items; the graph structure determines the menu structure.

Because lattice structures can become quite large, depending on the context that they were generated from, we assume for practicality that for any one menu representation, we will only be interested in the first three to five levels in the lattice. It becomes unreasonable from a human interface standpoint to expect the user to navigate down through more than a few layers of submenus at a time. However, it is certainly possible to keep track of one's position in the lattice structure as one navigates through the document structure, and regenerate practical menu items at each depth. This would be like going to a separate HTML page after several submenu selection, where the page simply presents more menus to select from, giving the users a break/pause in the process. A users personal desktop folders can contain nesting depth greater than five [35].

3.4   Labeling the Concepts

In order to make the menu items readable at a quick glance by the user, each concept in the extracted top layers needs to be assigned a concise text label, embodying the objects and attributes that the concept represents. Generating meaningful menu labels automatically is possible. For example, our Java program in [35] labels each node by the attributes the node contains, minus the attributes along the path to the node. Since different paths are possible, this leads to different labels but they link to the same object or document. For our example below we labeled most of the nodes automatically but some manually. In attempting to decide what labels are appropriate for which concepts, it is useful to use the heuristic of combining the attributes in the intent of the concept. For example, singleton object (or singleton attribute) generated concepts should use the name of the generating object as label. For more sizable menu structures where manual intervention is not feasible, we have explored the technique of unfolding lattice to trees [35] to streamline the menu-labeling process while retaining the benefits of FcAWN.

Note that automated labeling of menu items is a key advantage of FcAWN compared to the standard IR and ML (machine learning) techniques for clustering – if one were to use clustering techniques in the construction of menu structures – where for example canonical and humanly readable labels for cluster "centroids" (in the vector-space model) simply do not exist.

3.5   Building the Menu Hierarchy

Finally we generate the menu structure from this graph by taking concept labels that fall immediately below the top concept to be our top level menu items. In turn, the concepts that fall immediately below each one of these concepts will be taken to be more specific submenus of these menus. Again, we can use XML and Java to automate this process.

4   Case Study

We applied FcAWN to the design of the web-menu layout for Case Western Reserve University's Electrical Engineering and Computer Science (EECS) departmental website [36], strictly following the procedures described in the previous section.

Specifying objects and attributes. We selected 37 document areas and 13 attributes from the EECS website (see Appendix A). For this preliminary but substantial study we made a choice of stopping at document-kinds level. For example, "Courses", labeled object 9 in Appendix A, consist of over a hundred individual documents in our course-catalog. It may make sense to break the content further down into individual courses so that their respective topic areas are reflected in the context table. However, since our website is implemented in such a way that courses appear as a database table, the courses cannot be easily broken further into subject areas so it is difficult to get to the granularity level that the website implementation does not currently provide. This may be an aspect to be studied further.

There is also plenty of flexibility for attribute selection. We currently do not have a systematic procedure for obtaining attribute sets automatically. Document clustering may be one way to automate this process. The 13 attributes (A - M) in Appendix A are selected in an ad hoc manner according to intuition, using a combination of common-sense document categories, user categories, and menu-labels from the original site.

Document context. The context table is constructed by indicating which documents should have which attributes. For example, documents related to Graduate Study (object 11) should be related to Faculty (A), Research (B), Academics (D), Graduate (F), Students (H) Teaching (M), resulting in row 11 in Appendix A. In general, any page in our object set that involves research will have the Research attribute (B). Any page in our object set that involves news items in some way will have the News attribute (E). Checking this for all documents yields the context in Appendix A.

Generating the lattice diagram and menu-hierarchy. The formal context in Appendix A is the input data to a Java program [24] we developed to construct a visualizable lattice diagram and to convert to HTML and XML menu layout specifications accordingly. The context with 37 documents and 13 attributes generates a lattice with 116 nodes (see top of Appendix B). Among these, 13 appear in first level of the final menu layout (the bottom of Appendix B is a screenshot of the actually page, with user evaluation specific items embedded in it).

4.1 Discussion

Our case study demonstrated several advantages of FcAWN. Firstly, the menu structure was generated on the first try without much need for "tweaking" the context to "make a better fit" for our final menu hierarchy (we did eliminate some undistinguished concept nodes, however). Without much modification, the generated menu structure already makes sense. Related items are clustered together. For example *Research* menu items are grouped with other research items. Also, more specific menu items fall beneath more general ones. For example *Undergraduate Admissions* falls underneath the *Academics* submenu of the broader item of *Undergraduate*.

Secondly, the example shows that menus generated via FcAWN in this fashion are non-exclusive and need not conform to a strict tree structure. Essentially, this means that a given menu item is placed in *all* locations where it is likely to be found, rather than just one. This makes information access *complete*. To be more specific about the local structure given in Fig. 1 in the introduction, there are three submenus under *Research Resources*; but the *Research Resources* submenu, though not appearing on the root page, is accessible from both the *Research* and the *Resources* menu. Traditional tree-based menu layouts require that an item appear in the entire menu hierarchy *only once* in either one place or the other, but not both. Our model is not bound by this limitation. It allows the user to find a menu item in a location that is immediately most intuitive for him, rather than having to search through many menus to find the one location where the menu designer felt the menu item fit most logically, according to the designer's intuition. Because this property presents "duplicated" nodes in the menu structure, to avoid user confusion it becomes useful to use a menu displaying mechanism where not all submenus are revealed to the user at once.

Thirdly, in our menu labeling strategy we tried to avoid multiple attributes. To facilitate readability, we tried to use at most one conjunctive in the labeling of a menu item, such as *Student & Groups*, *Faculty & Staff* (note that in our original implementation faculty and staff are implemented in one table; therefore it is considered as a single document, numbered 16 in the table of Appendix A). If more depth in the menu structure is needed, we can use the "tree unfolding" technique introduced in our other work [35] to provide simple menu labels. It should be interesting to note that a conjunctive such as "&" in a menu label usually represents a *union*, instead of an *intersection*, of objects. For example, *News & Events* denotes web documents that is related *either to News, or to Events, or both*, and not simply the collection of documents that are *News Events*. The reading for the menu label *News & Events* should be: "Items related to *News* can be found here, and items related to *Events* can also be found here." Logical intersection (the logical conjunctive) should be captured by consecutive menu labels along a path, or by using nouns as adjectives (e.g. *Student Groups* instead of *Student & Groups*). Subsequent menu labels along a menu path from top down can be read as modifiers to the collection of objects captured by upper level menus. How conjunction and disjunction are captured by menu structures is a topic that may warrant further investigation, particularly in the context of FCA.

4.2   User Evaluation

As a formal method for menu design and construction, FcAWN is already a valuable tool. We would like to show further that the additional structural advantages brought about by FcAWN not only come from the theoretical analysis (as we have already done), but also are demonstrable by a rigorous user evaluation.

User evaluation of new interfaces has always been a challenge issue in computer science, partially due to the difficulty in obtaining enough unbiased data. It is important to design a realistic and informative statistical experiment, and perform adequate statistical analyses on the resulting data (hopefully unbiased) from the experiment. We have performed a preliminary user evaluation study on 30 users with 12 randomly-ordered navigation tasks of different difficulty levels (see screenshot on the lower part of Appendix B). Among the 30 users, half were randomly selected to perform the navigation tasks on the original site, and the other half on the FcAWN-site. Information on external factors such as users' knowledge of computers, their familiarity with the website, and their perceived level of difficulty in finding the answer to a question etc, have been collected and are used in our statistical data analysis to separate their respective contributions from the real contribution due to the design of a site (FcAWN vs. ad hoc). The performance metrics, or the response variables in statistics terminology, have been: (1) accuracy in menu-selection, (2) the number of clicks needed to find relevant information on a site, (3) the number of "backing ups" used in a session, and (4) ranking of session experience. A preliminary logistic regression analysis of the data (only on the number of users who gave up finding an answer) has demonstrated significant user performance improvement of the FcAWN site over the original site. The complete results of the user evaluation study are given in a separate paper [37].

5   Conclusion

There are currently few menu-design principles grounded directly on a mathematical theory. The contribution of FcAWN lies in the application of FCA as a formal method for web-menu design, a key modality for human-computer interaction. The basic idea underlying FcAWN is that the top layers of a concept lattice constitute a navigation-menu hierarchy. Building on algorithms that generate the coverage relation for FCA, FcAWN automatically generates a web-menu structure in XML and in HTML, which can in turn be built into standard web browsers.

Encouraged by both a theoretical analysis and a preliminary experimental user evaluation [37], we believe that FcAWN should be useful in general for building a navigation structure for a collection of items; files on a user's computer hard drive, discussion board messages, email collections, etc., can also benefit from our approach without changing the familiar user-interface modality while improving the navigation interfaces at the same time. Menu interface for other high-tech devices and consumer electronics may also benefit from a rigorous analysis using FcAWN.

References

1. R. J. Cole. *The Management and Visualization of Document Collections Using Formal Concept Analysis*. Ph.D. Thesis, Griffith University, Australia, 2000.
2. R. Cole, P. Eklund. Browsing semi-structured web texts using formal concept analysis. In *Proc. 9th International Conference on Conceptual Structures*, pp. 319 - 332, 2001.
3. R. Cole, P. Eklund, and G. Stumme. Document retrieval for email search and discovery using formal concept analysis. *Applied Artificial Intelligence*, Vol. 17, pp. 257 - 280, 2003.
4. M. Crampes, S. Ranwez. Ontology-supported and ontology-driven conceptual navigation on the World Wide Web. In: *Proceedings of the 11th ACM conference on Hypertext and Hypermedia*, San Antonio, Texas, USA, pp. 191 - 199, 2000.
5. P. Eklund, J. Ducrou, and P. Brawn. Concept lattices for information visualization: can novices read line-diagrams? In Peter Eklund (Eds.), Proceedings of ICFCA 2004, *Concept Lattices: Second International Conference on Formal Concept Analysis*, LNAI 2961, Sydney, Australia, pp. 57 - 73, 2004.
6. B. Ganter and R. Wille. *Formal Concept Analysis*. Springer-Verlag, 1999.
7. B. Ganter. *Beitraäge zur Begriffsanalyse*. Chapter Algorithmen zur Formalen Begriffsanalyse, BI-Wissenschaftsverlag, 1987.
8. B. Ganter and S. O. Kuznetsov. Stepwise construction of the Dedekind-MacNeille completion. In *Proc. 6th International Conference on Conceptual Structures,* pp. 295 - 302, 1998.
9. M. Hearst. User interfaces and visualization. Chapter 10, *Modern Information Retrieval*, Edited by Ricardo Baeza-Yates and Berthier Ribeiro-Neto, Addison-Wesley Longman Publishing Company, pp. 257 - 323, 1999.
10. P. Hitzler and GQ Zhang. A cartesian closed category of approximating concepts. *12th International Conference on Conceptual Structures (ICCS04)*, LNAI Vol. 3127, pp. 170 - 185, Huntsville, Alabama, USA, 2004.
11. T. Ho. An approach to concept formation based on formal concept analysis, *IEICE Trans. Information and Systems*, Vol. E78-D, No. 5, pp. 553 - 559, 1995. Ê
12. M. Ivory, and M. Hearst. Improving web site design. *IEEE Internet Computing*, Vol. 6 (2), pp. 56 - 63, 2002.

13. M. Ivory, R. Sinha, and M. Hearst. Empirically validated web page design metrics. In *ACM Conference on Human Factors in Computing Systems*, CHI Letters 3(1), pp. 53 - 60, 2001.
14. M. Ivory and M. Hearst. The state of the art in automated usability evaluation of user Interfaces. *ACM Computing Surveys*, Vol. 33 (4), pp. 173 - 197, 2001.
15. C. Joslyn, J. Oliverira, and C. Scherrer. Order theoretical knowledge discovery: a white paper. LANL Technical Report LAUR 04-5812, 2004.
16. M. Krötzsch, P. Hitzler, and GQ Zhang. A categorical view on algebraic lattices in formal concept analysis. Submitted to *Theoretical Computer Science*.
17. M. Krötzsch, P. Hitzler, and GQ Zhang. Morphisms in context. *13th International Conference on Conceptual Structures (ICCS'05)*, Kassel, Germany, 2005. In press.
18. C. Lindig. Fast concept analysis. In Gerhard Stumme (Ed.), *Working with Conceptual Structures* - Contributions to *ICCS 2000*, Shaker-Verlag, Aachen, Germany, pp. 152 - 161, 2000.
19. J. Moody and D. White, Structural cohesion and embeddedness: a hierarchical concept of social groups. *American Sociological Review*, Vol. 68(1), pp. 103 - 127, 2003.
20. D. A. Norman. Design principles for human-computer interfaces. *Proceedings of the SIGCHI conference on Human Factors in Computing Systems*, pp. 1 - 10, 1983.
21. R. Pollard. A hypertext-based thesaurus as a subject browsing aid for bibliographic databases. *Information Processing and Management*, Vol. 29 n.3, pp. 345 - 357, 1993.
22. U. Priss. Formal concept analysis in information science. *Annual Review of Information Science and Technology (ARIST)*, Vol. 40, 22 pages.
23. R. Rizzo, G. Fulantelli, M. Allegra. Browsing a document collection as an hypertext. *Proc. World Conference on the WWW and Internet*, San Antonio, USA, pp. 454 - 458, 2000.
24. G. Shen, Ye Tian, J. Sun and GQ Zhang. Concept lattices, clustering, and visualization using LaTeX. Manuscript, 2004.
25. G. Snelting and F. Tip. Understanding class hierarchies using concept analysis. *ACM Transactions on Programming Languages and Systems*, pp. 540 - 582, May 2000.
26. E. Stoica, M. Hearst. Nearly-automated metadata hierarchy creation. *In the Companion Proceedings of HLT-NAACL'04, Boston*, pp. 117 - 120, 2004.
27. D. Tudhope, D. Cunliffe. Semantically indexed hypermedia: linking information disciplines. *ACM Comput. Surv.* Vol. 31:4, 1999.
28. C. van Rijsbergen. *Information Retrieval*, Butterworth-Heinemann, Newton, MA, 1979.
29. R. Wille. Restructuring lattice theory: an approach based on hierarchies of concepts. In Ivan Rival, editor, *Ordered sets*, Reidel, Dordrecht-Boston, pp. 445 - 470, 1982.
30. K. Wolff. A First Course in Formal Concept Analysis. www.fbmn.fh-darmstadt.de/home/wolff/Publikationen, accessed May 25, 2005.
31. S. Yevtushenko. ConExp. http://sourceforge.net/projects/conexp
32. GQ Zhang. Chu spaces, formal concepts, and domains. *Electronic Notes in Computer Science*, Vol. 83, 16 pages, 2003.
33. GQ Zhang and G. Shen. Approximable concepts, Chu spaces, and information systems. In de Paiva and Pratt (Guest Editors), *Special Issue on Chu Spaces and Applications, Theory and Applications of Categories*, 2005. In Press.
34. GQ Zhang, J. Staiger, G. Shen, A. Troy, J. Sun. Web-menu design using formal concept analysis (Position Paper), In Pfeiffer Wolff and Delugach (Eds.) Conceptual Structures at Work, Shaker Verlag, pp. 141 - 145, 2004.
35. GQ Zhang and Y. Tian. ANOESys: An experimental system for automated content organization. *The 13th International Conference on Conceptual Structures (ICCS'05)*, Kassel, Germany, 2005. In press.
36. GQ Zhang, C. Hesse, L. White, M. Buchner, M. Mehregany. Roadmap for a departmental website. *EQ (Educause Quarterly)*, 2005. In press.
37. GQ Zhang, X.F. Wang, G. Shen, J. Sun. User evaluation of menu-interface design. In preparation.

A   Appendix. Tables and Diagrams

The table below includes documents (1 - 37) in the first column, attributes (A - M) in the second column, and the context (document-attribute relation), consisting of the remaining columns labeled by the attributes.

	Documents		Attributes	A	B	C	D	E	F	G	H	I	J	K	L	M
1	Overview	A	Faculty	×			×					×	×	×		
2	Guiding Principles	B	Research		×		×			×						×
3	Newsletters	C	Resources	×	×			×	×	×	×	×	×	×	×	×
4	Visitor Info	D	Academics								×					
5	Contact Info	E	News	×								×	×		×	
6	EECS in the Press	F	Graduate	×	×		×									
7	EECS Achievement Awards	G	Undergraduate	×			×								×	
8	EECS Seminar Series	H	Students	×	×		×	×	×							
9	Courses	I	About	×		×	×		×	×	×		×	×		×
10	Undergraduate Programs	J	Computer Science	×			×			×	×		×	×		×
11	Graduate Study	K	ECE	×	×		×		×		×					×
12	BS-MS Program	L	Staff	×	×		×		×	×	×					×
13	ENGR131	M	Teaching				×			×						×
14	Undergraduate Admissions						×			×	×		×	×		
15	Graduate Admissions						×		×		×		×	×		
16	Faculty and Staff			×	×						×	×	×	×	×	
17	Students and Groups									×	×	×	×			
18	EECS Photos			×							×	×			×	
19	Faculty Positions			×	×			×	×				×	×		
20	Research/Staff Positions				×			×	×						×	×
21	Student Job Board							×	×	×						
22	Research Areas				×							×	×	×		
23	Faculty Research Profiles			×	×							×	×	×		
24	MFL				×	×								×		
25	CCG				×	×							×			
26	MeRCIS				×	×								×		
27	Pathways				×	×							×			
28	AMANDA				×	×								×		
29	Dynamics				×	×							×	×		
30	Neuro-Mechanics				×	×								×		
31	GENIe				×	×								×		
32	Help			×		×					×			×		
33	Print/Scan/Fax/Make a CD			×		×					×			×		
34	Labs and Software				×	×					×			×		
35	Electronics Store					×					×			×		
36	Timecard System					×					×					
37	Request			×		×					×			×		

B   Appendix. Lattice Diagram and User Evaluation Screenshot

Displayed below is the lattice diagram automatically generated from the context in Appendix A using our LaTeXlayout tool [24].

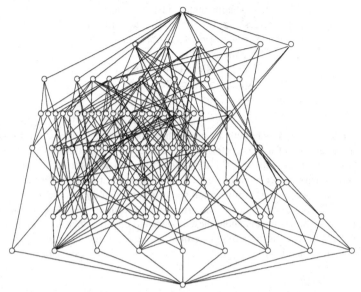

Appearing next is a screenshot of our user evaluation study starting page. Evaluation specific functions are embedded in the sites (duplicated) to be evaluated.

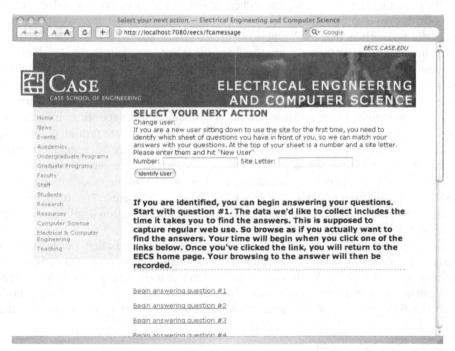

Supporting Resource-Based Analysis
of Task Information Needs

José Creissac Campos[1] and Gavin J. Doherty[2]

[1] Departamento de Informática,
Universidade do Minho, Braga, Portugal
jose.campos@di.uminho.pt
[2] Department of Computer Science,
Trinity College Dublin, Ireland
Gavin.Doherty@cs.tcd.ie

Abstract. We investigate here an approach to modelling the dynamic information requirements of a user performing a number of tasks, addressing both the provision and representation of information, viewing the information as being distributed across a set of resources. From knowledge of available resources at the user interface, and task information needs we can identify whether the system provides the user with adequate support for task execution. We look at how we can use tools to help reason about these issues, and illustrate their use through an example. We also consider a full range of analyses suggested using this approach which could potentially be supported by automated reasoning systems.

1 Introduction

Usability testing is a time consuming and expensive activity, often performed too late in the software development life-cycle. Thus it is interesting to look at analyses which may be performed early in the development life cycle, particularly if we can obtain leverage from design artifacts which are produced for other purposes within the development process. Task models (such as CTT models [12]) are an obvious type of artifact which may be produced at such an early stage. Task models on their own however, are not sufficient for the analysis of modern interactive systems, as the same basic task structure can be supported by many possible designs. The focus of this paper is on information needs; whether the right information is provided in an appropriate fashion at the right time. While there is an obvious and direct mapping between user tasks and their information needs, this is not the same as knowing how best to represent information, nor how to reconcile competing information requirements for multiple tasks within a given application, with fixed and possibly very limited screen "real estate" (as in mobile devices). We must also avoid confusing and inconsistent information displays where an excessive degree of task based adaptation is employed.

Thus we can see an opportunity for model-based techniques that can be applied early in development, as they can capture this information about proposed designs and be used to reason about the designs. Some behavioural models focus on the system and can be supported by automated reasoning systems. The capabilities of such models to explore issues related to interaction has been the focus of much work in the

S.W. Gilroy and M.D. Harrison (Eds.): DSVIS 2005, LNCS 3941, pp. 188–200, 2006.

past [13, 3, 14, 9]. Another family of techniques are based on task models as mentioned above. Again the use of such models in the analysis of interactive systems is well documented [6, 12]. Providing analyses which could help answer the questions regarding information needs detailed above would require us to augment our task models with models to account for system behaviour. The contribution of this paper is threefold:

1. To look at analyses which may be performed by checking an interactive system specification against a task model.
2. To examine the use of *resources* as a concept and model component to allow us to move beyond what may be achieved with interactor models.
3. To formalise and automate a portion of the analysis, reducing analyst effort, increasing the likelihood of finding problems and opening the door to more intelligent dynamic behaviour by applications.

2   Reasoning About System Designs

In previous work we have approached reasoning about system designs from two distinct perspectives. We have shown that using device models (with an emphasis on behaviour) and model checking, we can identify behaviours that might lead into undesirable situations [3]. We have also shown how using partial models of system, interface and user (with an emphasis on representation) we can analyse whether a representation is appropriate for a specific use [4].

In both cases we look mainly for situations where the properties under analysis would fail. It is mainly in such situations that design knowledge about the system will be generated. In the case of the first approach, the aim is to identify possible behaviours that would lead the system into undesirable states. The cognitive plausibility of the traces needs to be determined, and assumptions about user perception must be encoded into the properties under verification. A major issue is that non-plausible behaviour must be identified and filtered out, ie. cases where potential problems are flagged but which in fact correspond to implausible behaviour by the user. Task models can be introduced as a means of reducing these unwanted false positives, but at the cost of making the analysis consider normative behaviours only. While this approach helps determine situations where something wrong will or might happen, it tells us little about the degree of support the interface provides to its users in achieving their goals.

The second approach attempts to reason about whether there is a straightforward and accurate representation of information in the interface appropriate for the way it is used in the user's task. A failure to prove the equivalence between the different models involved will highlight problems in the representation, reflected in the mapping between the system's internal state and the mental model built by the users from the interface. However, this approach is difficult to apply to complex behaviours, as it does not directly support analyses of the changing set of information needs over a typical task performance.

Recent years have seen a move towards a more contextualised and situated view of interaction, where users react and adapt to a variety of information sources and stimuli in the "environment" in order to achieve their goals. This has been accompanied by a shift in the technology towards more pervasive and context-aware computing systems. This shift in emphasis places greater strain on the quality of the user interface, since it must provide sufficient appropriate information such that users can carry out their activities.

To address this problem we propose to relate tasks to the information and information representations that support them, and identify situations where support is not adequate. In order to do this, we take the following model components [2]:

- Device model—what is available at the interface, and how the interface behaves.
- Task model—how goals can be achieved.

The user's ability to infer a task model from the interface influences the execution gap in Norman's model [11]. At the very least, it is likely that the user will require information about the state of the system in order to decide on course of action and to check that the interaction is progressing as required. However, the nature of the information needs of the user may be more complex than this. One framework which allows us to think about the *nature* of information use is the resources model [15].

3   Resources for Action

The resources model is an interaction model whose aim is to support Distributed Cognition style analysis at an early stage of design, rather than as a means of understanding existing systems or prototypes. The model itself is simple; it views interaction as involving a number of information resources which can be characterised in terms of a number of different categories, depending on the role the information may play in interaction. Different interaction strategies on the part of the user (eg. goal-matching, plan following) will exploit different types of information, and place a different emphasis on such information. For those interested in developing mobile and context aware systems, the model is attractive since the information resources considered may be located in the environment, or provided by the system. The categories used to characterise information resources are as follows:

- *Plan*. A sequence of actions, events or states that should be carried out
- *Goal*. The required state of the world.
- *State*. A collection of relevant values of objects that feature in an interaction
- *Action-effect*. A relation between an action or event and its effect on the interaction.
- *History*. Actions, events or states already achieved in the interaction.
- *Possibilities*. The set of possible next actions of the user.

Thus we can posit a third starting point for our analysis—a model of user information needs, structured as resources needed for action.

A system comprised of a number of different devices, which together support the user in performing some complex task, with the user assessing the different devices according to his or her information needs, potentially requires a different form of analysis to reasoning about a user performing a task using a single device. An interesting aspect of a resource focus for the analysis is that it is consistent with such a heterogeneous multi-device view of interaction.

We view information elements in the interface as comprising resources, constituting not only information, but operations easily performed and encouraged by the representation. Such concepts can be incorporated into analytical models as perceptual and (logical) cognitive operations [4]. Modelling the use of information is itself an interesting problem; one possible approach would be to use the classification in the resources model to characterise information use.

Norman [11] explains the interaction process as a loop beginning with goal formation and ending with evaluation of the perceived response against the goal. When no strictly predefined plan exists, what the user will do depends solely on his or her evaluation of the system state and interpretation of the system behaviour. In this case we should provide resources appropriate to potential tasks and goals. We can also focus on actions themselves as a useful unit of analysis, without postulating detailed planning mechanisms. Instead, for possible actions which could be carried out as part of the user's activities we can ask if the action is properly resourced; is it possible to know if it is an appropriate action to take; what will the effect of the action be; will it bring the user closer to their goal; can the user evaluate how successful the action has been?

Resources take many shapes; but here we will focus on information presented at the interface, and actions available at the interface.

$$\text{Resource} = \text{Info}_{resource} + \text{Action}_{user} \tag{1}$$

We need to guarantee that user resource needs are met by the available resources in a dynamic task execution context. We need to ask what is the set of information resources which best suits the task at hand, at every stage, and under different (possibly concurrent) performance scenarios.

4   Device Model

In this section, we revisit the issue of device models, looking at how a standard device model (interactors) can be enriched with resource information. An interesting issue for further investigation would be to look at producing more dynamic interactive system specifications structured around the notion of resources themselves.

We can conduct our analysis using a range of behaviour modelling approaches. For simplicity and convenience, we use a domain specific language to model the systems: MAL interactors [3]. Figure 1 presents an example interactor.

We have discussed above how the concept of resource may help us to address a variety of questions regarding information needs in modern interactive systems; thus we have a question concerning how best to incorporate the notion of resources into an interactive system model.

In order to use automated reasoning support for the models we build, it is helpful to characterise what an interactor model is. An interactor defines a state space via its attributes, and the axioms define a relation on this state space labelled by the actions that cause the transitions:

$$\text{State}_i = \mathbb{P}\text{Attrib} \tag{2}$$

$$\text{Behaviour}_i = \mathbb{P}(\text{State}_i \times \text{Action} \times \text{State}_i) \tag{3}$$

interactor photocopier
attributes
     door: {open, closed}
     copying: boolean
     error: {ok, abc, bc, ac, c}
  |vis| display: {idle, copy, error_abc, error_bc, error_ac, error_c, door_open}
actions
  |vis| open close start checkA checkB checkC
     stop jam
axioms
     per(open) $\rightarrow$ door=closed
     [open] door'=open $\wedge$ $\neg$copying' $\wedge$ error'=error $\wedge$ display'=door_open
     per(close) $\rightarrow$ door=open
     [close] door'=closed $\wedge$ copying'=copying $\wedge$ error'=error $\wedge$ display'=idle
     per(start) $\rightarrow$ $\neg$copying $\wedge$ door=close $\wedge$ error=ok
     [start] copying' $\wedge$ door'=close $\wedge$ error'=ok $\wedge$ display'=copy
     per(stop) $\rightarrow$ copying
     [stop] $\neg$copying $\wedge$ door'=door $\wedge$ error'=error $\wedge$ display'=idle
     ...

Fig. 1. An example interactor

Available resources are associated with the modality that makes them available to the users. Different modalities might be selectable according to their appropriateness, eg. audio might be appropriate in one context (hands busy) and not in another (important meeting). Thus modalities are used to annotate appropriate attributes and actions. The resources define a state space (UI_{state}), which is a subset of the system state space defined by the interactor. Thus, for each user interface state we can identify a set of resources which are available at that point in the interaction.

$$UI_{state} = \mathbb{P}Resource \qquad (4)$$

It is important to realise that there is not an exact match between the information resources used in the modelling and the information made visible by interactors. Resources needed for an action may be provided by several interactors. Conversely, we specify the resources needed for an action, and much of the information provided by an interactive system might not be relevant to this particular task. For example, an engineer repairing a machine might use an onboard display of status (state) information, along with a PDA displaying procedure information for the repair (plan information in a resource based view). Both the machine status panel and the handheld may be displaying additional information not relevant to the repair task. Actions can be classified as user actions (those with a modality) or system actions (response to user action or autonomous action).

$$Action = Action_{user} + Action_{system} \qquad (5)$$

Different interface components and/or resources might become available or unavailable as the interaction progresses. Also, modalities might also change over time.

5   Task Model

A task model defines the set of interactions that, from a given set of initial states of the system, lead to the fulfilment of a goal. These interactions can be seen as sequences of actions (traces of behaviour).

$$\text{Task} = \mathbb{P}\text{State}_i \times \mathbb{P}\text{Trace} \tag{6}$$

As above, two types of actions can typically be identified at task level: user actions (representing physical actions performed by the user at the user interface), and system actions (representing changes to the user interface performed by the system). A hierarchical task model can be mapped down onto such a set of traces, which may be reduced by operational and planning constraints, if present. This set of traces could be large, depending on the degree of visibility on the underlying system state, and the number of different ways to achieve the task using the interface, further motivating the use of tools. As a first approach we can model traces as sequences of actions:

$$Trace = Action^* \tag{7}$$

For clarity we will be using ConcurTaskTree (CTT) models [12] to support the exposition of ideas. CTT is a commonly used notation for task representation and analysis. Note, however, that the approach is not specific to CTT, and in fact is extensible to other task modelling languages. Consider the CTT model in figure 2. The behaviour it models can be expressed by the following set of traces:

{present jam info→open door→check A→check B→check C→close door,
present jam info→open door→check B→check C→close door,
present jam info→open door→check A→check C→close door, }

As can be seen CTT abstract nodes are not represented since they are a structuring mechanism only. For concurrent tasks there may be many possible interleavings of the traces.

Let $(\text{State}_i, \text{Behaviour}_i)$ be an interactor, using the definitions above we can already perform a number of tests:

Action completeness.   All intended user actions are supported by the system.

$$\forall a \in \text{Action}_{user} \exists (s1, a, s2) \in \text{Behaviour}_i \tag{8}$$

This guarantees that all possible user actions the user might want to perform are possible in the system.

Predictability.   No user action has two possible effects.

$$\forall a \in \text{Action}_{user}, s \in \text{UI}_{state} \exists^1 (s1, a, s2) \in \text{UI}_{behaviour} \tag{9}$$

This definition demands that no two actions might have the same effect in the interface. This might be too strong in specific cases (for instance, due to moding). In that case we can use states from State_i instead of from $\text{UI}_{behaviour}$ only. This way we are requiring that no two action will have the same effect on the system's state.

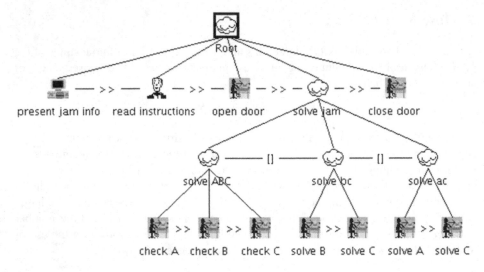

Fig. 2. An example task model

Task performance. The execution of a given task (s_t, ts) is possible if

$$\forall t \in ts\cdot, s \in s_t \text{trace\_poss}(s, t) \tag{10}$$

where

$$\text{trace\_poss}(s_t, t) \equiv \exists (s_t, head(t), s) \in \text{Behaviour}_i \land \text{trace\_poss}(s, tail(t))$$

The above type of analysis can be mechanised using model checking (cf. [2]), and indeed it would be difficult to perform in an accurate and complete fashion by hand. This analysis however, tells us only whether a given task is possible, not whether the system supports the user in performing it. To achieve this last goal, we need to consider the resources the system provides against the resources needed to perform the task.

6   Tasks and Resources

At specific stages in the interaction process, information resources will be needed by the user to decide on the course of action. It is this possibility of different courses of action that justifies using a set of traces to model a single task. In order to analyse this aspect we need to know whether the interface provides the adequate resources for the right choice to be made.

Using the models in the previous section would fail at this point because the process of decision is not explicitly represented in the traces. Hence, we must introduce another type of user action: choice actions (representing mental choices by the user regarding which physical action to take next).

$$\text{Action}_{user} = \text{Action}_{physical} + \text{Action}_{choice} \tag{11}$$

These actions exist in the CTT model as User Tasks. What needs to be done is to include them in the traces:

{present jam info→read instructions→open door→check A→check B→check C→close door,
  present jam info→read instructions→open door→check B→check C→close door,
  present jam info→read instructions→open door→check A→check C→close door, }

In order to analyse the system regarding its support for a given task we need to know what the task demands in terms of resources are. One obvious case is that each user action maps directly to the requirement that the resource corresponding to that action must be available at the interface at the required moment.

Additionally, for each user action in a task we must indicate what resources are needed (other more advanced options are discussed in section 8). For choice actions, there might be the need for some specific information to be present at the interface in order for the user to make the correct decision. For physical actions, besides the action being available, there might also be the need for some specific information to be present to prompt the user into performing the correct actions. We might consider whether information is made available at an earlier point in the task performance (trace) or whether it is visible at the current time. Focusing on resources, tasks become

$$\mathrm{Task}^{resourced} = \mathbb{P}\mathrm{State}_i \times \mathbb{P}\mathrm{Trace}^{resourced} \qquad (12)$$

where State_i represents the states from which the task can be performed, and traces include the actions, and the resource needs:

$$\mathrm{Trace}^{resourced} = \mathrm{Action}^{resourced*} \qquad (13)$$
$$\mathrm{Action}^{resourced} = (\mathrm{Action}_{user} \times \mathbb{P}\mathrm{Resource}) + \mathrm{Action}_{system} \qquad (14)$$

Hence, for each user action we can include a set of needed resources.

This information is not available at the original CTT model, and must be provided in order for the analysis to take place. Notice, however, that this is the type of information needed to carry out other types of analysis such as Cognitive Walkthroughs [8].

For example, if we go back to the example introduced in Figure 2 we can say that at the "read instructions" step the user needs the information about the type of jam to be present at the interface. We might also consider whether the user should be relied upon (or burden with the necessity) to remember the correct procedure. If we decide against that, all user actions after "read instructions" also require that information about the correct procedure be present at the interface. As an example, the trace for the ABC strategy becomes

present jam info→ (read instructions,{abc_error_info})→ (open door,{abc_error_info})→
(check A,{abc_error_info})→ (check B,{abc_error_info})→ (check C,{abc_error_info})→
(close door,{abc_error_info})

We can now verify if, for a given task (s_t, ts), the system always provides the needed resources. For that we must prove the following theorem:

$$\forall t \in ts, s \in s_t \cdot \mathrm{trace\_poss}^{resourced}(s, t) \qquad (15)$$

where

$$\text{trace\_poss}^{resourced}(s_t, t) \equiv$$

$$\exists_{(s_t, head(t), s) \in \text{Behaviour}_i} \cdot \quad (\text{is\_Action}_{system}(head(t)) \lor \pi_2(head(t)) \subseteq s_t)$$
$$\land \text{trace\_poss}(s, tail(t))$$

If this can be proved, then the needed actions and the specified information resources are available at each point in the task where they are needed. If not, then even if the task is possible, the user might find problems in performing it. While proving theorem 10 above would only guarantee that the task could be executed (nothing could be deduced regarding support to its execution), this analysis is comparable to a Cognitive Walkthrough type of approach, note however that we are attempting to make minimal assumptions about user cognition.

7   An Example

In this section we show how the approach can be applied to the running example in the context of the MAL interactors modelling and analysis work put forward in [3, 2]. Due to space constraints, we will not describe the modelling and analysis aspects in detail. Instead, we will focus on the impact of including resource related information into the analysis.

We use the model of a photocopier, already partially introduced in Figure 1, focusing specially on the handling of jamming problems. When a jam occurs, there are three different places inside the photocopier (A, B, C) which must be checked for paper. Depending on the type of jam a different sequence of actions must be performed. The photocopier has a display where this information is presented whenever a jam happens. Additionally the display can show information regarding the status of operation and of the door. Due to limited screen size, the display can only present one item of information at a time.

Using the model of the photocopier only we can already use i2smv and SMV to check whether it is possible to solve a jam problem. We will consider here the ABC jam error (all three places must be checked sequentially). First, we do a sanity check on the model and check whether a ABC jam is possible: EF(error=abc). What this formula states is that it possible to a a future state of the system where a ABC jam has occurred.

Next we check if the jam can be solved. This can be attempted by checking the following CTL formula: AG(error=abc −> AF(error=ok)). The property is not true. The model checker points out that the user might behave in a way which does not to solve the problem (for example, repeatedly opening and closing the door). At this stage we could introduce assumptions about user behaviour to the property being investigated. While this is useful in that it helps uncover those assumptions, it leads to hard to read properties. Also, since there are prescribed operating procedures for each type of jam, it would be interesting to analyse whether the interface adequately supports them.

We could use negation on the property to get a counter-example illustrating a strategy to solve the jam and compare it to our own pre-defined strategy. However, this will only be one possibility among many (usually the shortest, but that is not guaranteed), and we still have to consider the cognitive plausibility of the user following that particular strategy, and the degree of support given by the interface to the strategy.

Instead we will directly encode the strategy into the model in a way similar to [2]. We start by modelling the procedure as an interactor that performs the sequence of steps expressed in the task model. We then place the two models together using the following interactor:

> **interactor** main
> **includes**
> > photocopier **via** device
> > solve_abc_jam **via** task
> **axioms**
> > task.active → task.action=device.action
> > device.action=jam ↔ task.action=jam

What the axioms state is that: a) whenever the task is being performed, the system must behave according to the task description; b) if the device jams then the task model also processes that event (in order to activate the task).

We can now perform the tests proposed above. Testing the property AG(error=abc -> AF(error=ok)) we conclude that the strategy solves the problem. However we still do not know whether the strategy is supported by the interface. It might be, for example, that an action is required that in practice an user will have difficulty in identifying and performing. To address this, we include resource information in the task model. As has already been explained, we consider two types of resource needs:

- All of the needed action resources must be available when needed, otherwise it becomes physically impossible to perform the task.
- The strategy for solving the problem must be available during the solving procedure, otherwise the user will have to memorise the strategy or find some alternative means of externalising that knowledge.

Action resource verification is structurally guaranteed by the first theorem in the interactor above. If an action is not available when needed, task and device models cannot synchronize, and that behaviour deadlocks. Information resource needs are encoded using the following axiom:

$$\text{task.action} \in \{\text{open}, \text{checkA}, \text{checkB}, \text{checkC}, \text{close}\} \rightarrow$$
$$device.display = \text{error\_abc}$$

This axiom is an encoding of the resource testing condition of $\text{trace\_poss}^{resourced}$ from Theorem 15 above.

Using this we can conclude that the system does not support the strategy as the combined system/task model is not capable of performing the task. The source of the problem resides in the fact that once the door is open the information regarding the strategy needed for solving the jam problem is no longer available. This happens because the door open information replaces the jamming information. In this particular design, closing the door again would not help since according to the model the jam information is no longer displayed.

If we enhance the display to be able to present two items of information so that the door open item does not hide the jam item, then it is possible to verify the model, and conclude that all needed resources to solve the jam are available.

8   Conclusions

A resources based approach can help in identifying potential usability problems by exploring what should be available at the interface to support users. We have presented an approach to the inclusion of resource needs into an approach to mechanised reasoning over models of interactive systems. This analysis complements a more unconstrained style of analysis where all possible behaviours of the system are analysed.

In [10] an approach to checking tasks against system models is put forward. The analysis is based on the assumption that the task model identifies the perceptual operations performed by the users. These perceptual operations must then have corresponding output operations in the device model. A resources based approach allows us to break away from this tight coupling between task and system operations. We can concentrate on the users' needs, and inspect whether the system provides the relevant information resources at the user interface. Additionally, we believe that by considering different types of resources we can expand on the type of analysis that can be performed.

Other approaches exist that attempt to fold human factors considerations into model-based approaches to reasoning about usability. One possibility is to build an explicit model of the user as in programmable user models (eg. PUMA [1]) and executable cognitive architectures (SOAR [7], EPIC [5] etc.). While these may deliver more detail on cognitive and performance aspects, they also tend to be complex to build to an automatable state. Another approach is to encode assumptions about the user directly into the model (cf. [14]). In this case the separation between device model and user assumptions is not clear and can bias the user assumptions towards those that are needed to make the system work. By working with assumptions at task level, we have a clear separation between models, assumptions about users are expressed in terms of tasks and user interface, and not directly about the system. Additionally, the models are relatively easy to build. The concept of resources is straightforward to work with and provides a natural way for the HCI expert to augment a task model.

We have outlined many more possibilities for analysis than could be explored fully for this paper (especially in terms of tool support). Among the suggested possibilities for further work, we have considered the following:

- Development of a more flexible view of resources, including representational (perceptual) aspects.
- Action based analysis with task fragments and constraints as an alternative to canonical task trees, which can also be seen as the use of partial specifications of user behaviour.
- Tool support for analysis of multiple and concurrent tasks. Could we help find a compromise set of resources which supports all or most tasks? A related question would be understanding conflict and interference between different tasks.
- Modelling changing resource needs. Can we integrate the resource model characterisations (plan, possibility, action effect, etc.) into a modelling approach and match

against appropriate presentations? How can this be done within the framework of existing task languages?

- Dynamic availability of resources—can we come up with designs with better and fewer transitions between sets of resources. Modelling the availability is straight-forward, so this seems quite feasible.
- Encapsulating user interaction strategies, for example, when a user takes a side track to get some information. There are related questions about access to informa-tion in the history of an interaction which is required for a later action, and how this may be modelled.
- A new modelling approach directly based on resources. This is somewhat specu-lative but could lend itself towards intrinsically dynamic and adaptive interactive system specifications.

A final question pertains to the variety of possible analyses, how they relate to one another, and how they may be provided to the analyst as part of a coherent methodology.

Acknowledgements

The authors wish to thank Michael Harrison for his comments on earlier version of this work. Gavin Doherty would like to acknowledge the support of Enterprise Ireland in the form of an International Collaboration grant. José Campos would like to acknowledge the support of FCT (Portugal) and FEDER (EU) under contract POSC/EIA/56646/2004.

References

1. R. Butterworth, A. Blandford, D. Duke, and R. M. Young. Formal user models and methods for reasoning about interactive behaviour. In J. Siddiqi and C. Roast, editors, *Formal Aspects of the Human-Computer Interaction*, pages 176–192. SHU Press, 1998.
2. José C. Campos. Using task knowledge to guide interactor specifications analysis. In J. A. Jorge, N. J. Nunes, and J. Falcão e Cunha, editors, *Interactive Systems: Design, Specifica-tion and Verification — 10th International Workshop, DSV-IS 2003*, volume 2844 of *Lecture Notes in Computer Science*, pages 171–186. Springer, 2003.
3. José C. Campos and Michael D. Harrison. Model checking interactor specifications. *Auto-mated Software Engineering*, 8(3-4):275–310, August 2001.
4. Gavin J. Doherty, José C. Campos, and Michael D. Harrison. Representational reasoning and verification. *Formal Aspects of Computing*, 12(4):260–277, 2000.
5. D. Kieras and D.E. Meyer. An overview of the EPIC architecture for cognition and per-formance with application to human-computer interaction. *Human-Computer Interaction*, 12:391–438, 1997.
6. B. Kirwan and L. Ainsworth. *A Guide to Task Analysis*. Taylor and Francis, 1992.
7. J.E. Laird, A. Newell, and P.S. Rosenbloom. Soar: An architecture for general intelligence. *Artificial Intelligence*, 33:1–64, 1987.
8. Clayton Lewis, Peter Polson, Cathleen Wharton, and John Rieman. Testing a walkthrough methodology for theory-based design of walk-up-and-use interfaces. In *CHI '90 Proceed-ings*, pages 235–242, New York, April 1990. ACM Press.
9. Karsten Loer. *Model-based Automated Analysis for Dependable Interactive Systems*. PhD thesis, Department of Computer Science, University of York, 2003.

10. D. Navarre et al. A tool suite for integrating task and system models through scenarios. In C. Johnson, editor, *Interactive Systems: Design, Specification, and Verification*, volume 2220 of *Lecture Notes in Computer Science*, pages 88–113. Springer, June 2001.
11. Donald E. Norman. *The Psychology of Everyday Things*. Basic Book Inc., 1988.
12. Fabio Paternò. *Model Based Design and Evaluation of Interactive Applications*. Applied Computing. Springer Verlag, Berlin, 1999.
13. Fabio D. Paternò. *A Method for Formal Specification and Verification of Interactive Systems*. PhD thesis, Department of Computer Science, University of York, 1995.
14. John Rushby. Using model checking to help discover mode confusions and other automation surprises. *Reliability Engineering and System Safety*, 75(2):167–177, February 2002.
15. P.C. Wright, R.E. Fields, and M.D. Harrison. Analyzing human-computer interaction as distributed cognition: the resources model. *Human Computer Interaction*, 15(1):1–42, 2001.

Automatic Critiques of Interface Modes

Jeremy Gow[1], Harold Thimbleby[2], and Paul Cairns[1]

[1] UCL Interaction Centre (UCLIC), University College London,
31-32 Alfred Place, London, WC1E 7DP, United Kingdom
{j.gow, p.cairns}@ucl.ac.uk
[2] Department of Computer Science, University of Wales Swansea,
Singleton Park, Swansea, SA2 8PP, United Kingdom
h.thimbleby@swan.ac.uk

Abstract. We introduce a formal model of inconsistency-related mode confusion. This forms the basis of a heuristic methodology for critiquing user interfaces, using a matrix algebra approach to interface specification [12]. We also present a novel algorithm for automatically identifying modes in state-based interface designs, allowing a significant level of automated tool support for our methodology. The present paper generalises our previous work on improving state-based interface designs [5].

1   Introduction

Modes are an integral part of user interface design—only the simplest of interfaces may be entirely 'modeless'. But modes are often the focus of criticism for interface evaluations, and in the wider HCI literature. A key question for interface designers is: how can we distinguish between good and bad modes during the design process?

The concept of mode is extremely general, and the term 'mode confusion' covers a variety of interface problems. A general definition by Leveson [8] is that "a mode is a set of mutually exclusive system behaviours"—the system behaves a particular way in one mode, but not in another—and that mode confusion arises from divergent user and system models. Much of the mode literature has addressed the problems caused by abstraction of system details in the interface, or the presence of automation, e.g. in autopilots [3, 10], and classically in text-editing [11]. However, in this paper we address what Leveson calls inconsistent behaviour: users may expect an action to have a consistent effect within a given mode, and any exceptions to this may be a source of user error. Consistency is important for users to correctly learn how an interface works by generalisation, and inconsistent behaviour is harder to learn.

Consistency is a commonly cited principle of interface design, but a somewhat nebulous one. Miller and Potts emphasise the need for a formal definition of mode inconsistency [9]. We have previously proposed the identification and redesign of *partial behaviours* as a formal approach to consistent design [5], an approach that can be semi-automated to support the human designer/analyst. In this paper, we generalise this work to a process of identifying *action modes* and ensuring *consistent relationships* between them. Our specific contributions are a new formal model of consistency-related mode confusion (Sect. 3), a methodology for identifying modes and potential mode confusions (Sect. 4), and a novel algorithm that automates this process (Sect. 5).

S.W. Gilroy and M.D. Harrison (Eds.): DSVIS 2005, LNCS 3941, pp. 201–212, 2006.

2   Modes and Consistency

We can see the relationship between consistency and modes more clearly if we take a state-based view, which is compatible with Leveson's general definition given above: a mode is defined as a *set of states* in which a user interface behaves in a particular way. Clearly, it follows that we may be in several modes at once depending upon which behaviour we are considering.

Now suppose in mode M an action A typically exhibits a behaviour B. Following our definition, we can say there is another mode M' which is defined as 'the states in which A exhibits B'. The principle of consistency says that if we are in mode M then we should *always* be in mode M'. That is, M should be subset of M'. If there are a few exceptional states of mode M that are not in mode M', then the interface is inconsistent.

Partial behaviours give a formal description of a related consistency phenomena [5]: an algebra of events, including user actions, is used to specify interface behaviour. A *partial* behaviour is an algebraic property that is *usually but not always* true in a given mode—it indicates an inconsistency that may cause mode confusions. The methodology recommends redesign so that the property holds consistently throughout the mode.

This paper generalises our previous work on partial behaviours. We can characterise an 'interesting' (from a user's or designer's point of view) mode inconsistency as any relationship between modes that *almost* holds, and that the user is likely to perceive. That is, a simple relationship that holds for most states, but with a few exceptional states for which it does not. Clearly if it is true for only a few states then it is unlikely to be perceived; and if it is true for all states, there is no inconsistency. Provided the relation almost holds, experience is likely to lead the user to learn the relationship but

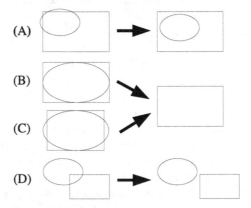

Fig. 1. Making mode relationships consistent. For two modes, represented by the ellipse E and the rectangle R, four examples of inconsistent relationships are shown: (A) mode E is almost a subset of R; (B) mode R is almost a subset of E, and E *is* a subset of R; (C) modes E and R are almost subsets of each other; (D) E and R almost completely separate modes. In each case, the transformation to a consistent relationship is shown.

not the exceptions, and their divergent user model can cause mode confusion. Moreover, a redesign of the user interface could make the relationship consistent and remove the source of errors. Figure 1 illustrates some inconsistent relationships between modes, and redesigns that enforce consistency.

3   A Model of Mode Inconsistency

As we only need consider mode relationships that the user is likely to (mis-)learn, we restrict ourselves to basic set theory. We have already discussed cases where one mode is a subset of, or equal to, another. Other relationships may also be mislearnt, but in our experience they can be explained in terms of subsets ($\subseteq$), providing we also use simple unions and complements of modes. For example:

- $A = B$ is equivalent to $A \subseteq B$ and $B \subseteq A$.
- A not intersecting with B is equivalent to $A \subseteq B^C$.
- $A_1, \ldots, A_n$ partitioning B is equivalent to $A_i \subseteq A_j^C$ for each $i \neq j$ and $A_1 \cup \ldots \cup A_n = B$.

In order to provide a model of mode inconsistency, we need to formalise the *almost subset* relation between sets of states.

3.1   Approximate and Near Subsets

In [5], we defined a partial behaviour as one that was true for a high proportion (called ρ below) of states within a mode. We take a similar, but more general, approach here. First, we define the the relation *approximate subset* $\underset{\approx}{\subseteq}$:

$$A \underset{\approx}{\subseteq} B \quad \leftrightarrow \quad \frac{|A \cap B|}{|A|} \geq \rho$$

This says that A is an approximate subset of B if the proportion of states in A that are also in B is at least ρ, where $0 \ll \rho < 1$, i.e. ρ is near 1. If the proportion is 1 then $A \subseteq B$ exactly.

The *nearly subset* relation $\underset{\sim}{\subseteq}$ is defined as an approximate subset excluding equality and actual subsets. Two modes A and B can be said to be inconsistent if and only if $A \underset{\sim}{\subseteq} B$ or $B \underset{\sim}{\subseteq} A$, where:

$$A \underset{\sim}{\subseteq} B \quad \leftrightarrow \quad \left(A \underset{\approx}{\subseteq} B \wedge A \not\subseteq B \right)$$

The definition of $\underset{\approx}{\subseteq}$ (and hence also $\underset{\sim}{\subseteq}$) is parameterised by the value ρ. Lowering ρ will increase the number of subsets which are classified as near subsets. In this paper, we take ρ to be a criterion, imposed by the designer. Instead, a design tool might determine a suitable ρ itself, or allow ρ to be dynamically adjusted by the designer; and, for example, sort near subsets by ρ for the attention of the designer. This practical question, while interesting for the design process, is irrelevant to our formal discussion.

3.2   Action vs Indicator Modes

So far, we have assumed that the user learns by experience the various interface modes and (possibly mislearns) the relationships between them. Our definition of mode — a set of states in which an interface behaves in a particular way — is deliberately general. However, the specific nature of the modes involved is likely to affect which modes and relationships are learnt by the user. In this paper we refine our model by distinguishing *action modes* and *indicator modes*.

Action modes are sets of states in which particular combinations of user actions, or other events, have a consistent effect. For a mobile phone this could be the sets of states in which a cancel button returns the user to an initial state, or in which a combination of two buttons work as a toggle for a keypad lock, or in which a specific protocol is used to enter text. The mode is determined by the state transitions for the given events. A specific action mode is something the user believes, but cannot directly observe. That is, given the history of user actions up to this moment, the user *believes* (from experience or training) that the system is in an action mode. This belief may inform the subsequent interaction. Note that each action mode is defined in terms of the system, not the user: a user may not understand the mode precisely, or even notice it exists! The aim here is to design systems that do not frustrate users that do notice these modes.

The second type of mode distinguished here are indicator modes. These are sets of states in which the interface sends or displays consistent feedback to the user. For instance, the set of states for which a particular LED is lit, or for which music is played (e.g., this could be the 'play mode' on a MP3 player). The user can (in principle) *see* that the system is in a given indicator mode.

The effects of mode inconsistency $A \underset{\sim}{\subset} B$ depends on the combination of mode types involved, as summarised in Table 1. In general, $A \underset{\sim}{\subset} B$ may be mislearnt as $A \subseteq B$. If the near-supermode B is an action mode, then the user may incorrectly believe that the action/effect association known to work in B will always work in mode A. In this case, the type of the near-submode A determines *when* this incorrect belief may be acted upon: if A is an action mode then this is whenever the user believes they are in A; if A is an indicator mode then it will be whenever the given indicator is observed.

If B is an indicator mode then errors may be caused when the indicator is absent: when A is an action mode the user may assume that the absence means the interface is *not* in mode A. This error is only made in the exceptional states which are the cause of the mode inconsistency. No errors are caused by an inconsistency in which both A and B are indicator modes.

Table 1. Types of user-interface divergence attributable to mode inconsistency $A \underset{\sim}{\subseteq} B$

Mode A	Mode B	User belief	Interface state
Action	Action	In B	In A and not in B
Indicator	Action	In B	A observed and not in B
Action	Indicator	Not in A	In A and B not observed
Indicator	Indicator	—	—

When defining compound modes via union and complement, we make the simplifying assumption that modes are only combined with others of the same type, with the combined mode being of that type. For example, the union of two indicator modes is an indicator mode. We speculate that users are less likely to reason about modes defined as a combination of event behaviours and indicators.

3.3   Using the Model

The model of mode inconsistency presented above is heuristic because it does not suggest a specific consistent redesign, only a performance characteristic, namely the values of ρ and the counts of inconsistent modes. Furthermore, a more consistent redesign (i.e., fewer inconsistent modes or a larger ρ with the same modes) is not guaranteed to improve the interface: other design constraints may be violated — for example, redesign might replace three benevolently inconsistent modes with two atrociously inconsistent modes. However, redesign to reduce inconsistent modes has an underlying rationale, and there is an *expectation* that it will tend to improve the interface design other things being equal. Using a design tool, a designer could easily experiment with redesigns and the trade-offs they represent, once problems are indicated.

4   A Method for Mode Analysis

Analysis requires the designer to already know which modes to examine. Indicator modes are part of the interface design and hence need to be provided, at least implicitly, by the designer. Action modes are intrinsic to and implicit in the interface design and are therefore more difficult to find. In this section, we provide a methodology for finding action modes. The process we describe here can be automated and, in the next section, we provide an algorithm to do this.

Our approach is based on an algebraic specification of the interaction of states and user actions, as described in [12, 4]. We formally define an action mode as the largest set of states for which one of these algebraic properties is true. We also assume that the interface design is formally described as a finite state machine (FSM). Alternatively, it could be translated into an FSM from a higher-level formalism, perhaps one of many standard state-based notations for system specification, such as Statecharts [6] or Promela [7].

4.1   An Algebraic Model

We start with an FSM model of the user interface design, from which we generate a specification algebra. The FSM is defined as

- A set of states S
- A set of events E, including the actions available to the user
- A transition relation $trans : S \times E \times S$

An equivalent formulation could use a transition function $S \rightarrow powerset(S)$ instead. Also, we optionally have a set of indicator modes M_I.

A familiar FSM concept is the Boolean *transition matrix*, which defines all the transitions from every state to every other state. Instead, we define the *button matrix* for each event e as the transition matrix of the finite state machine restricted to transitions of event e. This is the basis of a very productive approach for a variety of user interface issues [12].

States are represented as row vectors, with each element corresponding to an individual state that the interface could be in. Hence, each particular state corresponds to a vector with a single non-zero entry, whereas groups of states — such as modes — may be represented as arbitrary vectors.

Formally, we use $||.||$ to denote the mapping from elements of the FSM to matrix algebra. So we distinguish between a state $s \in S$ and its vector $||s||$ and between an event $e \in E$ and its matrix $||E||$. Also, for any indicator mode $m \in M_I$ there is a vector $||m||$. Note that simulating the FSM corresponds to matrix multiplication: $trans(s, e, s')$ if and only if $||s||.||e|| = ||s'||$.

4.2 Specifying Action Modes

We describe the specification language for defining event/state properties (and hence action modes) using standard BNF notation:

$$
\begin{aligned}
\text{P} ::=\quad & \text{E} \equiv \text{E} \quad | \quad \text{S} \equiv \text{S} \quad | \quad not(\text{P}) \quad | \quad undo(\text{E}) \\
\text{E} ::=\quad & Nothing \quad | \quad \text{e} \quad | \quad \text{E.E} \quad | \quad \neg\text{E} \quad | \quad \text{E} \vee \text{E} \quad | \quad \text{E} \wedge \text{E} \quad | \quad go(\text{S}) \\
\text{S} ::=\quad & All \quad | \quad None \quad | \quad \text{s} \quad | \quad \text{S.E} \quad | \quad \neg\text{S} \quad | \quad \text{S} \vee \text{S} \quad | \quad \text{S} \wedge \text{S}
\end{aligned}
$$

The simple semantics of the language is defined using matrix algebra: states (S) evaluate to vectors, events (E) evaluate to matrices, and there are simple calculable propositions (P) about them. The language operators correspond to simple vector/matrix operations. Equivalence ($\equiv$) is between either states or events, defined as entry-wise equality between the vectors/matrices. The proposition $undo(E)$ holds if the matrix $||E||$ is invertible. $Nothing$ is an event which does nothing, and evaluates to the identity matrix. All and $None$ are the set of all states and no states, which evaluate to the vector with all non-zero elements and with all zero elements respectively. $E_1.E_2$ is the event E_1 followed by E_2. $S.E$ is the set of states reached from S via E. Both are evaluated by matrix multiplication. The event $go(S)$ takes any state to the set of states S.

The remainder of the operators are Boolean: $\neg S$, $S_1 \vee S_2$ and $S_1 \wedge S_2$ are respectively the states not in S, those in S_1 or S_2 and those in S_1 and S_2. Event $\neg E$ causes only those transitions not taken by E. Event $E_1 \vee E_2$ represents transitions caused by E_1 or E_2 (their combined functionality), while $E_1 \wedge E_2$ represents those caused by both (their common functionality).

This specification language is of limited expressiveness. In themselves the algebraic properties are not a sufficient basis for all the kinds of usability analysis we may want to do. However, they can be used to state and calculate simple behaviours of events and states. Moreover, the simplicity of the language allows us to easily construct properties that define action modes.

4.3   Mode Analysis

Mode analysis using these algebraic properties is a three stage process. First, the interface designer must formulate properties that correspond to intended features of specific parts of the design. For example, they could specify that a cancel button returns the user to initial menu state $MainMenu$ and that along with the $*$ button it toggles the keypad lock:

$$Cancel \equiv go(MainMenu) \qquad Cancel.Star.Cancel.Star \equiv Nothing$$

For another device they might specify that a play button starts music playing, i.e. enters one of the set of states $Music$, and that the play and volume functions work independently:

$$Play \equiv go(Music) \qquad Play.(+Vol \vee -Vol) \equiv (+Vol \vee -Vol).Play$$

Each of these properties defines an action mode, i.e. the set of states in which the property is true. Although formulating them is a skilled task, they are essentially quite simple and within the capabilities of many interface designers given appropriate tool support. Indeed, they can also generated automatically for the designer to review using the algorithm described in the following section.

Given a set M_A of action modes, each defined by an algebraic property, the next stage is to form a revised set of modes M'_A by taking complements, unions and intersections of the modes in M_A. The same process is repeated for the indicator modes M_I, to give a set M'_I. Finally, pairs of modes from $M'_A \cup M'_I$ are compared using the $\underset{\sim}{\subseteq}$ relation, avoiding pairs of indicator modes. Any inconsistent pairs are flagged as candidates for redesign.

5   Automating the Method

To support the designer in applying our mode consistency methodology, we now present a novel algorithm that can automatically find algebraic properties/action modes to 'feed into' the analysis. The algorithm can also be used to generate action specifications as part of a more general design methodology [12]. We have developed MAUI, a Java/XML prototype design tool that supports specification with and automatic generation of such properties [4]. A prototype implementation of this mode analysis technique has been made in MAUI, which we intend to use for an evaluation of this methodology. Early results suggest it can handle realistic interface designs.

The algorithm can only generate a restricted subset of specification properties. Specifically, those of the forms:

$$A_1.....A_n = B_1.....B_m \qquad C_1.....C_p = go(s)$$

for $A_i, B_i, C_i \in E$ and $s \in S$. It generates these properties up to a bound N on the maximum product length (i.e. on n, m and p), which is set by the designer. The algorithm is exponential in N, but we have found practical examples can easily be computed. A more sophisticated implementation, e.g. [2], could be used should computational resources become a problem.

5.1   Automation—Finding Equivalences

Given the set of events E we want to combine individual events into composite actions, represented by the set of terms $\mathcal{T}_E$ formed by matrix multiplication. This is an infinite set, and we limit ourselves to investigating a finite subset $\mathcal{T}_E^N$ (for some $N > 0$), defined inductively as:

$$\frac{e \in E}{e \in \mathcal{T}_E^1} \qquad \frac{t \in \mathcal{T}_E^k \quad e \in E}{t.e \in \mathcal{T}_E^{k+1}}$$

The first step is to partition $\mathcal{T}_E^N$ into a set of equivalence classes $\mathcal{C}_E^N$, defined by equivalence between events. Formally $\mathcal{C}_E^N = \{C_1, \ldots, C_m\}$ such that $\bigcup C_i = \mathcal{T}_E^N$ and for $a \in C_i$ and $b \in C_j$, $||a|| = ||b||$ iff $i = j$. There is also a *representative* function $\phi : \mathcal{C}_E^N \rightarrow \mathcal{T}_E^N$ which selects a distinguished element from an equivalence class, i.e. $\phi(C) \in C$.

Computing the equivalence classes involves the gradual construction of $\mathcal{C}_E^N$ and ϕ, a process we describe here in pseudo-code, to give an clear description of the algorithm. An actual implementation will be able to make numerous efficiency savings over the 'code' here (at the expense of being more obscure). For brevity, our code uses various global data structures: the set of events E, a function `matrix` from terms to matrices (both given as inputs), the set of novel terms `Novel`, the set of unique events `Unique`, the set of equivalence classes `EQC` and a function `rep` which maps each class C to its representative element $\phi(C)$. The purpose of the algorithm is to compute `EQC` and `rep`.

The main algorithm depends on three functions: `classify` is used to place a new term in an appropriate equivalence class (see Figure 2); `redundant` tests whether a term has a subterm that has already been computed (see Figure 3); and `newTerms` computes the new terms introduced to $\mathcal{C}_E^N$ when n is increased by one (see Figure 4). The algorithm that computes $\mathcal{C}_E^N$ for $N > 1$ is shown in Figure 5. It calls `newterms`

```
classify(term t) {
  if (exists c in EQC and matrix(rep(c)) = matrix(t))
      put t in c;
  else
      new class c';
      put c' in EQC;
      if (matrix(t) = matrix(go(s)) for state set s)
          put go(s) in c';
          r = go(s);
      else
          r = t;
      fi
      put t in c';
      extend rep so that rep(c') = r;
      put r in Novel;
  fi
}
```

Fig. 2. The `classify` function

```
redundant(term t):bool {
  red = false;
  for (c in EQC)
      for (q in c)
          if (not(q == rep(c)) and t == pq) red = true;
  return red;
}
```

Fig. 3. The redundant function

```
newTerms(int n) {
  Seeds = Novel;
  Novel = {};
  for (t in Seeds)
      for (e in Unique)
          if (not(redundant(t.e))) classify(t.e);
}
```

Fig. 4. The newTerms function

```
computeEquivClasses(int n) {
  C = {Id};
  r(C) = Id;
  EQC = {C};
  Novel = {};
  for (e in E)
      classify(e);
  Unique = Novel;
  if (n > 1)
      i = 1;
      do
          newTerms(i);
          i++;
      until
          (i > n) or Novel = {};
}
```

Fig. 5. The main algorithm for computing equivalence classes

for successive values of n, until the bound is reached or until no new novel terms are introduced by this cycle. In the latter case we say the equivalence classes are *saturated*: the classification for any larger term can be computed algebraically from the existing classification, and so further classification is pointless. Note that the algorithm is presented in a simple form and considerable efficiency savings could be made, e.g. by using a dynamic programming approach to build up terms during the classification.

5.2   Automation—Identifying Modes

Having computed the equivalence classes $\mathcal{C}_E^N$ for the set of terms T_E^N, we can generate algebraic properties that define action modes. Global properties of the interface can be found by equating a term with its class representative, but here we are interested in the non-global properties that define modes. Formally, pairs of equivalence classes C_1, C_2 are compared to see if there is a set of states m such that

$$go(m).\phi(C_1) \quad \equiv \quad go(m).\phi(C_2)$$

i.e. that matrices for C_1 and C_2 are equivalent for the rows corresponding to the states of m. If this holds, then m is an action mode defined by the property $\phi(C_1) \equiv \phi(C_2)$.

This process may return unmanageably many modes for any non-trivial interface, and the potential modes must be pruned in some way: a minimum mode size for m can be enforced, or a bound on size of property (we treat repetitions of the same event as a single event, e.g. $e.e$ is e^2.) Another technique is to generalise a set of similar modes into a single mode, e.g. $e \equiv f$ for mode m_1, $e.e \equiv f$ for m_2 and $e.e.e \equiv f$ for m_3 can be generalised to $\exists N. e^N \equiv f$ for mode $m_1 \wedge m_2 \wedge m_3$. Finally, the designer should be able to review and filter the generated modes to select those they judge useful for further analysis.

6 Discussion

Several authors have used formal methods to model mode problems, in particular those caused by abstraction and automation [3]. Rushby used model checking to find divergence between user and system models [10]. In a similar vein, Bredereke and Lankenau provided a more rigorous characterisation of mode confusion [1]. In contrast, our model addresses a different form of mode confusion — specifically caused by inconsistency — and does not require a user model. Other types of mode confusion might be better understood with similar formal models that complement existing heuristic approaches, such as [8].

Inconsistency-related mode confusion is a familiar heuristic concept in HCI. Miller and Potts take a formal approach to avoiding such mode confusions in the context of cockpit interfaces [9]. They prove lemmas in PVS stating that certain switches always act as toggles. In our approach this is expressed as a simple algebraic property, e.g. $A.A = Nothing$. Not only is this a clearer representation, we also formally characterise inconsistent violations of this property, as well as many others. Moreover, we have provided a method for automating this analysis.

The scalability of automating our approach is an issue: the 'combinatorial explosion' will render our automatic analysis impractical for large enough systems. As discussed above, this can be mitigated with more sophisticated implementations. Comparable limits in model checking have been pushed back so that extremely large state systems can now be analysed. More importantly, even a restricted amount of system analysis may reveal interesting mode inconsistencies.

Our priority for further research is the evaluation of the theory and methodology described here, using the prototype implementation in MAUI [4]. This is initially being done by testing the theory on a corpus of interface designs. Our notion of inconsistency could be refined by measuring near-subsets based on a weighting of interface states. As users will spend more time in some states, these will bias their perception of interface behaviour, and therefore their learning (and mislearning) of mode relationships. There is also scope for extending the classification of mode types beyond action/indicator.

Modifying a design is a rather open-ended activity and is of course best suited to human designers. A tool can however still make very useful suggestions for reducing mode inconsistencies. We intend to extend our techniques to suggest possible mode redesigns as well as improving the identification of existing mode inconsistencies. A design tool can establish or check many other sorts of property. Further work should explore convenient ways to express a large range of such properties — and in a way that is 'designer friendly' rather than logic-driven.

We have various parameters to our methodology as constants: the minimum bound for inconsistency ρ, the maximum product size N, and the minimum mode size. These could, instead, be 'sliders' on the design tool: the designer could adjust the slider to get the level of detail (pedantry?) that they want to work with. Perhaps — and we look forward to trying this — it would be insightful to visualise the effects of these parameters by drawing graphs. Further research may develop ways to automatically determine values that give a 'reasonable' description of the interface design.

7   Conclusions

We have presented a general, formal model of inconsistency-related mode confusion and an accompanying methodology for mode analysis, a significant amount of which can be automated. The model is general enough to provide a framework for further study into consistency and mode confusion.

We have argued here that inconsistent modes are an important user interface feature that are likely to cause users problems. Generally, they should best be avoided unless there are contra-indications due to the nature of the user's task. Unfortunately inconsistent modes are a non-trivial implicit feature of user interfaces and therefore not easily avoided by diligent designers; fortunately, as this paper shows, they can be enumerated automatically by appropriate tools, such as the MAUI system, which we are in the process of evaluating.

The approach has the potential to give ordinary designers useful usability insights: a simple specification language is used and, with appropriate tool support and automation, we anticipate that little training would be required.

Acknowledgements. Jeremy Gow is funded by EPSRC grant GR/S73723/01. Harold Thimbleby is a Royal Society Wolfson Research Merit Award Holder.

References

1. J. Bredereke & A. Lankenau (2002), "A rigorous view of mode confusion." In Anderson, Bologna & Felici (eds), *Computer Safety, Reliability and Security, Proc. SAFECOMP 2002.* LNCS 2434, Springer, pp19–31.
2. E. M. Clarke, E. A. Emmerson & A. P. Sistla (1999), *Model Checking.* MIT Press.
3. A. Degani (1996), "Modelling human-machine systems: On modes, error and patterns of interaction." PhD thesis, Georgia Institute of Technology.
4. J. Gow & H. Thimbleby (2004), "MAUI: An interface design tool based on matrix algebra." In Jacob, Limbourg & Vanderdonckt (eds), *Computer-Aided Design of User Interfaces IV, Proc. CADUI 2004.* Kluwer.

5. J. Gow, H. Thimbleby & P. Cairns (2004), "Misleading behaviour in interactive systems," In Dearden & Watts (eds), *Proc. 18th British HCI Group Annual Conference (HCI 2004)*, Volume 2.
6. D. Harel & A. Naamad (1996), "The STATEMATE semantics of Statecharts," *ACM Transactions on Software Engineering and Methodology*, **5**(4):293-333.
7. G. J. Holzmann (2003), "The SPIN model checker," Addison-Wesley.
8. N. G. Leveson, L. D. Pinnel, S. D. Sandys, S. Koga & J. D. Reese (1997), "Analyzing software specifications for mode confusion potential." In Johnson (ed.) *Proc. Workshop on Human Error & System Development*, Glasgow, pp132–146.
9. S. P. Miller & J. N. Potts (1999), *Detecting Mode Confusion Through Formal Modeling and Analysis*. NASA Contractor Report, NASA/CR-1999-208971.
10. J. Rushby (2002), "Using model checking to help discover mode confusions & other automation surprises," *Reliability Engineering & System Safety*, **75**(2):167–177.
11. H. Thimbleby (1982), "Character level ambiguity: Consequences for user interface design," *International Journal of Man-Machine Studies*, **16**:211–225.
12. H. Thimbleby (2004), "User interface design with matrix algebra," *ACM Transactions on Computer-Human Interaction*, **11**(2):181–236.

Quantitative Measurement of Quality Attribute Preferences Using Conjoint Analysis

Kwang Chun Lee, Ho-Jin Choi, Dan Hyung Lee, and Sungwon Kang

Information and Communications University,
119 Munjiro, Yuseong-Gu, Daejeon, Korea
{statkclee, hjchoi, danlee, kangsw}@icu.ac.kr

Abstract. Conjoint analysis has received considerable attention as a technique for measuring customer preferences through utility tradeoffs among products and services. This paper shows how the method can be applied to the area of software architecture to analyze architectural tradeoffs among quality attributes. By eliciting customer utilities through conjoint analysis, software engineers can identify and focus on the useful quality attributes, which will increase the chance of delivering satisfactory software products to the customers. This paper proposes a quantitative method of measuring quality attribute preferences using conjoint analysis and demonstrates its efficacy by applying it to the Project Management Center (PMCenter) project. The proposed method is complementary to the Architecture Trade-off Analysis Method (ATAM) in that ATAM relies on customer's feedback to elicit important quality attributes, whereas this method can be used to actually measure the utilities of quality attributes in a quantitative manner. Furthermore, our method provides a new framework for choosing architecture styles and design patterns based on customer's preferences of quality attributes.

1   Introduction

Software architecture has become an important area of research and practice within software engineering over the past 15 years [15]. Software architecture is critical for designing high-utility software products because it is an artifact that specifies early design decisions that would greatly affect subsequent development. Before enormous organizational resources have been committed, it would be extremely desirable to have an adequate method to determine whether quality goals can be achieved by the architecture [14]. The ATAM method developed by the Software Engineering Institute aims to assess the consequences of architectural decisions by using quality attributes-based scenarios [15]. However, the ATAM method lets architectural decision go into the heart of architecture construction without giving quantitative measurement of customer's utility. We believe that by being able to measure the degrees of utilities to the customer we can design higher quality architectures and ultimately provide higher quality products to the customer.

The aim of this paper is to propose a quantitative measurement method of quality attribute preferences using conjoint analysis, and to explore its potential impact on the development of software architecture. Measuring customer's utility quantitatively is aligned with the development of high-utility software architecture. The remainder of

S.W. Gilroy and M.D. Harrison (Eds.): DSVIS 2005, LNCS 3941, pp. 213–224, 2006.
© Springer-Verlag Berlin Heidelberg 2006

the paper is structured in six parts. After this introduction, Section 2 is devoted to the explanation of the concept of software architecture and the ATAM method. Quality attributes play an important role in evaluating software architecture, but when combined with conjoint analysis, they can deliver more useful information. In Section 3 we explore conjoint analysis, followed by a study of the literature and the conjoint analysis process. In Section 4 the conjoint analysis in ATAM has been shown. It provides a new mechanism for quantitative utility measurement of quality attributes in ATAM. In Section 5 the results of PMCenter project are presented. Finally, Section 6 is the conclusion.

2   Software Architecture and ATAM

Users naturally focus on specifying their functional, or behavioral, requirements, but there is more to successful software development than just delivering the right functionality. They are known as software quality attributes, or quality factors, and are parts of the system's nonfunctional requirements [12]. These functional and non-functional requirements are inputs to following software development life-cycle. Recently many researchers and practitioners have realized the importance of software architecture before moving toward detailed design phase. When systems are constructed from many components, the organization of the overall system-the software architecture- presents design issues to software engineers [4].

The Architecture Tradeoff Analysis Method (ATAM) developed by the Software Engineering Institute (SEI) at CMU is a method for evaluating architecture-level designs that considers multiple quality attributes such as modifiability, performance, reliability and security in gaining insight as to whether the fully fleshed-out incarnation of the architecture will meet its requirements [9]. ATAM aims to identify architectural elements affecting quality attributes such that it helps to discover software architecture with high utility to customers. In particular, quality attributes facilitate communications among stakeholders.

Even though ATAM has opened a new formal communication channel to deliver satisfactory software architecture to customers, it still assumes that customers are intelligent enough to provide sufficient and reliable information to software architects. In addition to it, measurement process and methods for customer utility have not been clearly documented. Therefore, ATAM aims to deliver high utility software architecture to customers, but it still lacks the ability to measure customer utility in a quantitative manner. Choosing appropriate architectures from the recent activity in cataloging architecture styles or design patterns which provides a broad palette of quality attributes and quantitative measurement of quality attribute preferences under the ATAM framework increases the possibility of delivering high utility software to customers.

3   Conjoint Analysis

A customer decision process can be interpreted as a black box as shown in Fig. 1. Inputs are product attributes, external factors, and market information. Outputs are purchase decisions and related market behavior. In order to understand a customer decision process correctly, it is necessary to model cognitive mechanisms explicitly and then use

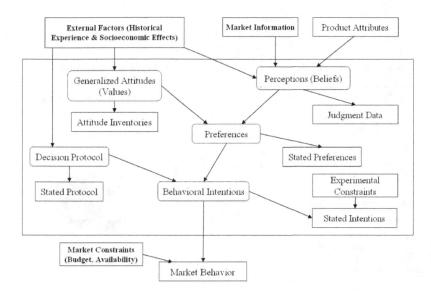

Fig. 1. Path diagram for the customer decision process adopted from [12]

experimental data to fit this model. Once the model is fitted to the data, a customer behavior prediction can be done through simulation.

Since data is a valuable resource in terms of data collection cost and subsequent benefits, it is necessary to separate data collection with information extraction as shown in Fig. 2. Goal-driven or model-driven data collection is a good example. The purpose-driven data collection provides analysts with much more information and high-fidelity knowledge sources.

The purpose of utilizing models is to make it easier for stakeholders to understand customers correctly. If there are data on customer behavior linked to products or market information, statistical approach can be one of potentials. Recently many researchers and practitioners are paying special attention to data mining associated with data ware-house. Powerful computing and huge storage have made technical break-throughs in data-driven decision support. It is necessary to discover applicable methods in revealing customer preference in software architecture in regard to software data characteristics such as sparsity and small observations.

Multi-attribute utility models or Analytical hierarchy process (AHP) can be a candidate, but they are not suitable for software architecture design because designing software architecture involves complex processes associated with many stakeholders communications, whereas both approaches emphasized small numbers of decision makers facing high-level decisions [7]. Conjoint analysis is based on the judgmental approach with defined data collection process. Self evaluation with well-defined data collection procedure enables customers to reveals their intentions. In addition, results of conjoint analysis can be used to simulate market share and effects of product penetration and cannibalization with the help of expert systems.

Conjoint analysis is an additive model with compensatory multi-attributes. It assumes that the utility for a product can be expressed as a sum of utilities for its attributes

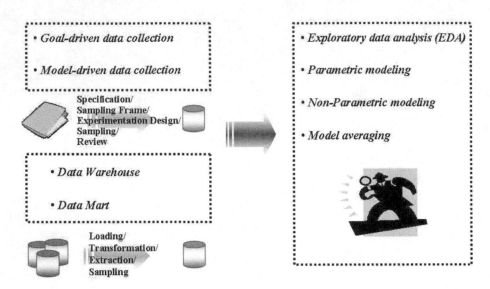

Fig. 2. Data collection and information extraction

and utilities can be measured by customers overall evaluation of products. Furthermore estimates of the utilities can be used to predict market share through simulation. Each quality attribute has different functional form to overall utility.

$$U = u_1(QA_1) + u_2(QA_2) + \cdots = \sum_{i \in attributes} u_i(QA_i) \qquad (1)$$

The conjoint analysis can provide a complementary approach in measuring customer utility in a quantitative manner. The conjoint analysis can measure customer utility quantitatively and objectively through well-defined process. In addition to it, it is not necessary for customers to understand ATAM or software system itself. Since the conjoint analysis delivers suitable design sets, the only thing that customers should do is to specify their preferences through ranking or comparisons, and then the defined conjoint analysis process will reveal the hidden customer preferences. Benefits from understanding customer preferences will lead to the development of high-quality software architecture and the smooth transition for the later part of software development life-cycle.

4   Conjoint Analysis in ATAM

Conjoint analysis serves as a go-between to elicit customer architectural preference. Even if customers don't have domain knowledge in quality attributes, architects can figure it out by applying conjoint analysis to ATAM. In order to utilize conjoint analysis in ATAM, four components such as quality attributes, experimental design, scenario generation, and analysis are needed as shown in Fig. 3. Based on quality attributes, architects make appropriate design plans to elicit architectural preference. In the scenario generation phase the design plans are tailored and elaborated to fit customer tastes.

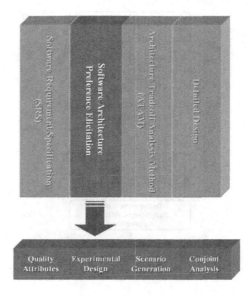

Fig. 3. Conjoint analysis in ATAM

Customers evaluate them and fill out request form. In the final phase, statistical data analysis reveals customer architecture preference.

4.1 Process of Conjoint Analysis

Conjoint analysis is one of many techniques for handling situations in which a decision maker has to deal with options that simultaneously vary across two or more attributes [7]. The seminal paper by Luce and Tukey [11] and the experimental design papers by Addelman [1] and Plackett and Burman [13] provided key theoretical underpinnings and motivation for developing conjoint analysis.

In this paper, a typical conjoint analysis process [3] has been adopted and tailored for quantitative measurement of quality attributes preference not only to maintain process stability of conjoint analysis but also to embrace architecture quality attributes in the following framework. The process of conjoint analysis consists of six steps as shown by Fig. 4.

Quality Attribute Selection. The first step of the conjoint analysis is to define the quality attributes. The SEI had research on refining quality attributes [10]. These quality attributes can be candidate attributes for the conjoint study. Depending on target systems (e.g. web-based system or real-time system), different sets of quality attributes can be defined.

In addition, goal of target system affects quality attributes selection. For instance, there are conflicts between modifiability and performance since as real-time Java removed many functionalities to make it lighter, performance sometimes needs trade-offs of maintainability, configurability and so on. The priori information can be utilized to perform effective and efficient research design and reduce redundant subsequent tasks.

Fig. 4. Conjoint analysis process tailored for preference analysis of quality attributes

Determination of Quality Attribute Levels. The second step is to determine the levels of quality attributes as shown in Fig. 5. Since quality attribute consists of quality attribute levels, quality attribute levels should be mutually exclusive and collectively exhaustive. In that case the quality attribute levels are sufficient to represent the quality attribute. One of quality attributes, performance, can be made of capability, concurrency, and processing time. Levels of quality attribute may be defined in different ways in order to identify customer preferences accurately.

In addition, it should be realistic to ensure realism of the scenarios when presented to customers. Compared with prototype-based presentation, the scenarios-based presentation has implicit limitations, such that it should deliver sufficient and clear information through effective message mechanism. For example, utilizing visual images or audio-video media associated with textual information may overcome limitations and deliver more realistic and detailed scenarios to help customers reveal preferences correctly and easily.

Determination of Quality Attributes Combinations. The third step involves determining the combinations of quality attributes. If a customer is asked to rank too many architecture profiles, he/she will be exhausted by evaluating nearly similar and too many profiles. To avoid such wear-out and reduce the number of evaluating scenarios to a more manageable level, fractional-factorial designs are frequently used with orthogonal plans [5][6]. According to Pareto's hierarchical ordering principle, the number of important factors is small and lower order factors are more likely to be important than higher order factors. Therefore, this approach is useful and relatively straightforward in that more often than not, quality attribute combinations are determined with fractional-factorial and orthogonal plans.

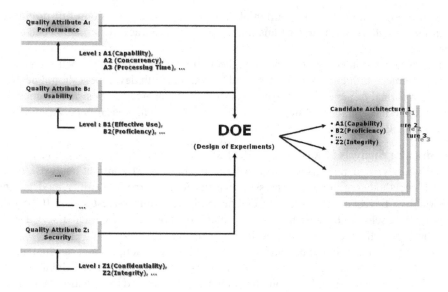

Fig. 5. Candidate architecture generation using quality attributes and levels

Orthogonality is a strong assumption and sometimes unrealistic since two or three quality attributes are correlated and they become critical for software quality. Therefore, other design schemes to detect these patters are necessary. If priori information is not available, designs to investigate which quality attributes are significant are used in order to screen out potential factors out of trivial many factors. Once significant factors are discovered, fractional designs are used to investigate interaction patterns among quality attributes. The two-stage design strategy is desirable for relaxing orthogonal assumption and identifying interactions.

Determination of Approach to Obtaining Customer Judgements. The fourth step is to determine an approach to obtaining customers judgements. There are various ways to obtain customers judgement such as rating, ranking, etc. One of popular presentation methods is to show profile cards or paragraph descriptions to customers. Pictorial materials or actual prototypes are frequently used to enhance realism in representing product characteristics. Once these stimuli are represented, customers are asked to obtain ranking and rating scales judgement for each of stimuli.

Profiles do not contain all the attributes, such that fractional-factorial designs are typically used. Attributes are divided carefully, such that profiles contain partial and different attributes. Besides, paired comparisons are common in computer-assisted methods [6]. In computer-aided cases, customers are asked to reveal their preference by selecting only one out of two candidates and repeat this process in a similar manner.

Determining How Judgements Will Be Aggregated. The fifth step involves determining how judgements will be aggregated. If there are multiple respondents, it is necessary to determine how those judgements are collected and represented. When dealing with different customers, data pooling of similar respondents' conjoint full-profile responses through clustering algorithms can increase the accuracy of estimation and avoid biases.

If software engineers aim to develop high-quality software products focused on multiple customers, influence of customers and interaction with developers should be dealt with in a formal framework. A Bayesian approach can provide a consistent framework to figure out this situation. However, it will be skipped in this research because there is only one stakeholder.

Conducting Analysis of Responses. The last step is to conduct analysis of responses. Usually analysis of responses has been fixed in the earliest conjoint analysis. Three analysis methods are popular: regression-based methods, random-utility models, and hierarchical Bayesian estimation. In our method the ordinary-least-square (OLS) regression was selected because the preference judgment is an approximate interval scale and the partworths are represented as dummy variables [8].

Statistical models should be validated through hold-out samples and residual analysis. In design phase, samples are divided into two parts: modeling and validation samples. Since the residual analysis contains important and omitted information, it provides a clue for improving models.

5   Case Study

In this section, we apply our method to an industry software development project[1]. The client of the project wants to have a software project management system named PMCenter (Project Management System), which supports overall management activities. The PMCenter consists of project planning, monitoring, controlling, and measure analysis.

Since conjoint analysis is good at revealing customer preferences on quality attributes, a conjoint study has been set up after reviewing the ATAM quality attributes and meeting customers. After looking at web-based system characteristics, five quality attributes were chosen. They are performance, usability, availability, modifiability, and security. Attributes and levels are summarized in Table 1.

Since full-profile analysis, which utilizes all quality attributes instead of partial quality attributes, has the advantage that the respondent evaluates each profile holistically and in the context of all other stimuli, full-profile approach has been selected [8]. The possible scenarios from the selected attributes and levels gave rise to 48 ($3\times2\times2\times2\times2=48$). Since evaluating the 48 scenarios was time-consuming for customers, an experimental design method has been adopted. In order to ensure the absence of multicollinearity, an orthogonal main effects design has been adopted through SPSS ORTHOPLAN[2] and 8 scenarios has been generated. Each scenario has been evaluated and ranked by a customer. Based on the defined design and customer responses, ordinary-least-square (OLS) regression model has been fitted to estimate importance of quality attributes.

---

[1] ICU-CMU (Information and Communications University - Carnegie Mellon University) MSE (Master of Software Engineering) Studio Project developed a prototype system of the web-based project management system for Korea Telecom (KT).

[2] Copyright © 2004, SPSS Inc.

Table 1. Attributes and levels in the PMCenter

Atributes	Levels
Performance	Capability, Concurrency, Processing Time
Usability	Efficient Use, Proficiency/Testing
Availability	Fault Tolerance, High Availability
Modifiability	Cost of Change, Prevention of Ripple Effect
Security	Confidentiality, Integrity

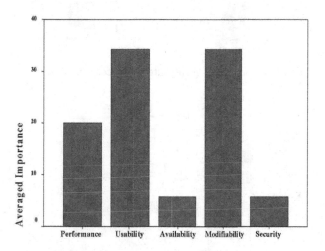

Fig. 6. Importance of quality attributes

The conjoint analysis results show that the customer paid special attentions to the quality attributes of usability and modifiability, whereas availability and security are not regarded as important to the customer as summarized in Fig. 6. In addition to utilities of quality attributes, importance of quality attributes by levels provided in-depth investigation of quality attributes as shown in Fig. 7. Those findings recommended that software architect should regard the two quality attributes (usability and modifiability) as the key quality attributes to best align PMCenter architecture with customer needs.

Since it is clear that what the customer wants is a web-based system with high usability and modifiability, the PMCenter project team designed architectures to maximize these quality attributes and put relatively small weight on security and availability with a palette of architecture styles and design patterns. The layered architecture combined with Model-View-Controller (MVC) pattern supported usability and modifiability compared with other architecture styles or design patterns. The component and connector view of architectural decision is shown in Fig. 8. The layered architecture combined with Model-View-Controller (MVC) pattern supported usability and modifiability. The middle tier, which is located between clients and data server provides service by getting

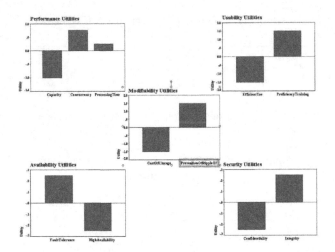

Fig. 7. Importance of quality attributes according to levels

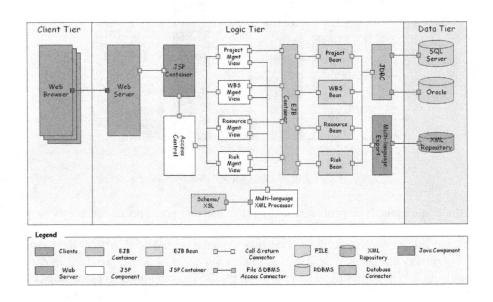

Fig. 8. PMCenter: Web-based Project Management System

request from the client and performing proper operation cooperating with data server. The processing of request of client is divided between controller and view components. View components are JSP pages that create the HTML response pages that determine the user interface when rendered by the browser. Controller components do not handle any presentation issues, but rather, process all the HTTP requests from clients. They are responsible for generating any EJB logic beans or objects used by the view components, as well as deciding, according to the user's actions, which view component to forward the request to. Controller components have been implemented as Servlet. Model components represent enterprise data and the business rules that govern access to and updates of this data. In addition, the quantitative results of conjoint analysis promoted an architectural design of high utility to the customer and facilitated communications among team members when making important design decisions.

6   Conclusion

The conjoint analysis has been used in revealing customer preferences among the quality attributes for choosing appropriate architecture styles or design patterns and constructing software architecture in the web-based project management system. After conducting the ATAM process, we constructed a utility tree with stakeholders including the customer. Important quality attributes from the utility tree are in accordance with the result of conjoint analysis, viz. usability and modifiability. In addition, conjoint analysis identified interesting points. From the customer viewpoints software architect should pay special attention to prevention of ripple effects because the customer put more weights on robust software architecture, rather than concerns on rework.

When adopting in commercial off-the-shelf (COTS) based software system development, it is more likely to be successful. The COTS products are dealing with mass market such that it is necessary to understand customer preference. The traditional interview method can deliver biased investigation results by selecting inappropriate samples and limited communication channels. Variants of conjoint analysis can overcome these weak points and facilitate successful COTS product development.

Since conjoint analysis is relatively new in Human-Computer Interaction (HCI) and software engineering, this method has been applied in custom-built software systems. The result has shown a positive impact on quality attribute preference measurement. Conjoint analysis can be one method that enables us to develop more competitive software products by measuring customer preferences, facilitating smooth transitions, and developing high-utility products.

References

1. Addlelman, S.: Orthogonal main-effect plans for asymmetrical factorial experiments. Technometrics, Vol. 4 (1962) pp.21–46
2. Armstrong, S.: Principles of Forecasting, Kluwer Publishing (2001)
3. Churchill, G. and Lacobucci, D.: Marketing research: methodological foundations, 8/e, South-Western College Pub. (2002)
4. Garlan, D. and Shaw, M.: An introduction to software architecture, CMU/SEI-94-TR-21, ESC-TR-94-21. (1994)
5. Green, P. E. and Srinivasan, V.: Conjoint analysis in consumer research: issues and outlook, Journal of Consumer Research, Vol.5 (1978) pp.103–23.
6. Green, P. E. and Srinivasan, V.: Conjoint analysis in marketing: new development with implications for research and practice, Journal of Consumer Research, Vol.5 (1990) pp.103–23.
7. Green, P. E., Krieger, A. M., and Wind, Y.: Thirty Years of Conjoint Analysis: Reflections and Prospects, Interfaces, 31:3, Part 2 of 2 (2001) pp. S56–S73.

8. Hauser, J. R. and Rao, V.: Conjoint analysis, related modeling, and applications. In Advances in Marketing Research: Progress and Modeling, Norwell, MA, Ed. Kluwer Academic Publishing (2004).
9. Kazman, R., Klein, M., and Barbacci, M.: The architecture tradeoff analysis method, 4th Int'l Conference on Engineering of Complex Computer Systems (ICECCS98), pp. 67–78. T Longstaff, H. Lipson, J. Corriere, Eds. IEEE Computer Society (1998).
10. Kazman, R., Klein, M., and Clements, P.: ATAM: method for architecture evaluation. Technical Report CMU/SEI-2000-TR-004, Software Engineering Institute, Carnegie Mellon University (2000)
11. Luce, R. D. and Tukey, J.: Simultaneous conjoint measurement: a new type of fundamental measurement, Journal of Mathematical Psychology (1964) pp. 1–27.
12. McFadden, D.: The choice theory approach to market research, Marketing Science Vol 5, No 4. (1986)
13. Plackett, R. L. and Burman, J. P.: The design of optimum multifactorial experiments, Biometrika, Vol. 33 (1946) pp. 305–325
14. Shaw, M. and Garlan, D.: Software architecture: perspectives on an emerging discipline, Prentice Hall, (1996)
15. Smith, D. and Merson, P.: Using architecture evaluation to prepare a large web based system for evolution, Proceedings of the 5th IEEE Int'l Workshop on Web Site Evolution, (2003)
16. Wiegers, K. E.: Software requirements, 2/e", Microsoft Press, (2003)
17. Wittink, D. R. and Cattin, P.: Commercial use of conjoint analysis: an update", Journal of Marketing, 53 (1989) pp. 91–96.
18. Wittink, D. R., Vriens, M, and Burhenne, W.: Commercial use of conjoint analysis in Europe: results and reflections", International Journal of Research in Marketing, Vol. 11, (1994) pp. 41–52.

A Model-Based Design Process for Interactive Virtual Environments

Erwin Cuppens, Chris Raymaekers, and Karin Coninx

Hasselt University, Expertise Centre for Digital Media (EDM)
and Transnationale Universiteit Limburg,
Wetenschapspark 2, 3590 Diepenbeek, Belgium
{erwin.cuppens, chris.raymaekers, karin.coninx}@uhasselt.be

Abstract. Nowadays, interactive systems are not limited to the desktop. On the one hand they are deployed onto handheld and embedded devices, and on the other hand they evolve into interactive virtual environments which are controlled by direct manipulation interaction techniques. However, the development of these virtual environment user interfaces is not a straightforward process and thus not easily accessible for non-programmers. In this paper, we envision a model-based design process for these highly interactive applications, in order to bridge the gap between the designer and the programmer of the application. The process is based on both requirements of model-based user interface developments processes, and virtual environment development tools and toolkits. To evaluate the envisioned approach, a tool was created that supports the described process, and a case study has been performed.

1 Introduction

Virtual Environments are computer generated three-dimensional environments that create the effect of an interactive world in which the user is immersed. For several years our lab has performed research on interaction techniques within these environments and for this purpose several virtual environment applications have been developed that support the use of various interaction techniques. Although Interactive Virtual Environments (IVEs) offer a lot of advantages, the use of these applications is not very widespread. There are several possible reasons for this, including the fact that the development process of an IVE is not easily accessible for non-specialists.

In order to investigate alternative methods to facilitate the development of IVEs, we initiated the VR-DeMo project (Virtual Reality: Conceptual Descriptions and Models for the Realization of Virtual Environments). Within this project we elaborate on the possible use of conceptual modelling and high-level interaction descriptions in the IVE design process. We believe that the introduction of a conceptual level will facilitate the development of IVEs for programmers as well as designers.

In this paper we propose a *model-based approach* for the development of IVEs. Nowadays, model-based techniques are mainly used in multi-device user interface (UI) development processes. The description of a UI by means of declarative models offers three major advantages [16]:

S.W. Gilroy and M.D. Harrison (Eds.): DSVIS 2005, LNCS 3941, pp. 225–236, 2006.

1. The models provide an abstract description of the UI.
2. The models facilitate the creation of methods to design and implement the UI systematically.
3. The models provide the infrastructure required to automate the UI design and implementation processes.

We believe that the advantages of model-based design can aid in bridging the gap between the application programmers and the IVE designers because the IVE can be described in a way that is abstracted from its implementation.

The majority of the current Model-Based User Interface Development (MBUID) tools focus on topics such as WIMP and speech interfaces. Because of these specific points of interest, most tools are limited to dialog and web-based user interfaces and do not elaborate on direct manipulation techniques. In contrast, user interfaces for IVEs typically focus on the topic of direct manipulation, since interaction mostly happens by means of one (or more) specific interaction techniques or metaphors. Because of these differences, we have to examine which of the existing models or algorithms are useful for the model-based design of IVEs.

In the remainder of this paper we will elaborate on the envisioned model-based design process. First, an overview of some MBUID environments and processes will be given, followed by a discussion of several existing VE development tools and toolkits. Afterwards we will describe the analysis that was made in order to gather the requirements necessary for model-based design of an IVE. Once the most important requirements had been determined, they were used to specify a model-based design process that has benefits of both development approaches. Finally this process has been implemented within a tool, called CoGenIVE (Code Generation for Interactive Virtual Environments). Evaluation of CoGenIVE will be done using a case study in which a virtual shop will be designed and generated. An overview of the tool and the case study is given in Sect. 4. We will conclude our paper by analyzing the result of the case study and present ongoing work in Sect. 5.

2   Model-Based IVE Development: The Requirements

Before we could specify a model-based design process and develop a code-generation tool to facilitate this process, it was of great importance to determine the requirements necessary for the process and the supporting tool. Since we tried to combine two different development approaches, namely MBUID and the toolkit-based development of IVEs, we had to examine both the MBUID processes and tools, and the virtual environment development tools and toolkits. The results of this analysis are presented in this section.

Based on the advantages and properties of the examined tools and processes, we determined the requirements necessary to specify our design process and development tool.

2.1   Model-Based User Interface Design Processes and Tools

Although several MBUID environments exist, most of these tools focus on different topics and use alternative design processes.

A first process is defined within the Cameleon Reference Framework [3]. This framework defines UI development steps for multi-context interactive applications. The process contains four steps, starting from tasks and concepts, evolving via abstract and concrete UIs into the final user interface. After each step the user is able to manipulate any of the generated artefacts.

Originally, the Cameleon framework was created by Coutaz et al. in order to specify plasticity of user interfaces [2], but nowadays several other projects such as UsiXML [20], a user interface description language for the specification of multimodal user interfaces, also make use of the framework.

The TERESA tool [14] developed by Paternò et al. is also based on the Cameleon framework and focusses on the development of multi-device user interfaces. The process used in the TERESA tool is described as *One Model, Many Interfaces*. This means the design process starts with an abstract description of the tasks the interactive system has to support, and gradually transform the descriptions into different concrete user interfaces. In particular, the process starts with a task model and through a number of transformations the specific interface for each of the different devices is generated.

The goal of DynaMo-AID [4] developed by Clerckx et al. is the development of context-sensitive multi-device user interfaces. DynaMo-AID uses a process elaborating on the Dygimes framework [13]. Similar to the process used by the TERESA tool, DynaMo-AID starts from a task model representing tasks for different contexts of use, in particular the ConcurTaskTree notation [15]. The first step in the process is extracting the different task sets and derive the dialog model from them. The following step is the generation of an abstract UI out of the task sets and the generated dialog model. This abstract UI will be converted into a concrete UI when the interface is deployed on the target device.

Mobi-D [18] is a highly interactive development environment that starts with a user-task elicitation stage and offers testing possibilities for the generated user interfaces. The user-task elicitation exists of an informal task description that evolves into a formal task outline with help from the designer. Next, the developer starts interacting with Mobi-D in order to create the user-task and domain model. In the following step the presentation and dialog model are defined and finally a prototype of the UI will be created. Once generated, Mobi-D aids in the evaluation of the generated prototype interfaces.

Although model-based design processes have proven their value in dialog or web-based interfaces, none of these seems to be directly usable in order to design interaction within a VE. Highly interactive interfaces, like an IVE, contain several direct manipulation techniques and are therefore not considered.

The overview of these design processes however, shows several common properties which we will take into account in our own design process. Each process *starts with a task related model* and evolves towards the final user interface using an *incremental approach*. After each step in the design process, the designer has the possibility to *modify the generated artefacts manually*. One property that was not really emphasized but nevertheless is very important, is the fact that the process should be *iterative* in order to easily alter, regenerate and evaluate a prototype UI. Finally, it is essential that *manual changes from the designer are preserved* when the user interface is regenerated.

2.2   VE Development Tools and Toolkits

We are aware that several tools and toolkits to facilitate the IVE design process already exist, but the number of processes particularly conceptualized for the entire development of an IVE is rather limited. We believe several reasons exist to explain this scarcity. For example, the complexity of interaction in a VE, the wide variety of input and output techniques, the lack of suitable standard notations.

One approach trying to support the design of IVEs is the Marigold toolset [21]. The focus of the process lies in the systematic design, evaluation and refinement of interaction techniques by means of extensive visual tool support. The Marigold toolset consists of two tools: the Hybrid Specification Builder, in which the designer can specify interaction techniques using the Flownets notation [19]; and the Prototype Builder, in which parts of code can be specified in order to support different devices, and provide interaction with world objects.

Although the process appears to resolve several issues concerning the design of interaction techniques, it also raises some questions. At first, describing interaction using the Flownets notation is no straightforward process and the diagram tends to become very large, even for rather simple interaction metaphors. A second issue concerns the usability of the Prototype Builder for non-programmers since it requires code editing and uses concepts such as input and output variables.

Nowadays, standardization in the field of IVE development is limited to file formats, such as VRML and X3D. Because of the lack of standards concerning interaction techniques and development methodologies, there is a wide variety of toolkits, all trying to facilitate the development of these applications. Most existing toolkits are programming API's, concentrating on the technical details of the application and in most cases focussing on specific development issues. As a result, most toolkits are not easily accessible for non-programmers.

CaveLib [6] is a low-level API, used for the creation of VR-applications in projection based set ups. CaveLib especially aims at multi-display and network applications and thus offers no direct support for any specific scene graph technology.

VRJuggler [7] is a more high-level approach to develop and run VR-applications. It is an open source platform that introduces a software layer between the application and the device interface to provide a hardware-independent programming API. By means of a graphical user interface, the designer can combine code-blocks (chunks) in order to use input and output devices in his application (which has to be coded by hand). The chunks that are available within VRJuggler contain several functionalities (e.g., scene graph technology, openGL output, input with the 3D mouse or other input devices, CAVE support, tracking).

The OpenManip framework [1] provides support for direct object manipulation techniques such as selection and manipulation of scene objects, independent of the underlying scene graph technology.

Alice [5] offers an alternative for these technical toolkits is. It is a graphical programming environment, solely for the creation of IVE simulators. The created simulations use the DIVER platform as a rendering engine and device handler. Because of its graphical notation, even environment designers without any programming experience can use Alice in order to create a virtual scene containing some basic animations. More complex behavior can be accomplished by means of Python scripting.

In contrast with the MBUID tools described in Sect. 2.1, the presented toolkits do not immediately show common characteristics. Kulas et al. identified several research challenges concerning the development of virtual and augmented reality development tools and design processes [12]. The most important issue concerning the development tools is the wide variety of existing toolkits, each focusing on a specific part of the final application. Combining several toolkits is not straightforward since the output of one tool can, in most cases, not be used as input for another tool. Therefore, it is important that several design issues can be integrated within the same tool. Challenges concerning the design process are the specification of a formal process and the possibility of rapid prototyping in order to experiment with different variations of the UI in quick succession.

2.3 Selected Requirements

When combining the advantages and requirements of both design processes and development tools, we achieve the following specifications for our model-based design process and the supporting tool:

Selected Requirement 1. The process should evolve incrementally, from an abstract (user-task) description and high-level models into a concrete interface and low-level code.

Selected Requirement 2. The process should be iterative: once a prototype UI has been generated and evaluated, the designer should be able to alter the models and regenerate the interface.

Selected Requirement 3. Since an IVE consists of several direct manipulation techniques, it should be possible to design these interaction techniques by means of an additional description model. In the remainder of this paper we will refer to these description models as *Interaction Description Models*.

Selected Requirement 4. In order to be useful for non-programmers, the process should automatically generate the code for the described IVE.

Selected Requirement 5. When the code is regenerated after certain models have been altered, it is essential that manually edited code is preserved.

Selected Requirement 6. In order to be useful, graphical tool support and assistance should be offered in order to design the high-level description models and check their correctness.

3 Model-Based IVE Development: The Process

Based on the requirements gathered in Sect. 2, we propose a model-based approach for the design and development of IVEs. The process is based on some existing models and algorithms which are adapted in order to support the direct manipulation and interaction techniques that are typical for IVEs.

In this section, our envisaged design process will be described and Sect. 4 will present a tool developed in order to support the proposed process.

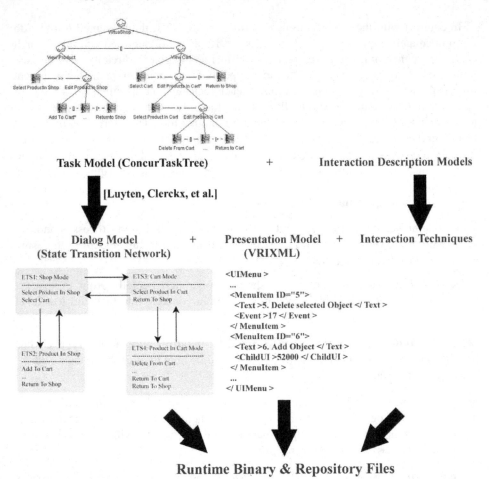

Fig. 1. Envisaged design process

A schematic overview of our process is shown in Fig. 1. The first step is the creation of a task model of our IVE. This **Task Model** is done by means of the ConcurTaskTree (CTT) notation [15] (as shown in the top-left part of Fig. 1). The CTT notation, elaborated by Paternò, is a widely used notation which uses a graphical syntax and offers both a hierarchical structure and support to specify temporal relations between tasks. Four types of tasks are supported in the CTT notation:

1. *Application tasks*—tasks completely executed by the application.
2. *User tasks*—tasks performed by the user; usually they are important cognitive activities.
3. *Interaction tasks*—tasks performed by the user interacting with the system by some interaction techniques.
4. *Abstract tasks*—tasks which require complex activities whose performance cannot be unequivocally allocated.

Sibling tasks at the same level in the hierarchy of decomposition can be connected by temporal operators (e.g., choice ([]), enabling (>>), disabling ([>)).

Since we are designing *Interactive* Virtual Environments, we will concentrate on the interaction tasks within the application. A possible example of an interaction task in the leaf-nodes of a CTT is object selection. In a 2D user interface this is a straightforward task in which the user selects an item from a given list by means of a mouse. In an IVE however, this task becomes more challenging since the interaction techniques in a virtual environment are not limited to keyboard and mouse input. Several well-known selection techniques are grabbing, ray-casting and gogo-selection [17].

Because of the complexity of most interaction tasks in 3D environments, we propose the usage of a graphical notation to describe these interaction techniques in more detail. Attaching these **Interaction Description Models** (IDM) to an interaction task in the CTT has two advantages. Firstly, the design process of the IVE becomes more flexible since an IDM offers the possibility of altering the used interaction technique for an interaction task, without having to adapt the task model or any other model in the design process. A second advantage results from the fact that by using an IDM to define specific interaction tasks, the design of a task model for an IVE becomes similar to that of a 2D user interface.

Once the task model is designed, the algorithm described by Luyten, et al.[13] can be used to automatically extract the application's **Dialog Model** from the CTT. The dialog model is based on the enabled task sets which are derived from the application's task model. An Enabled Task Set [15] (ETS) is defined as: *"a set of tasks that are logically enabled to start their performance during the same period of time"*. The resulting ETSs can be mapped onto the different application states, containing all interaction tasks that can be executed in that state. The transitions between the application states are the same as those in the state transition network that represents the dialog model.

After the dialog model is extracted, the different states of the application are connected to the interaction techniques, defined by the IDMs. Further, the designer has to merge the dialog model with the **Presentation Model**. In our process, the presentation model is represented by VRIXML, a description language used to specify interface elements for the resulting IVE. A small extract of a VRIXML menu is shown in Fig. 1. More examples and a motivation for the creation of this user interface description language can be found in [8].

Once the entire design process is completed, the specified models are used to automatically **generate a runtime binary** of the virtual environment application. In addition, the process generates some repository files that can be interpreted by the application at runtime. These repository files offer more flexibility and typically contain descriptions of the user interface elements (VRIXML files) in order to alter them even after the application is generated.

One of the selected requirements, determined in Sect. 2 was "In order to be useful, graphical tool support and assistance should be offered in order to design the high-level description models and check their correctness". To fulfill this requirement we created a development environment that supports the design process that was described in this section. The functionalities of this tool, together with a case study, will be presented in Sect. 4.

4   Model-Based IVE Development: Tool Support

In order to assess the practical use of the envisaged approach, presented in Sect. 3, we started with the development of a design tool, called CoGenIVE (Code Generation for Interactive Virtual Environments). This tool has been used to develop a case study, called VirtuaShop. The VirtuaShop application contains several states in which the user can navigate through the shop, select and drag objects into his shopping cart and check the properties of the products by means of the user interface elements.

The process that has been presented in section 3 describes an incremental top-down design and development process for IVE applications (Sel. Req. 1). The implementation of the presented approach for the realization of virtual environments is based on an event-driven framework that has been presented by De Boeck et al. [9]. This bottom-up approach allows gradual extension of the tool with additional high-level descriptions and models, while a basic version of the tool covers essential design development steps such as code generation.

As stated in the requirements gathered in Sect. 2 it is highly recommended to provide graphical tool support for a description language or model. In particular, when creating the **Presentation Model**, the graphical design of user interface elements is supported by CoGenIVE. Within the tool it is possible to *draw* the interface elements while the result is automatically saved in the VRIXML file-format (Sel. Req. 6).

The use of VRIXML offers more flexibility to the application designer since it becomes possible to alter the design and behavior of the user interface elements after the application has been created. In Fig. 2, a menu and a dialog are shown that are described by means of VRIXML.

Following the design of the presentation model, we extended CoGenIVE with the **Dialog Model**. Using this model, the designer can specify the different program states, the possible transitions between these states and the tasks available to the user in each of the states. The designer can also attach one of the created user interface elements to each of the states.

Figure 3 shows the state transition network that represents the VirtuaShop application. The application contains four modes and several of these modes have a user interface element attached to them in order to provide the necessary interaction.

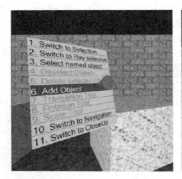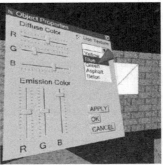

Fig. 2. VRIXML user interface elements

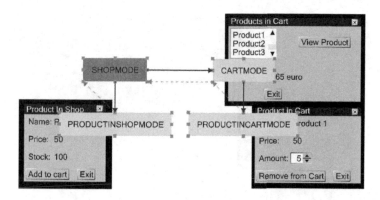

Fig. 3. VirtuaShop States (dialog model) and the connected UI elements (presentation model)

The next step in the development of our tool was supporting the *Code Generation Process*, based on the models (Sel. Req. 4). The generated application code is built upon an event-driven framework and it is possible to execute the application without further code editing. However, it is likely that the application developer has to perform some minor changes or add some application specific code. These adjustments can best be done with traditional software development tools and in order to support these post-generation adjustments, CoGenIVE generates a MS Visual C++ project file that can be used for further development. In order to support an iterative design process (Sel. Req. 2), we designed the tool in such a way that manual code changes are preserved whenever a model is updated and the application is regenerated (Sel. Req. 5).

5   Preliminary Results and Ongoing Work

The size of the VirtuaShop application is about 2500 lines of code of which 2000 lines are generated fully automatic. The other 500 lines contain the implementation of the interaction technique, certain dialog behavior and the implementation of the application specific tasks. The design of the application (requirements analysis, discussion and creation of the models in CoGenIVE) took about half a day and the manual implementation and debugging of the application details took another day and a half. So, in total the creation of the VirtuaShop application took about two days. In contrast, the development of such an application without the CoGenIVE tool could easily take up to two weeks.

In Fig. 4, screenshots of CoGenIVE, as well as the generated VirtuaShop application, are shown [1]. The application shows a shop product being *dragged* into the shopping cart. Since specification of interaction techniques is not yet supported by CoGenIVE, we had to implement them by hand. The majority of this code, however, will also be generated, once a suitable Interaction Description Model is developed and integrated within CoGenIVE (Sel. Req. 3).

---

[1] More screenshots and demonstration videos can be found at
http://research.edm.uhasselt.be/ ecuppens/CoGenIVE/

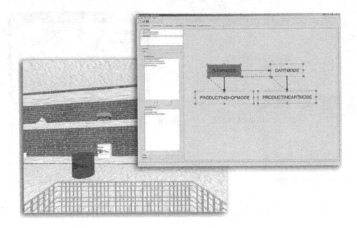

Fig. 4. VirtuaShop and CoGenIVE

Currently, we are evaluating some existing notations like InTml [11], ICon [10] and Statecharts, in order to find a notation that can serve as an Interaction Description Model.

In addition, we are extending CoGenIVE by integrating the ConcurTaskTree notation and the dialog model extraction algorithm described by Luyten et al. [13].

6   Conclusions

In this paper we have presented a model-based approach for the design of Interactive Virtual Environments, as well as the development of a tool that supports the envisioned design process. The tool, called CoGenIVE, is developed while keeping in mind several requirements that are typical for existing model-based design processes and VR tools or toolkits. As a case study for the tool we designed an interactive virtual shop. Early evaluations of CoGenIVE by means of VirtuaShop have shown that a large part of the application code can already be generated automatically based on the dialog and the presentation model of the application. The current version of CoGenIVE already meets most of the determined requirements but in order to maximize the amount of generated code some requirements still have to be implemented.

Acknowledgments

Part of the research at EDM is funded by EFRO (European Fund for Regional Development), the Flemish Government and the Flemish Interdisciplinary institute for Broadband technology (IBBT). The VR-DeMo project (IWT 030284) is directly funded by the IWT, a Flemish subsidy organization.

The authors would like to thank Tom De Weyer for his valuable contribution in the development of CoGenIVE and Tim Clerckx for his input on model-based user interface development techniques.

References

1. Michael Braitmaier, Manfred Weiler, and Thomas Ertl. Openmanip: An extensible cross-scene-graph framework for direct object manipulation. In *Proceedings of Eurographics Partner Event OpenSG 2003 - Concepts and Components of Software Frameworks for Interactive 3D Graphics*, pages 65–72, Darmstadt, Germany, April 1–2 2003.
2. Gaelle Calvary, Joëlle Coutaz, and David Thevenin. A unifying reference framework for the development of plastic user interfaces. In Murray Reed Little and Laurence Nigay, editors, *EHCI*, volume 2254 of *Lecture Notes in Computer Science*, pages 173–192, Toronto, Canada, May 10–14 2001. Springer.
3. Gaelle Calvary, Joëlle Coutaz, David Thevenin, Quentin Limbourg, Laurent Bouillon, and Jean Vanderdonckt. A unifying reference framework for multi-target user interfaces. *Interacting with Computers*, 15(3):289–308, 2003.
4. Tim Clerckx, Kris Luyten, and Karin Coninx. Dynamo-AID: a design process and a runtime architecture for dynamic model-based user interface development. In *Pre-Proceedings of EHCI-DSVIS'04*, pages 142–160, Tremsbüttle Castle, Hamburg, Germany, July 11–13 2004.
5. Conway, Pierce, Pausch, Steve Audia, Tommy Burnette, Dennis Cosgrove, Kevin Christiansen, Rob Deline, and et al. Alice: Lessons learned from building a 3D system for novices. In *Proceedings of CHI'2000*, pages 486–493, The Hague, The Netherlands, April 1–6 2000.
6. C. Cruz-Neira. *Virtual Reality Based on Multiple Projection Screens: The CAVE and its Applications to Computational Science and Engineering*. PhD thesis, University of Illinois, Chicago, May 1995.
7. C. Cruz-Neira, A. Bierbaum, P. Hartling, C. Just, and K. Meinert. Vr juggler - an open source platform for virtual reality applications. In *40th AIAA Aerospace Sciences Meeting and Exhibit 2002*, Reno, Nevada, January 2002.
8. Erwin Cuppens, Chris Raymaekers, and Karin Coninx. VRIXML: A user interface description language for virtual environments. In *Developing User Interfaces with XML: Advances on User Interface Description Languages*, pages 111–117, Gallipoli, Italy, May 2004.
9. Joan De Boeck, Chris Raymaekers, Erwin Cuppens, Tom De Weyer, and Karin Coninx. Task-based abstraction of haptic and multisensory applications. In *Proceedings of EuroHaptics 2004*, pages 174–181, Munchen, DE, 2004 June 5–7.
10. Pierre Dragicevic and Jean-Daniel Fekete. Input device selection and interaction configuration with ICon. In Ann Blanford, Jean Vanderdonckt, and Phil Gray, editors, *Proceedings of IHM-HCI 2001*, pages 443–448, Lille, France, 2001. Springer-Verlag.
11. Pablo Figueroa, Mark Green, and James H. Hoover. InTml: A description language for VR applications. In *Proceedings of Web3D 2002*, pages 53–58, Tampe, Arizona, USA, February 24–28 2002.
12. Christian Kulas, Christian Sandor, and Gudrun Klinker. Towards a development methodology for augmented reality user interfaces. In Emmanuel Dubois, Philip D. Gray, Daniela Trevisan, and Jean Vanderdonckt, editors, *MIXER*, volume 91 of *CEUR Workshop Proceedings*, 2004.
13. Kris Luyten, Tim Clerckx, Karin Coninx, and Jean Vanderdonckt. Derivation of a dialog model from a task model by activity chain extraction. In Joaquim A. Jorge, Nuno Jardim Nunes, and João Falcão e Cunha, editors, *Interactive Systems: Design, Specification, and Verification*, volume 2844 of *Lecture Notes in Computer Science*, pages 191–205. Springer, 2003.
14. Giulio Mori, Fabio Paternò, and Carmen Santoro. Design and development of multidevice user interfaces through multiple logical descriptions. *IEEE Transactions On Software Engineering*, 30(8):1 – 14, August 2004.

15. Fabio Paternò. *Model-Based Design and Evaluation of Interactive Applications*. Springer, 1999.
16. Paulo Pinheiro da Silva. User interface declarative models and development environments: A survey. In *Interactive Systems: Design, Specification, and Verification*, pages 207–226, Limerick, Ireland, UK, June 5–6 2000. 7th International Workshop, DSV-IS 2001, Springer-Verlag.
17. I. Poupyrev, S. Weghorst, M. Billinghurst, and T. Ichikawa. Egocentric object manipulation in virtual environments: Empirical evaluation of interaction techniques. In *Proceedings of EuroGraphics 1998*, Lisbon, Portugal, August 31 – September 4th 1998.
18. Angel R. Puerta. A model-based interface development environment. *IEEE Software*, 14(4):40–47, 1997.
19. Shamus Smith and David Duke. The hybrid world of virtual environments. *Computer Graphics Forum*, 18(3):297–308, September 1999.
20. Jean Vanderdonckt, Quentin Limbourg, Benjamin Michotte, Laurent Bouillon, Daniela Trevisan, and Murielle Florins. UsiXML: a user interface description language for specifying multimodal user interfaces. In *Proceedings of W3C Workshop on Multimodal Interaction 2004*, Sophia Antipolis, France, July 19–20 2004.
21. James Willans and Michael Harrison. A toolset supported approach for designing and testing virtual environment interaction techniques. *International Journal of Human-Computer Studies*, 55(2):145–165, August 2001.

Mapping ConcurTaskTrees into UML 2.0

Leonel Nóbrega[1], Nuno Jardim Nunes[1], and Helder Coelho[2]

[1] Department of Mathematics and Engineering, University of Madeira,
Campus da Penteada, 9000-390 Funchal, Portugal
{lnobrega,njn}@uma.pt
[2] Department of Informatics of the Faculty of Sciences,
University of Lisbon, Bloco C6, Piso 2, 1749-016 Lisboa, Portugal
hcoelho@di.fc.ul.pt

Abstract. ConcurTaskTrees (CTT) is one of the most widely used notations for task modeling, specifically tailored for user interface model-based design. The integration of CTT with a de facto standard modeling language was already identified as an important issue, but there is no consensus about the best approach to achieve this goal. The purpose of this paper is to examine the relative strengths and weaknesses of control and data flow specification in UML 2.0 Activity Diagrams to represent CTT semantics. The analysis is driven by the definition of pattern-based activities for the temporal operators in CTT. In this paper, we propose an extension of the UML 2.0 abstract syntax that fully supports the concepts behind CTTs and provides an adapted graphical notation for a UML-like representation.

1 Introduction

Task modeling is a central and familiar concept in human-computer interaction (HCI) but it is seldom used in object-oriented software engineering (OOSE). A task model details users' goals and the strategies adopted to achieve those goals, in terms of actions that users perform, the objects involved in those actions and the underlying sequencing of activities [1]. Task models capture the dialog model of interactions and are crucial for enabling model-based approaches for building interactive systems. The UML insufficiencies for interaction design are widely recognized [2, 3] and the integration of task model represent a step further in its limitations. The ConcurTaskTree notation, is one of the most widely used notations for task modeling, specifically tailored for model-based user interface design and its integration with UML has been already identified as a desirable goal.

Integrating CTT with UML can be generally achieved through the following approaches:

- Using the UML extension mechanisms (profiles), to represent elements and operators of a CTT model by an existing UML notation.
- Extending the UML metamodel, introducing a separate user task model, and establishing relationships between the CTT elements and existing UML elements.

The first solution is feasible and was already proposed in [2]. This approach represents CTT as stereotyped class diagrams. Constraints associated with UML class,

S.W. Gilroy and M.D. Harrison (Eds.): DSVIS 2005, LNCS 3941, pp. 237–248, 2006.

association and dependency stereotypes are defined to enforce the structural correctness of the CTT models. The major drawbacks to this proposal are the expressiveness of the notation and the semantic validation of the CTT temporal constraints in terms of UML class diagrams.

The second solution is outlined in [3] and covers the definition of UML for Interactive Systems. The approach proposed describes the integration points between UML models and task models in a complementary way. Yet, a unified integration at the semantic and notational levels should be provided in order for an effective incorporation of task models into UML.

In this paper we propose a different approach that enables the integration of CTT with UML through the extensions of UML 2.0 activity diagrams. Our approach takes advantage of the new characteristics of the UML 2.0 semantics, in particular the separation of statecharts and activity diagrams, which enables a better definition of the temporal operators underlying CTT, without compromising the usability of the notation. We strongly believe the enhancements in the UML 2.0 activity diagrams, finally enabled an effective integration of CTT into UML. The solution presented here could provide a common ground for effectively bringing task modeling into software engineering, promoting artifact interchange between tools and practitioners in SE and HCI.

The paper is organized as follows. Sections 2 and 3 briefly introduce ConcurTaskTrees and UML 2.0 Activity diagrams. Section 4 reports the evaluation of UML Activities Diagrams to express CTT semantics. Section 5 presents an extension of UML abstract syntax in order to support CTT concepts and the underlying notation. Finally, Sect. 6 concludes the paper.

2 Overview of ConcurTaskTrees

ConcurTaskTrees is a notation that has been developed by taking into account the previous experience in task modeling and adding new features in order to obtain an easy-to-use and powerful notation to describe the dialogue in interactive systems. CTTs are based on a graphical notation that supports the hierarchical structure of tasks, which can be interrelated through a powerful set of operators that describe the temporal relationships between subtasks. The formal semantics of the temporal relationships in CTT are defined using Labeled Transition System (LTS) formalism. In addition, CTTs allow designers to indicate a wide set of optional task attributes, such as category (how the task performance is allocated), type, manipulation of objects, frequency, and time requested for performance.

The CTT notation is supported by CTTE (the ConcurTaskTrees Environment), a set of freely available tools supporting editing and analysis of task models. The CTT notation is widely recognized as one of the most popular task notations in the HCI field, it is used for teaching and research purposes in several universities, and there is also evidence of usage in development projects. The CTT environment includes a simulator and a number of features enabling, for instance, designers to dynamically adjust and focus their attention on subsets of large task models, while analyzing large specifications.

Figure 1 illustrates a simple task model in CTT (provided in CTTE distribution). As we can see from the example, task models are represented in CTT as inverted trees (the task structure); each task can differ in type (user task, interactive task, abstract task and system task). The temporal relationship between subtasks at the same level is represented through lines annotated with the different temporal relationships. For a full description of CTT refer to [4].

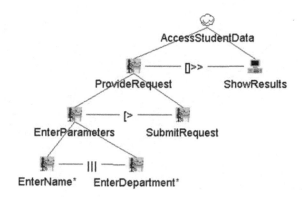

Fig. 1. Example of a ConcurTaskTree

3   Overview of UML 2.0 Activity Diagrams

Since the early versions of the standard, UML adopted Harel statecharts as the key notation to represent the dynamical aspects of software intensive systems. In addition, the UML 1.x versions also included activity diagrams, defined as a subset of statecharts. Activity diagrams have since become one of the key diagrams of the UML, in particular for business process modeling and user modeling [5].

Recognizing the problems with UML 1.x activity diagrams, in UML 2.0, activities where redesigned to follow "Petri-like" semantics thus separating activity diagrams from statecharts. Among other benefits, this widens the number of flows that can be modeled, especially those that have parallel flows of control [6]. The fundamental unit of behavior specification of an Activity Diagram is an Action. An action takes a set of inputs and converts them to a set of outputs, although either or both sets may be empty. There are three types of actions, namely:

1. Invocation Actions, used for performing operations calls, signal sending and accept event actions.
2. Read and Write Actions, for accessing and modifying objects and their values.
3. Computation actions, transforming input values into output.

Besides actions, an activity diagram can also contain control nodes, object nodes, activity edges and activity groups. In Fig. 2 we represent a subset of the UML 2.0 activity diagram notation, which is of particular interest to the discussion in this paper.

Among the possible activity groups we highlight the Interruptible Activity Region due to its intensive use in this paper. This type of group is described as an activity group that supports termination of tokens flowing in the portions of an activity [6]. The termination of all tokens occurs when a token leaves an interruptive region via an interrupting edge. A token transition is never partial; it is either complete or it does not happen at all [6].

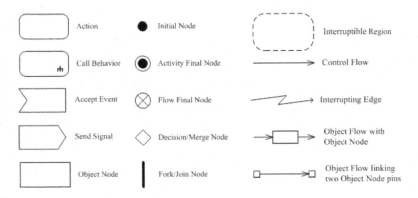

Fig. 2. UML 2.0 notation for Activity Diagrams

4   Mapping CTT into UML 2.0 Activity Diagrams

The analysis of the UML activity diagrams to represent CTT semantics is provided in terms of the behavior obtained by applying a temporal operator between two tasks. For the purpose of the evaluation of the approach described in this paper, one can consider atomic tasks (i.e., tasks that are not refined into subtasks) or composed tasks (resulting from application of temporal operators to subtasks). We highlight these definitions because they are slightly different from the original concepts in CTT. A CTT task is either an atomic task or the task resulting from applying a full sequence of operators to all sibling tasks. Furthermore, the composition of tasks (via temporal operators) requires a definition of starting and terminating conditions of composed tasks. For instance, in the following sequence T1|=|T2>>T3, the T3 task only becomes enabled either after termination of the T1 or T2 tasks (depending upon the selected order). This particular type of dependency between tasks implies that we have to express the start and termination of composed tasks in terms of the start and termination of the tasks being composed. In our UML 2.0 based approach we use signals to control the aforementioned conditions. We assume that an atomic task signals its own start and termination of execution. Hence, the composition of tasks must take into account the precedence of temporal operators. For instance, the sequence T1|||T2[>T3 must be considered as (T1|||T2)[>T3 and not as T1|||(T2[>T3). To prevent this problem, we consider the following sequence of operator precedence: >>, [>, |>, |||, |=|, [].

In our UML 2.0 approach, a CTT task is mapped into an Action, if it is atomic, and into a Call Behavior Action, otherwise. Finally, from the UML 2.0 semantics, a task is enabled if it possesses a token and is otherwise disabled.

In the following subsections we examine the UML semantics for each CTT temporal operator. All the operators descriptions used were taken from [7].

4.1 Independent Concurrency (T1 ||| T2)

Description. Actions belonging to two tasks can be performed in any order without any specific constraint.

Proposed UML 2.0 mapping. The independent concurrency is captured by a Fork node to create two independent flows of control for each task and a Join node to synchronize them. The start of the composed task T1|||T2 corresponds either to the start of T1 or of T2. This condition could be modeled using two Accept Event actions for the start signals of T1 and T2 and, once one of these actions succeeds, a signal Start T1|||T2 is produced, through a Send Signal action. An interruptible region is necessary because only one signal must be produced. The termination of the composed task occurs when both tasks signal their termination and must wait for both signals before sending a signal that corresponds to the termination of task T1|||T2.

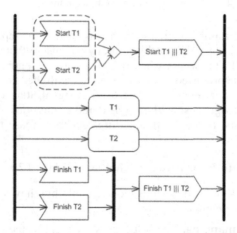

Fig. 3. UML specification for Independent Concurrency temporal operator

4.2 Choice (T1 [] T2)

Description. It is possible to choose from a set of tasks and, once the choice has been made, the task chosen can be performed; the other tasks are not available at least until the chosen task has been terminated.

Proposed UML 2.0 mapping. In this case both tasks must be enabled at the beginning but once one of them starts its execution the other must be disabled. This can

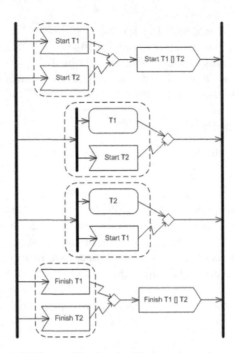

Fig. 4. UML specification for Choice temporal operator

modeled using an interruptible region with the task and an Accept Event action for the Start signal of the other task. Using this strategy we ensure that only one task is executed. The start of T1[]T2 occurs when one of the tasks sends its Start signal (only one Start signal will be produced). The same occurs with the task termination.

In Fig. 4, two Accept Event actions are used to signal Start T1 (and also to signal Start T2). In fact both signals should be considered as only one. This simplification is adopted here and in the following figures, in order to increase the readability of the diagrams.

4.3   Concurrency with Information Exchange (T1 | [] | T2)

Description. Two tasks can be executed concurrently but they have to synchronize in order to exchange information.

Proposed UML 2.0 mapping. The solution is identical to the one presented for the independent concurrency operator. Additionally, a Central Buffer node must be used for information exchange purposes.

4.4   Order Independence (T1 | = | T2)

Description. Both tasks have to be performed but when one is started then it has to be finished before starting the second one.

Proposed UML 2.0 mapping. The solution for this operator is similar to the choice operator. The difference is that when a task is disabled (due to the execution of the other), we must wait for the termination of the execution, before enabling the task again. Moreover, both tasks must be executed before the send of Finish T1|=|T2 signal.

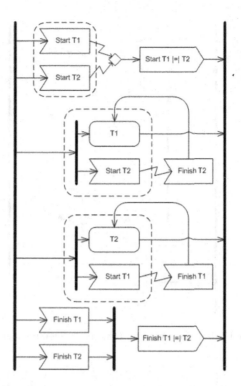

Fig. 5. UML specification for Order Independent temporal operator

4.5 Deactivation (T1 [> T2)

Description. The first task is definitively deactivated once the first action of the second task has been performed.

Proposed UML 2.0 mapping. If task T1 executes normally, T2 must be disabled after the completion of task T1. This case is ensured by grouping task T2 and an Accept Event action for Finish T1 signal in an interruptible region. The other case, when T2 aborts the execution of T1, is modeled using an interruptible region and an Accept Event action for Start T2 signal. Thus, if T2 starts its execution T1 will be interrupted. The start of T1[>T2 corresponds to the start of T1 or the start of T2 without starting T1. The termination corresponds to the termination of one of the two tasks.

4.6 Enabling (T1 >> T2)

Description. In this case one task enables a second one when it terminates.

Proposed UML 2.0 mapping. In this case a control flow is used to connect both tasks. The start of T1>>T2 corresponds to the start of T1 and the termination corresponds to the termination of T2.

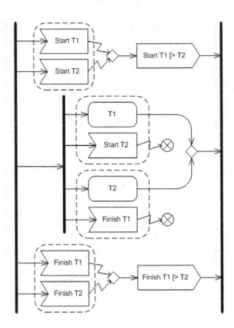

Fig. 6. UML specification for Deactivation temporal operator

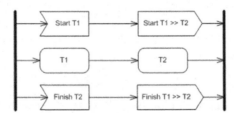

Fig. 7. UML specification for Enabling temporal operator

4.7 Enabling with Information Passing (T1 []>> T2)

Description. In this case task T1 provides some information to task T2 other than enabling it.

Proposed UML 2.0 mapping. Similar to the enabling operator, assuming, in this case, an object flow between tasks T1 and T2.

4.8 Suspend-Resume (T1 |> T2)

Description: This operator gives T2 the possibility of interrupting T1 and when T2 is terminated, T1 can be reactivated from the state reached before the interruption.

Proposed UML 2.0 mapping: There is no evidence in the UML 2.0 specification that any behavior supports the resume functionality. Therefore, this operator is not supported by existing UML semantics.

4.9   Iteration (T*)

Description. The task is performed repetitively.

Proposed UML 2.0 mapping. This unary operator has a straightforward mapping in UML. The Start signal occurs at first execution of task T1 and a flow loop is created for task T1.

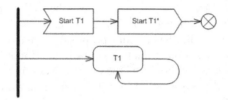

Fig. 8. UML specification for Iteration operator

4.10   Finite Iteration (T1(n))

Description. It is used when designers know in advance how many times a task will be performed.

Proposed UML 2.0 mapping. A finite iteration can be mapped into UML using a local variable for counting the iterations. The start of the iteration begins with the first execution of task T1 and termination is signaled after n occurrences of the Finish T1 signal. We use in this case an exception rule to the normal execution in Activities—if an AcceptEventAction has no incoming edges, then the action starts when the containing activity or structured node does. In addition, an AcceptEventAction with no incoming edges is always enabled to accept events, no matter how many such events it accepts [6].

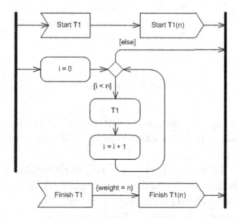

Fig. 9. UML specification for Finite Iteration operator

5 An UML Notation for ConcurTaskTrees

In the previous section we described how the new UML 2.0 standard can successfully support the CTT semantics by taking advantage of the redesigned activity diagrams. However, even a simple task tree results in very complex sets of activities with a remarkable number of actions and control nodes. This is a well-known problem with statechart-like notations: they become unreadable as the number of states increases. Although semantically correct, the previously described UML mappings to the CTT temporal operators will be completely useless even for a simple task model. This was one of the major problems with the previous proposals to map CTTs into the UML: in order to propose a useful solution to the mapping of temporal relationships one would compromise the semantic correctness and the other way around.

The existing graphical representation for CTTs, based on a hierarchical structure, is one of the most significant factors of its success. The hierarchical structure reflects the logical approach of most designers, allowing the description of a rich set of possibilities that is both highly declarative, and generates compact descriptions [4]. In what follows we propose to solve this problem with a small increment to the UML abstract syntax. With this approach the concepts required for modeling CTTs can be added to the UML. In the following figures we detail this original approach to extend the UML abstract syntax.

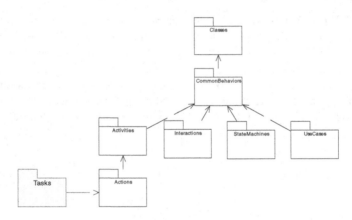

Fig. 10. Package dependencies

As we can see from Fig. 10, in order to isolate the extensions from the actual UML specification, we create a new Package named Tasks to contain the new concepts required for task modeling.

Figures 11 and 12 detail the Task package. We introduce three new concepts: TaskTree as a specialization of the Activity concept; Task for modeling the concept of task; and TaskEdge for modeling temporal operators. These new concepts allow the creation of a specialized type of Activity Diagrams for modeling task trees (we name these diagrams Task Tree Diagrams).

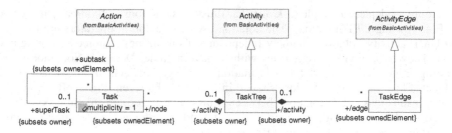

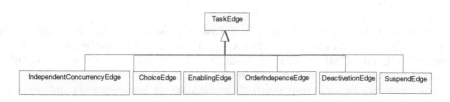

Fig. 11. Tasks Package

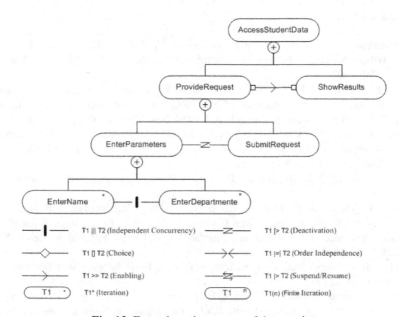

Fig. 12. Tasks Operators

In order to ease connection with the existing UML 2.0 notation, we decided to maintain a very close relationship between the new task concepts and the existing activity diagrams. Figure 13 illustrates the extension to the UML 2.0 abstract syntax and provides an example for each of the previously described temporal relationships.

Fig. 13. Example and summary of the notation

Figure 13 depicts a simple task tree that illustrates our approach (already presented in Fig. 1, using CTT notation). The notation used for temporal operators are inspired by UML activity notations, namely Independent Concurrency, Choice and Deactivation. They have obvious similarities with Fork/Join Node, Decision Node and Interrupting Edge, respectively. For information exchange between tasks, we adopt the Object Flow and Pin notation shown in the link between ProvideRequest and ShowResults tasks. The relations between a task and its refinement subtasks are inspired by the notation for showing a Package and its contents in the same diagram, providing an adequate hierarchical representation.

6 Conclusions

We showed in this paper that the ConcurTaskTrees semantics can be expressed in terms of UML Activities semantics, allowing a truly unified integration of task model concepts within the UML framework, fostering co-evolutionary development of interactive systems, providing a common ground to effectively bring task modeling into software engineering and promoting artifact interchange between tools and practitioners in SE and HCI. The Petri-net like semantics of UML 2.0 Activities represents a clear improvement over previous versions thus bringing this new opportunity to integrate CTT with UML. The extensions and the adapted notation described here keep the expressiveness and effectiveness of CTT's notation and reduce the difficulty of acceptance of another notation. Finally, activity-based semantics for CTTs can take full advantage of existing work on verification and execution of activities diagrams and promotes the inclusion of task modeling in model-based approaches.

References

1. van Harmelen, M., Artim, J., Butler, K., Henderson, A., Roberts, D., Rosson, M. B., Tarby, J. C., Wilson, S.; Object Models in User Interface Design, 29(4), SIGCHI Bulletin, New York, ACM, 1997
2. Nunes, N. J., Cunha, J. F.: Towards a UML profile for interactive systems development: the Wisdom approach, in Proceedings of UML´2000 Conference, Kent – UK, A. Evans, S. Kent, B. Selic (Eds.), Springer Verlag LNCS 1939, New York (2000) pp. 101–116
3. Paternò, F: Towards a UML for Interactive Systems, in Proceedings of Engineering for Human-Computer Interaction HCI'2001, LNCS 2254, pp. 7–18, M. Reed Little, L. Nigay (Eds.), Springer Verlag (2001).
4. Paternò, F: Model-Based Design and Evaluation of Interactive Applications, Springer Verlag (1999)
5. Patricio, L., Cunha, J. F., Fisk, R., Nunes, N. J.: Designing Interaction Experiences for Multi-Platform Service Provision with Essential Use Cases in Proceedings of the 9th international conference on Intelligent user interface: Short Papers, Funchal, Madeira, Portugal pp. (2004) pp. 298-300
6. OMG: UML 2.0 Superstructure Specification, Revised Final Adopted Specification (ptc/04-10-02) October 8 (2004)
7. Mori, G., Paternò, F., Santoro, C.: CTTE: Support for Developing and Analysing Task Models for Interactive System Design, IEEE Transactions on Software Engineering, Vol. 28, No. 8, IEEE Press, (2002) pp. 797-813

Goal-Oriented Design of Domain Control Panels

Christophe Ponsard[1], Nadiya Balych[2], Philippe Massonet[1],
Jean Vanderdonckt[2], and Axel van Lamsweerde[2]

[1] CETIC Research Center, Charleroi, Belgium
[2] Université Catholique de Louvain, Belgium

Abstract. Goal-oriented methodologies have demonstrated some adequacy for modelling composite systems, from high level desired properties to operational requirements on responsible agents. This paper shows how to derive a user interface for human agents from such a model, especially with respect to the monitor and control capabilities of those agents. A goal-oriented widget taxonomy was elaborated in order to facilitate selecting widgets that are appropriate for each element of the underlying domain model. A user-friendly tool for building user interfaces, supporting the retrieval of adequate components and their fine tuning at a graphical level, was developed and deployed on the animator of the Objectiver/FAUST requirements toolbox.

1   Introduction

For many years, Model-Based Interface Development Environments (MB-IDEs) have been largely driven and inspired by the same suite of typical models such as: task, domain, user, abstract user interface, concrete user interface, final user interface, platform, etc. [17][2]. Among these, two classic models typically initiate the development process: the domain and task models. The former has been largely used during the past decade to automatically generate a graphical user interface. The later was defined to address some shortcomings. Today, it represents the most common model that drives the development process to foster user-centered design. These models have demonstrated some relevance, some convenience, and some efficiency in producing user interfaces for a very specific type of interactive system: information systems, where the User Interface (UI) mainly consists of a predefinition of forms, windows, menu bars, pull-down menus, etc. Typical information systems could be developed in Interface Builders such as Microsoft Visual Basic, C++, Java or Web applications. Traditional MB-IDEs have demonstrated the feasibility of the approach for such systems.

But when it comes to developing the UI of a complex, reliable system that is not an information system (e.g., a control system, a simulator), in particular when the UI cannot consist of predefined widgets with a predefined behavior, it seems more difficult to reuse the same suite of models. Since in this case these models have not been expanded enough to capture sufficient information to initiate the development process, perhaps other models need to be used.

In addition, the task model is widely recognized and used in the Human-Computer Interaction (HCI) community, whereas the Software Engineering (SE) and more specifically Requirements Engineering (RE) community, tends to ignore such a model and

S.W. Gilroy and M.D. Harrison (Eds.): DSVIS 2005, LNCS 3941, pp. 249–260, 2006.
© Springer-Verlag Berlin Heidelberg 2006

rather prefer to exploit models that are more traditionally used in their field. This paper investigates whether the shortcomings of most MB-IDEs for complex, reliable, time constrained interactive systems could be developed following a model-based approach, but based on another suite of models than those which are traditionally used in HCI.

In particular, the task model usually represents in HCI the user's viewpoint by recursively decomposing the task into sub-tasks that are connected with temporal operators to end up with leaf tasks. Of course, each task is associated with one or several goals that need to be achieved when the task has been carried out. In contrast, in RE, a goal model represents the system's viewpoint by specifying a decomposition of goals into sub-goals that are linked together with several operators to end up with leaf goals assigned to an agent.

As in HCI, the initial goal model does not come alone. It is then related to three other models that progressively capture relevant information for the other aspects: object model, agent model, and operation model (Sect. 2). These models are frequently used in the area of RE which provides capabilities to reason about human agent interface design with respect to the requirements under its responsibility (Sect. 3). Therefore, when it comes to specifying the components of the final user interfaces, i.e. the widgets to be used, instead of having a widget classification that is based on the task and/or the domain, the widget ontology should also be revisited. It should provide a rich framework to select the most appropriate combination of displays/controls for each agent to realize its goals (Sect. 4). Then, an animator should provide agent-oriented animations in the same way as the task can be simulated in traditional MB-IDEs [14][1] (Sect. 5). Finally, related work will be reviewed to highlight the contribution and limitations of our approach.

Throughout this paper, a non-trivial train system will be used as running example. Although simplified for fitting the size constraints of this paper, this system is based on implementations taken from real world railway signaling systems.

2   Background: Goal-Oriented Modeling

This paper considers goal-oriented modelling with the KAOS language which is organised in 4 models: (i) the central model is the *goal model* which captures and structures the assumed and required properties; (ii) the *object model* captures the relevant vocabulary to express the goals; (iii) the *agent model* takes care of assigning goals to agents in a realizable way; (iv) the *operation model* details, at state transitions level, the work an agent has to perform to reach the goals he is responsible for.

2.1   Building the Goal and the Object Models

Although the process of building those 4 models is intertwined, the starting point is usually a number of key properties of the system to-be. Those are expressed using *goals* which are statements of intent about some system (existing or to-be) whose satisfaction in general requires the cooperation of some of the agents forming that system. *Agents* are active components, such as humans, devices, legacy software or software-to-be components, that play some role towards goal satisfaction. Some agents thus define

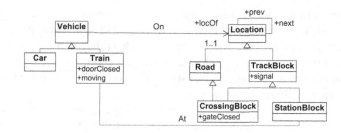

Fig. 1. Object Model

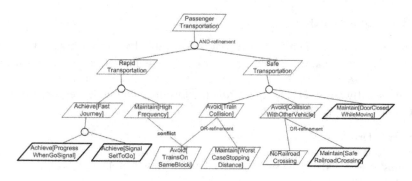

Fig. 2. Portion of the Goal graph

the software whereas the others define its environment. Goals may refer to services to be provided (functional goals) or to the quality of service (non-functional goals). Goals are described informally in natural language (InformalDef) and are optionally formalized in a real-time temporal logic (FormalDef) [3][8][12].

In our example, the goals relate to safety of transportation: avoiding collision between trains, with other vehicles (especially at railroad crossings), securing passenger (eg., by closing doors when moving). This goal can be stated as follows:

Goal Maintain[DoorsClosedWhileMoving]
    InformalDef: Doors should be closed when the train is moving.
    FormalDef: $(\forall tr : Train)\ tr.moving \Rightarrow tr.doorClosed$

In the above formulation, we have identified the *Train* entity with its *moving* and *doorClosed* attributes. Those are incrementally added to the structural model which captures passive (entities, relationships and events) and active objects (agents).

Unlike goals, *domain properties* are descriptive statements about the environment, such as physical laws, organizational norms or policies, etc. (eg., a train requires some distance to come to stop—law of inertia).

A key characteristic of goal-oriented requirements engineering is that *goals* are structured and that guidance is provided to discover that structure and refine it until agents can be found to realize those goals in cooperation. In KAOS, *goals* are organized in AND/OR refinement-abstraction hierarchies where higher-level goals are in general strategic, coarse-grained and involve multiple agents whereas lower-level goals are in general technical, fine-grained and involve fewer agents [4]. In such structures, *AND-refinement* links relate a goal to a set of subgoals (called refinement) possibly conjoined with *domain properties*; this means that satisfying all subgoals in the refinement is a sufficient condition in the domain for satisfying the goal. *OR-refinement* links may relate a goal to a set of alternative refinements.

Figure 2 shows the goal structure for our system. It was set up starting from a few initial goals and by asking respectively "WHY" and "HOW" questions to discover parent goals (such as *Maintain[SafeTransportation]*) and son goals (such as *Maintain[DoorClosedWhileMoving]*).

2.2   The Agent Model

Goal refinement ends when every subgoal is realizable by some individual *agent* assigned to it, that is, expressible in terms of conditions that are monitorable and controllable by the agent [10]. A *requirement* is a terminal goal under responsibility of an agent in the software-to-be; an *expectation* is a terminal goal under responsibility of an agent in the environment. For example:

Agent TrainDriver
  Kind: Human
  ResponsibleFor: Maintain[DoorClosedWhileMoving], Achieve[TrainProgress...
  Monitors: *Block.signal*
  Controls: *Train.moving, Train.doorClosed, Train.blockOf*

In our design, all agents are part of the automated system except the train driver, a human which stays in control of the moving state and the location of the train. The *door and motor controllers* are running on board of the train, while the *signal controller* and the *gate controller* are ground-based. In our case study, a very important problem to reason about is the way to relay ground and board information w.r.t their monitor/control needs. Figure 3 shows the *agent interface view* which displays the flow of monitored/controlled information among agents.

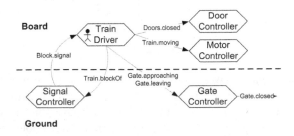

Fig. 3. Agent Interface Model

2.3   The Operation Model

Goals are operationalized into specifications of operations to achieve them [3]. An *operation* is an input-output relation over objects; operation applications define state transitions along the behaviors prescribed by the goal model. The specification of an operation is classical with precondition (necessary), postcondition (target state) and trigger condition (sufficient). An important distinction is also made between (descriptive) domain pre/postconditions and (prescriptive) pre-, post- and trigger conditions required for achieving some underlying goal(s). For example, the *OpenDoors* operation may be specified as follows:

Operation OpenDoors
  Input: tr:Train/doorClosed
  Output: tr:Train/doorClosed
  DomPre: $tr.doorClosed$
  DomPost: $\neg tr.doorClosed$
  ReqPre: for $SafeRailroadCrossing \; \neg tr.moving$
  ReqTrig: for $FastPassengerTransfert \; (\exists st : Station) \; at(tr, st)$

A goal operationalization is a set of such specifications. For example, to be complete, our operationalization of the goal *DoorClosedWhileMoving* would also require to strengthen the *StartTrain* operation.

3 Overview of the Panel Design Process

Designing a control panel from a correctly refined and operationalized model can be done in a systematic way as the model, and more specifically the agent sub-model, captures all the relevant information. The overall process is the following:

- For each human agent in the goal model, retrieve all the requirements under his responsibility
- For each human agent in the agent model, identify all the information he has to monitor and to control w.r.t the realization of those requirements.
- For each human agent in the in the operation model, identify the operation(s) under the performance of that agent and through which he may affect controlled elements.
- For each monitored element, select an appropriate *display* widget and map it on the monitored element.
- For each controlled element, select an appropriate *control widget* and map it on the related operation(s).

In our example, the *TrainDriver* is responsible for the goal *Maintain [DoorClosed-WhileMoving]*. The agent model shows he has to control both the *doorClosed* state and the *moving* state. The *TrainDriver* is also responsible for other goals such as *Maintain[ProgressWhenGoSignal]* and *Maintain[StopOnRedSignal]* which requires the ability to monitor *Signal* and again to control the *moving* state. For the controlled part: *doorClosed* and *moving* are boolean attributes whose control is achieved through the *Start/Stop* and *OpenDoors/CloseDoors* pair of operations. In this case, an adequate control widget is a two-state switch for which each transition has a corresponding operation in the model. It also provides feedback on the controlled state.

As human agents are limited in many ways, it is important to check for the effective monitorability/controlability of the considered information. *Lack of monitorability* may be caused by limitation in perception capabilities (eg. danger of missing/misinterpreting track information at high speed), limited focus (eg. looking at track signals and on-train controls), etc. *Lack of controllability* may be caused by limitation in response time (eg. emergency braking at high speed), high load, etc. Those specific properties can be taken into account when reasoning about the realizability of the design of the system using a number of available techniques (obstacle[20], agents tactics[10]). For example, when reasoning about the monitorability of block occupation, direct physical perception of track signals is only possible at low speed. High speed would be an obstacle which can be resolved by a more elaborate system design, with in-cabin reporting and relying on ground-cabin communications. *Human agents can also forget things and make mistakes*: the KAOS framework can model and reason about this using knows/belief predicates in goal formulations. The reasoning can be done directly, at refinement time, or more preferably later, using obstacle analysis[20] performed on an ideal model to evaluate possible consequences and mitigate them.

4   Building the Widget Taxonomy

In order to facilitate the design of interactive panels with respect to the underlying goal model, several real-world control panels were studied in a number of domains such as transportation, industrial control and domestic use. They helped in the definition of a widget taxonomy in terms of goals (being able to monitor/control state, to report dangers, etc.) instead of directly being focused on data or tasks. So far, several widget taxonomies have been investigated, but based on other models such as domain model [21] or a task model [13]. In those existing taxonomies, widgets are classified according to the underlying data or domain model they can manipulate, but do not differ whether the data are involved as input, output, or w.r.t their impact on system goal. Rather, in the present taxonomy, it is possible to directly map the previously identified goals and sub-goals (especially the leaf goals) to the widget they can best represent.

The resulting taxonomy is partially shown in Fig. 4. It is structured much in the same spirit as a KAOS model: the first level of the classification is a generic model capturing the goals the UI should address. Each goal is refined until relevant widget classes are identified. Those are then structured based on a more traditional data type hierarchy. At the bottom of the figure, some typical instances are illustrated.

In the resulting taxonomy, a number of *conceptual attributes* were identified such as display/control/alarm kind (goal level) and the type of data shown (data level). Based on the study of several widget instances, a number of *graphical attributes*, not part of the taxonomy, were also identified: those help in tuning the visual aspect: layout, divisions, labels, units, etc. For the speedometer dial shown on the left of Fig. 5, conceptual attributes are: display modality, continuous data range; graphical attributes are: angular layout, subdivisions, unit. All those features are captured by a single concept which is the "computer version" of that widget and of other "dial" widgets sharing the same conceptual attributes. It is implemented by a corresponding class. In this work, the Java language was used together with a JavaBeans interfacing mechanism and the Swing graphical toolkit.

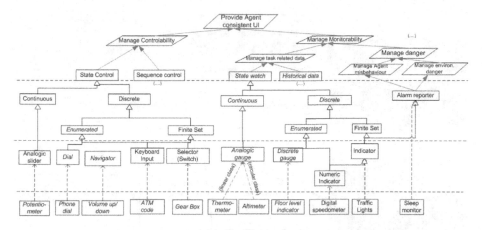

Fig. 4. Widget Taxonomy

Fig. 5. Physical (left) and modeled (right) dials from various domains

5   Deployment on a Requirements Animator

An important aspect of using models from the beginning of the development process, especially for complex systems like interactive monitoring and supervision systems, is the capability to execute the elicited models in some way to animate a first version of the future system for validation purpose. So, it is crucial that the underlying models are expressive enough to obtain a running interface. For instance, the Visual Task Model Builder [1] mainly exploits the task model to animate the ordering of tasks in time. This is certainly interesting but is not detailed enough to obtain a working prototype that is executable enough to demonstrate non-trivial interaction sessions. Similarly in CTTE [14], it is possible to animate the task model to see possible orderings of tasks in time, but the task model is not expressive enough to demonstrate a complete executing of a task. For this purpose, we wanted to exploit all underlying models as exposed in Section 2 to obtain an animator that is really working without coding or modeling more aspects.

The FAUST requirements animator supports the animation of KAOS goal-oriented models [19], [16], [18]. Relying on the Objectiver RE platform[15], the FAUST animator helps in the design of the system model, by the ability to generate and replay execution traces and in the validation, by allowing domain experts to interact with an executable model using a familiar UI. The existing animator supports the compilation of operationalized goal-models into finite state machines (FSM) which are then run in a simulator engine on a server. Several client actors can then connect on that simulator to

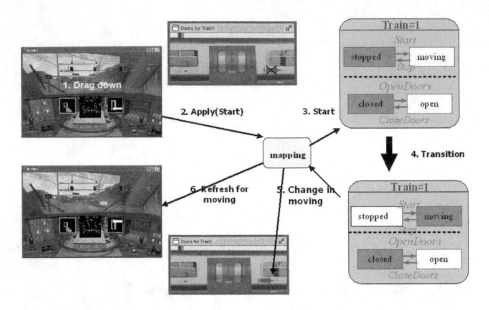

Fig. 6. An Animation Scenario

interact with the model in a multi-user way, enabling interesting validation scenarios to be played. The animator is complemented by a monitor which reports goal violations.

Presently, the animator suffers from a three important shortcomings: (1) the lack of control using domain specific interfaces, (2) the lack of consistent agent-based UI (currently an animator actor is not specially bound to an agent in the model, it may not give enough monitor/control or too much) and (3) the lack of a support for the development of such interfaces.

The first and second points were addressed in the previous sections. On the tool side, the composition and mapping is supported by a visual tool allowing the animation designer to assemble the panel by performing queries on the widget library for mapping each relevant variable. The tool was implemented in Java with the Swing graphical library. It supports composition by drag-and-drop of components on the panel. A JavaBeans based property editor is available for instantiating the available widgets and tuning their graphical rendering. A number of common widgets are also proposed for domains such as automotive, railroad, aerospace and industrial control.

The integration within the animator is achieved using a mapping component which manages the consistency between the underlying conceptual model (ie. states and transitions of the generated FSM) and the UI (controls and displays) of the animation. To achieve maximal flexibility, it can be defined at type level and tuned at instance level. The mapping is fully described in [19] and can be roughly summarized as follows:

- *Display widgets* are mapped on state elements (which are also linked to instances of the object model). The type of the widget and the underlying state should be compatible.

- *Control widgets* are mapped on an operation which is applied when a user action is performed. The performer is the human agent associated with the enclosing panel. Operation arguments are derived from the input capabilities of the widget (eg., rate of acceleration) and from other observable states (eg., current speed used as set point for a cruise control). Additional constraints can also be expressed using instance information (eg., speed applies to train controlled by the agent).

Figure 6 shows a typical animation scenario in two steps, respectively at top and bottom of the figure. The control panel, the lateral view of the train and the FSM instances are displayed from left to right. The user playing the "driver" role makes a request to start the train (1). It is forwarded to the simulator (2,3) which accepts it (the guard being enabled because doors are closed). After the resulting transition (4), the train is now moving and a state refresh is triggered on the control panel (speedometer) and the lateral view ("forward" arrow) (5,6).

In the above scenario, note that if the doors were opened when requesting the start, that user action would have been rejected. This could also be signalled at the UI level using information widgets. This is an interesting feature for modelling automated backup mechanisms behind a human agent.

6   Related Work

FAUST and its animator, as outlined in this paper, mainly differs from existing MB-IDE approaches in the sense that four models are borrowed from requirements engineering. Therefore, these models address functional (FR) and non-functional requirements (NFR) in the different models as opposed to solely some NFR in task-based approaches. For instance, it is possible in FAUST to automatically execute the underlying models to obtain a genuine dialog whereas in traditional MB-IDEs, this dialog model should be generated from the task model, which represents a complex task. Furthermore, FAUST is based on all types of requirements, whereas traditional MB-IDEs mainly focus on user's viewpoint and requirements, such as portability, usability, etc. They decompose the task into sub-tasks, but without considering seriously FR such as domain constraints, robustness, reliability, performance, avoiding of conflict. Such properties are automatically obtained by construction and by generation in the FAUST process, whereas they usually need to be done by hand in MB-IDEs, based on the existing models [21].

Most animations exploit the task model [1] [13], whereas FAUST exploits all four models. Other animation approaches combine system modelling and domain-based visualization:

- *State-machines based* approaches, such as in Statecharts or UML state diagrams. Tools like Statemate and Rhapsody allow those FSM to be executed and coupled with graphical views. Recent work in the area explores reactive animations [5] in order to combine and merge efforts in reactive design (using statecharts) and animation techniques (such as Flash). Our approach has a similar purpose but focuses more on earlier steps: our FSM are less structured but are consistent with goals. Both approaches and tools look essentially complementary and definitively worth combining.

- *Tabular-based* approaches, such as SCR and RSML and supported with tools like SCR-toolset [7] and SpecTRM [9]. They focus on the system and model the input-output relation with a number of tables. The SCR animator has a visual composer with a library of display and control widgets which can be mapped on table variables. However the SCR library lacks a conceptual structure.
- *Labeled transition system (LTS)*. LTSA, an LTS animator relies on scenebeans, a descriptive XML-based animation framework [11]. It provides low level animation primitives (similar to SVG or Flash) which are easy to deploy and reuse even with other underlying modelling languages.
- In existing MB-IDEs approaches, the model that is usually chosen for representing the dialog, such as a state-transition diagram, a statechart or a Petri net, should be added and constructed by exploiting merely the task model, which leaves the problem typically underspecified. It is therefore the responsibility of the designer to manually choose the right design options and to tweak the dialog model to obtain a version that is detailed enough to work.

The above approaches are based on operational specifications and lack the ability to capture the goals, model the environment or reason about agents. Another goal-oriented approach is Formal Tropos which also has an animator but without visualization capabilities [6].

Finally note the focus in this work is on the the design of display/control panels for control systems—other approaches attempt to be more generic.

7   Conclusion and Future Work

In this paper, we exposed how goal models, borrowed from requirements engineering, can help in the design of control panels by providing a property driven paradigm as alternative to traditional data-oriented or task-oriented paradigms. A method to design consistent control panel user interfaces from goal models was proposed as well as a goal-oriented widget library to assemble them. The result has then been deployed on a requirements animator as a tool for designing agent-oriented animations. The work has been tested on a number of case studies such as a baggage lockers and a safety injection system. It is now being validated on a larger industrial case: a floor door system for an automated train.

FAUST and its animator mainly differ from existing MB-IDEs in that they exploit models borrowed from Requirements Engineering to produce a fully executable UI. In this way, we can also say that the underlying models are executable and dynamic, but they are also more expressive to the point that the dialog and a complete animation can be automatically generated. In addition, it is possible in existing MB-IDEs to apply model-checking techniques to verify properties of interest, such as IFIP Dialog principles, but they need to be run by a human operator. In contrast, here, there is no direct need to rely of these techniques because the resulting interface satisfies the FR and NFR by construction. It is impossible to produce a UI that is not compliant with the constraints imposed by the various models. In the case the requirements were somehow flawed/incorrect in the first place, the goal-directed methodology provides means to detect that because a conflict or inconsistency is likely to become apparent as the refinement/agent assignment/operationalization process would fail at some point. Finally, the most interesting difference is that the first model, i.e. the goal model, contains both FR and NFR intertwined, as opposed to user goals only in traditional task-based models.

In the end, both approaches should not be presented as alternatives but rather as complementary: the focus is here more upstream in the design process and based on property refinement rather than task refinement. The resulting operation model can be seen as a task model which can be handled by standard HCI techniques. The benefit of using the presented RE-based approach is the access to interesting reasoning techniques about the system, its environment and the interactions across their borderlines which impact the UI. This calls for a more in-depth comparison of HCI and RE approaches and the ways they can cross-fertilize.

At short term, we envision to address a number of limitations. Currently, our work focuses mainly on control systems with agents responsible for a small part of the system. We would like to support supervising agents which have global monitoring/control capabilities on the system (eg., train dispatcher). Better structuring mechanisms are also needed for mapping more elaborated data type and helping in the reuse of preassembled sub-panels. We also plan to provide an integration of the goal monitor to reports alarms at interface level.

Acknowledgement

This work is financially supported by the European Union (ERDF and ESF) and the Walloon Region (DGTRE).

References

1. M. Biere, Birgit Bomsdorf, and Gerd Szwillus. The visual task model builder. In *Chapter 20, in Proceedings of CADUI'99*.
2. G. Calvary, J. Coutaz, D. Thevenin, Q. Limbourg, L. Bouillon, and J. Vanderdonckt. A unifying reference framework for multi-target user interfaces. *Interacting with Computers*, 15(3), June 2003.
3. A. Dardenne, A. van Lamsweerde, and Stephen Fickas. Goal-directed requirements acquisition. *Science of Computer Programming*, 20(1-2):3–50, 1993.
4. R. Darimont and A. van Lamsweerde. Formal refinement patterns for goal-driven requirements elaboration. In *4th FSE ACM Symposium, San Francisco, 1996*.
5. S. Efroni, D. Harel, and I. Cohen. Reactive animation. In *Proc. 1st Int. Symposium on Formal Methods for Components and Objects (LNCS 2852)*, 2002.
6. A. Fuxman, L. Liu, M. Pistore, M. Roveri, and P. Traverso. Specifying and analysing early requirements in tropos. *Requirements Engineering Journal*, 2004.
7. C. Heitmeyer, J. Kirby, and B. Labaw. Tools for formal specification, verification, and validation of requirements. In *Proc. COMPASS '97, Gaithersburg, 1997*.
8. R. Koymans. *Specifying message passing and time-critical systems with temporal logic, LNCS 651*. Springer-Verlag, 1992.
9. G. Lee, J. Howard, and P. Anderson. Safety-critical requirements specification and analysis using spectrm. In *Proc. 2nd Meeting of the US Soft. Syst. Safety WG, 2002*.

10. E. Letier and A. van Lamsweerde. Agent-based tactics for goal-oriented requirements elaboration, 2002.
11. J. Magee, N. Pryce, D. Giannakopoulou, and J. Kramer. Graphical animation of behavior models. In *Proc. ICSE'2000, Limerick*, 2000.
12. Z. Manna and A. Pnueli. *The Reactive Behavior of Reactive and Concurrent System.* Springer-Verlag, 1992.
13. G. Mori, F. Paternó, and C. Santoro. Design and development of multi-device user interfaces through multiple logical descriptions. *IEEE TSE*, 30(8), August 2004.
14. F. Paternó. Model-based design and evaluation of interactive applications. In *Springer Verlag*, November 1999.
15. The Objectiver RE platform. http://www.objectiver.com.
16. C. Ponsard, P. Massonet, A. Rifaut, J.F. Molderez, A. van Lamsweerde, and H. Tran Van. Early verification and validation of mission critical systems. In *8th FMICS Workshop, Linz*, 2004.
17. A.R. Puerta. A model-based interface development environment. *IEEE Software*, 14(4), July/August 1997.
18. The FAUST toolbox. http://faust.cetic.be, 2004.
19. H. Tran Van, A. van Lamsweerde, P. Massonet, and C. Ponsard. Goal-oriented requirements animation. In *12th IEEE Int.Req.Eng.Conf., Kyoto*, September 2004.
20. A. van Lamsweerde and E. Letier. Handling obstacles in goal-oriented requirements engineering. *IEEE Transactions on Software Engineering, Special Issue on Exception Handling*, 26(10), October 2000.
21. J. Vanderdonckt. Advice-giving systems for selecting interaction objects. In *Proc. of 1st Int. Workshop on UI to Data Intensive Systems, Edimburgh*, 1999.

Future Challenges of Model-Based Design

Sandra Basnyat, Joan De Boeck, Erwin Cuppens, Leonel Nóbrega,
Francisco Montero, Fabio Paternò, and Kevin Schneider

When we consider models in model-based design (MBD) approaches in the HCI field, we can say that the first generation of tool for user interface construction was based on database models. The second generation of MBD approaches includes models such as the user model, task model, cognitive model, system model etc. However, the third generation of models is the one facing current and future challenges. In this summary report, we present our discussion on the future challenges of MBD.

We begin by discussing users, which are complex entities that must be considered in User Centred Design (UCD) approaches and in MBD approaches. Much of their behaviour can impact the models they are represented in. Emotions can change the way people perform tasks for example. Users are not perfect, not always predictable and can perform in an erroneous manner. MBD is usually considered from an error-free perspective however boundaries much be extended to account for errors. Since we are dealing with humans to achieve UCD, we are dealing with fuzzy information, emotions, behaviour, actions etc. These types of information are difficult to capture in the models we are creating. To what extent are we able to model quality aspects of UI design and incorporate experience in models, or should we accept that there are limitations in MBD approaches. How can we obtain more aesthetically pleasing UIs by extending the use of models?

In the field of software engineering, MBD approaches are a big success. For example, UML is widely accepted. However there seems to be a gap between models used in software engineering and MBD approaches used in HCI. Perhaps our models are not accessible, usable and maybe we use too many different models. There are also issues of integration between models while maintaining consistency between them. We need to bridge this gap and have mutual recognition of contributions from different communities. Requirements gathering is an important aspect when bridging the gap between MBD in different communities. MBD should provide support for a wider variety of interaction techniques including virtual reality, haptic touch, multimodality, gesture and voice recognition etc and since we generally model from a single-user perspective, MBD must also cater for multi-user environments which are commonly found in safety-critical systems.

UCD is generally an iterative process. In MBD, there is an issue of redesign within models. Modifying models should require little effort. Moreover, models would be useful if they were reusable. There are many other aspects that are generally not addressed in MBD that could improve future UIs including, working with guidelines, patterns, templates and incorporating non-functional requirements in models such as safety.

S.W. Gilroy and M.D. Harrison (Eds.): DSVIS 2005, LNCS 3941, p. 261, 2006.
© Springer-Verlag Berlin Heidelberg 2006

Supporting Values Other Than Usability and Performance Within the Design Process

Nick Chozos, Jennifer G. Sheridan, Özcan Mehmet, Amir Naghsh,
Kwang Chun Lee, and Ann Blandford

When we design computerised systems, we mainly focus on meeting values such as efficiency, reliability, usability and performance among other obvious design requirements. However, computer technologies have evolved to such a level that they have redefined the way humans, companies, organizations, and even society operate, a fact which suggests design has to consider more than just achieving usability and performance. Through experience it has been realised that the way in which technology intertwines with the social and human elements requires that design focuses on supporting human and social values as well.

These values vary across domains of application, whether it is safety-critical systems, management information systems, the internet, games, performance arts and so on. Rather than discussing values according to domain of application, we have decided to consider the role of technology in terms of its interaction with the user, the organization and society.

The value of usability mainly concerns the user, where the designer's goal is to design a system that the user can understand, manage and control to a desirable standard. At the level of Human–Computer Interaction, there is a great number of values which are considered as able to enhance and improve both the user's personal satisfaction and experience, and overall performance, which is probably the most obvious of all desired design values. Research has been investigating design approaches towards facilitating values such as creativity, aesthetics, and even fun. Although the benefits of adding these values to an application are recognised, it will take time before they are considered to be as important as usability for companies.

Discussion around design values is far more complicated when considering companies and organizations. Perhaps they can all be summarised under 'quality', however quality has many dimensions. On the technical side, reliability, dependability, expandability and other "–ities" are achievable and measurable to a certain extend. However, as mentioned in the beginning of our discussion, when considering other values apart from usability and performance, we have focused on values which are not given enough attention, mainly of a human and social nature. Assuring privacy and fairness, as well as reconciling cultural differences, are some of the challenges of design. It should be noted though that we are not referring only to the design of technology; in order to design technology towards meeting these values, organizations have to evolve towards considering these values as priorities that will affect their performance and financial growth.

The last notion highlights the relevance of ethics to design. Especially since the emergence of the World Wide Web, the debate around ethics and computing is constantly growing. The WWW offers a great amount of creativity; however, it is almost

S.W. Gilroy and M.D. Harrison (Eds.): DSVIS 2005, LNCS 3941, pp. 262–263, 2006.
© Springer-Verlag Berlin Heidelberg 2006

completely unregulated, facilitating even criminal activities. Furthermore, accidents have occurred due to systems' failure originating from 'poorly' designed systems, suggesting ethically un-sound design. The Internet and computer technology in general have, and are, reshaping morality of our times, constantly challenging the role of the designer. It could be suggested that ethics is one of the most important values to be supported by the design process. However, ethics does not only demand professionalism from the side of the designers, but from many other stakeholders that are involved, such as adopting organizations, users and even the government and regulatory agents.

Ambience and Mobility

Gavin J. Doherty, Lydie du Bousquet, José Creissac Campos, El Mustapha El Atifi,
Gilles Falquet, Mieke Massink, and Carmen Santoro

Mobile users generate a number of new problems by changing the context of interaction with the system. While context has always been relevant to interaction, the fact this can change, and the fact that tasks may be dependant on these contexts adds a new dimension to the design problem. Furthermore in some cases applications should be able to adapt to be pertinent to the current context, adding to the complexity of the applications to be constructed. With regard to "ambient" interaction, where systems are attempting to intelligently and unobtrusively help the user, understanding the user's intentions and providing relevant and adequate responses is a new problem. Furthermore, supporting the construction of such applications provides an additional challenge.

From a design perspective, an important activity is to determine what part of the context is relevant for the tasks of the user or for that particular application. We considered what level of detail and complexity for context models is necessary for design. In terms of modelling the context it was felt that there is a need for useful abstractions for reasoning about aspects of context of relevance to the user, but also aspects of context which the sytem may be responding and adapting to. Particular problems identified in this regard were context switching and context superposition. Where these are complex enough to justify tool support, there are issues to be addressed regarding the types of models which are appropriate for specification and validation purposes.

One can question whether a specific and seperate model to express the context is necessary, and particularly whether augmentations of task models could be sufficient. The answer to this may depend on the complexity of the situation being considered. Possible additional dimensions to be addressed by context models would include real time issues, modes, adaptative interfaces, user models, domain models and device models. Another issue which may be resolved through the use of models is to examine multiple applications existing in the same context, potentially using the same context infrastructure. For ambient applications knowledge of user intentions may be required to propose appropriate behaviour by the system. How can we model user intentions for the purposes of building such systems? It was proposed that there might there be typical mistakes to avoid, and methods or patterns for providing particular kinds of ambient "service". A final question concerns how user intentions may be dependant on the context, and whether this can be incorporated into models.

S.W. Gilroy and M.D. Harrison (Eds.): DSVIS 2005, LNCS 3941, p. 264, 2006.

Outdated Ideas of the Design Process and the Future of Formal Models, Methods and Notations

Dominic Furniss, Alan Dix, Christophe Ponsard, and Guo-Qiang Zhang

This topic implies that the future of formal techniques is tied to outdated ideas of the design process, perhaps of the 'waterfall model' variety, in contrast to more informal, fast and iterative techniques such as agile methods, which tend to be prototype-centric and less analytical. Indeed, these more agile techniques appear to be gaining importance where industry is moving towards more mobile and ambient technologies. A future challenge of formal techniques is how they could contribute to these areas, and how they can fit into the less formal conceptions of the design process. It is also important to understand industrial design contexts and fit with their conduct rather than trying to impose radical changes.

The diverse toolbox of formal techniques can be used to add value in design. Formal techniques differ in the extent of their formalness, from strict mathematical models to less formal notations and diagramming techniques. There is wide variation both in their application to different contexts and in the investment in terms of the formalness involved in applying a particular technique. Both of these should be considered by the designer when choosing a technique to add value to a design process. It was recognised that a future challenge was to better communicate when to use a particular technique, what bits of it and how much.

Formal techniques can be used for a variety of different purposes, including model checking, developing an understanding of a situation, and communication within design groups and stakeholders. Each plays a part in different design contexts, and it is up to the designers to deploy these techniques correctly. Importantly, the process of applying a formal technique develops an understanding of the situation in the designer, beyond any representation they may create. The application of the model/method/notation by the designer necessarily shapes the situation someway; this interplay between the designer, situation and representation leads them to reconceptualise the situation by noticing certain properties and features within it, which ultimately develops their understanding of it.

The value of formal techniques is likely to be realised differently in different contexts, and so their potential is tied to the values of the context in question. For example, the value of guaranteeing the safety of a system will be higher in critical environments than in website development. It is therefore likely that formal methods will be successful in some contexts and less so in others. Adding value in different contexts is no doubt a critical factor for potential adoption. In addition, the value of formalisms tend to be evident only long after use; getting more immediate perceived/actual benefit is critical to future adoption of formal methods.

The extent to which formalisms will be utilised continues to depend on the values of the design context and the value they can give to the design process and designer. It appears there is still work to be done in adapting, developing, and communicating these techniques to increase the perceived/actual value they provide.

S.W. Gilroy and M.D. Harrison (Eds.): DSVIS 2005, LNCS 3941, p. 265, 2006.

Author Index

Lecture Notes in Computer Science

For information about Vols. 1–3894

please contact your bookseller or Springer